Boston's Cardinal

RELIGION, POLITICS, AND SOCIETY IN THE NEW MILLENNIUM

Series Editors: Michael Novak, American Enterprise Institute, and Brian C. Anderson, Manhattan Institute

For nearly five centuries, it was widely believed that moral questions could be resolved through reason. The Enlightenment once gave us answers to these perennial questions, but the answers no longer seem adequate. It has become apparent that reason alone is not enough to answer the questions that define and shape our existence. Many now believe that we have come to the edge of the Enlightenment and are stepping forth into a new era, one that may be the most religious we have experienced in five hundred years. This series of books explores this new historical condition, publishing important works of scholarship in various disciplines that help us to understand the trends in thought and belief we have come from and to define the ones toward which we are heading.

Political Memoirs, by Aurel Kolnai, edited by Francesca Murphy
Challenging the Modern World: Karol Wojtyla/John Paul II and the Development of Catholic Social Teaching, by Samuel Gregg
The Scepter Shall Not Depart from Judah: Perspectives on the Persistence of the Political in Judaism, by Alan L. Mittleman
In the World, But Not of the World: Christian Social Teaching at the End of the Twentieth Century, by Andrew L. Fitz-Gibbon
The Surprising Pope: Understanding the Thought of John Paul II, by Maciej Zieba, O.P.
A Free Society Reader: Principles for the New Millennium, edited by Michael Novak, William Brailsford, and Cornelis Heesters
Beyond Self Interest: A Personalist Approach to Human Action, Gregory R. Beabout, et al.
Human Nature and the Discipline of Economics: Personalist Anthropology and Economic Methodology, Patricia Donohue-White, et al.
The Free Person and the Free Economy: A Personalist View of Market Economics, Anthony J. Santelli Jr., et al.
Meaninglessness: The Solutions of Nietzsche, Freud, and Rorty, by M. A. Casey
Boston's Cardinal: Bernard Law, the Man and His Witness, edited by Romanus Cessario, O.P.
Don't Play Away Your Cards, Uncle Sam: The American Difference, by Olof Murelius, edited by Jana Novak
Society as a Department Store: Critical Reflections on the Liberal State, by Ryszard Legutko

Boston's Cardinal

Bernard Law, the Man and His Witness

Edited by
Romanus Cessario, O.P.

With a biographical introduction
by Mary Ann Glendon

LEXINGTON BOOKS
Lanham • Boulder • New York • Oxford

LEXINGTON BOOKS

Published in the United States of America
by Lexington Books
4720 Boston Way, Lanham, Maryland 20706

12 Hid's Copse Road
Cumnor Hill, Oxford OX2 9JJ, England

British Library Cataloguing in Publication Information Available

Library of Congress Cataloging-in-Publication Data Available

ISBN 0-7391-0340-7 (cloth)
ISBN 0-7391-0341-5 (pbk.)

Printed in the United States of America

∞™ The paper used in this publication meets the minimum requirements of American National Standard for Information Sciences—Permanence of Paper for Printed Library Materials, ANSI/NISO Z39.48–1992.

Contents

Preface

+

From his ordination on the eve of the Second Vatican Council to his current prominence as one of the most influential leaders of the Catholic Church, Bernard Francis Law has witnessed and participated in many of the struggles and events that have shaped American and Church history. As a young priest-journalist in strife-torn Mississippi of the 1960s, he became an outspoken advocate for racial justice and an enthusiastic expositor of the teachings of Vatican II. From 1973 to 1985, he pioneered in developing the understanding of the role of the post-conciliar bishop in Springfield–Cape Girardeau, Missouri. As Archbishop of Boston, he has gained world-wide prominence for his eloquent advancement of religiously grounded moral positions on the major issues of our times. It thus seems fitting and proper, in the year of Bernard Law's seventieth birthday, that the rich materials contained in his speeches, homilies, and columns be made available to persons interested in the role of the Catholic Church in a pluralistic modern society.

The writings collected in this volume have been organized under headings that correspond to the principal public roles that a bishop is required to exercise: *Advocate for the Common Good, A Moral Voice in the Modern World,* and *A Pastor Speaking to the Faithful.* Together with the introductory biographical essay by Mary Ann Glendon, these materials provide a capsule glimpse of a modern bishop in action, as well as a revealing portrait of the man many consider to be the quintessential post–Vatican II bishop.

The job description of bishops is of great antiquity. It reaches back to the beginnings of Christianity, when many gave witness through martyrdom. One can discern the outreach of bishops to civil society in the first moments when the Church attained an established public status. From as early as the fourth century, bishops have figured prominently in both Church and city. It is because of this role in both spiritual and temporal affairs that a bishop is sometimes referred to as a Pontifex, or bridge builder. A long line of Church leaders—including Ambrose, Augustine, and Gregory the Great—have acted upon their obligations toward both ecclesial communion and civil commonweal, and the list of notable Churchmen who have been bridge builders under various configurations of civil and religious authorities continues to the present day.

The challenge for every bishop is particularly acute in times of rapid social and economic change. In our own time, Pope John Paul II has been the outstanding model of "teaching, sanctifying, and governing" as he seeks to fulfil the imperative to transform everything that exists in accordance with the image of God who created not only human persons but the world order in which they dwell. No wonder, then, that Bernard Law has found a model and a patron in the Pontifex Maximus—Pope John Paul II.

As one peruses the writings collected in the present volume, it is easy to see why Bernard Law has been called a "gatherer of peoples" and "a negotiator for God." His ministry as priest and bishop has been characterized from its outset by a vivid sense of the unity of the human family, a passion for healing divisions, a deep love of Church, a zeal for evangelization, a special sympathy for persons suffering in body or mind, and by Gospel-inspired activism on behalf of the weakest and most vulnerable members of society. An unusual multicultural childhood prepared him well for a vocation that would be lived out in the era of globalization, and for a key role in relations with Latin America. One of the hallmarks of his vocation from the beginning has been outreach across racial, religious and national boundaries. "Boston's Cardinal" is not only a Cardinal for the new Boston, but one who has never lost sight of the relation between the local and the universal Church.

Bernard Law's political vision, in conformity with the social teachings of the universal Catholic Church, transcends conventional party lines and categories. He has been a consistent supporter of a role for government in providing decent living conditions, a staunch defender of human life from the moment of conception until natural death, a proponent of experimentation with the intermediate structures of civil society to deliver social services, an articulate opponent of capital punishment, a major player in preparing the way for relations with a post-Castro Cuba, and a leader in the effort to provide debt relief to poverty-stricken nations.

It is hoped that the reflections by "Boston's Cardinal" on these and other topics will be of value to all persons who are interested in the Church, her leaders, and the role of religion in public life.

Finally, the Editor would like to express his gratitude to those who have helped to bring this volume to a successful completion, especially Kaye Woodward, Secretary to Cardinal Law; Robert Johnson-Lally,

Archivist of the Archdiocese of Boston, and his staff; and the Dominican Nuns of the Monastery of Our Lady of the Rosary, Buffalo, New York.

Romanus Cessario, O. P.

15 August 2001
Boston, Massachusetts

Biographical Introduction

Bernard Cardinal Law
Gatherer of Peoples

Mary Ann Glendon

On Mother's Day in his seventieth year, Boston's Bernard Cardinal Law processed to the altar of Holy Cross Cathedral, clapping in time to chants and drums. He was presiding over an African liturgy organized by members of Boston's Nigerian and Kenyan communities, and throwing himself into it with obvious gusto. The stained glass of the old church, glowing with spring sunlight, found an unaccustomed reflection that morning in the resplendent costumes of visiting worshippers. The usual Sunday crowd, catching the mood, joined in an exuberant rendition of the Gloria. It was a fitting day for a homily that took its cue from the Book of Revelation: "Behold, I make all things new." The Cardinal called for new attention to the problems of the African continent, and for renewed respect and support for mothers everywhere—expectant mothers, grandmothers, single mothers, mothers on welfare. He recalled his own mother "who taught me the meaning of love from my first conscious moments and even before." He asked those present to strengthen their resolve to build a civilization of love and peace at home and abroad. The ceremony was emblematic of the priesthood of Bernard Law—rooted in the local Church, yet celebrating the universal Church in all its diversity; deeply spiritual, yet embracing the joys and sorrows of everyday life.

For Bernard Francis Law, the Church was one of the few fixed points on the frequently shifting landscape of an unusual childhood. He was born on 4 November 1931, in Torreòn, Mexico, to Bernard A. and Helen Stubblefield Law. Captain Law, a pioneering aviator, had been an Army pilot in World War I and a barnstormer in the southwestern United States before settling in that small Mexican city to run an airline company. The elegant Miss Stubblefield had come to Torreòn from her home state of Washington to spend a vacation with her uncle's family. The couple were of different generations (he was forty and she was twenty) and religions (he a Catholic of Scots descent and she a Welsh Presbyterian), but they shared a love of literature and music. Their only child, Bernard, spent his early years speaking Spanish and English in a home filled with books and the sounds of his mother's piano. He learned to play the piano himself, and developed an enduring love of Bach, choral music, and Beethoven's quartets.

By the time young Bernard graduated from high school, he was an "American" in the expansive sense of the word. He had lived in Mexico, Colombia, Panama, and the Virgin Islands, with occasional periods of residence in the mainland United States. When the airline in Torreòn fell victim to the depression, the Laws moved to New York City where Captain Law turned his talents for a time to writing short stories, and a popular illustrated book on military airplanes. The family returned to Latin America when Bernard was eight, this time to the Colombian port city of Barranquilla, where his father became station manager for a Pan Am subsidiary. They remained in Colombia until the United States entered World War II, at which time the Captain went back into the Army, emerging as a colonel. Mother and son lived on Army bases until war's end, when Colonel Law rejoined Pan Am, which sent him first to the Virgin Islands and then to Panama where Bernard began high school. The whole family, however, had fallen in love with the people and the natural beauty of St. Thomas. Thus, when the governor of the U.S. Virgin Islands invited Colonel Law to head the islands' development authority, he readily accepted.

That multicultural childhood put young Bernard ahead of his generation where race relations were concerned. At Charlotte Amalie's high school on the island of St. Thomas, all but one of his teachers were black, and he was one of a handful of white students. Yet he felt totally accepted by his classmates who elected him class president in their senior year. He was, of course, aware of the situation on the mainland—the race riots in northern cities and the practice of segregation on the basis of color. In his

Bernard A. and Helen Stubblefield Law

Bernard Francis, age 4, and Helen Law

Bernard Francis Law, age 2 in Torreòn

high school valedictory address, he celebrated the special atmosphere of the Virgin Islands. In St. Thomas, he said, "the ugly marks of ignorance-bred prejudice are not rampant here as in other less fortunate places. . . . Acceptance does not depend on race, color, or creed. [A person] is free to develop his innate abilities, he may aspire to any height." The islands would have to be vigilant, he continued, to maintain their special character as they pursued economic development. "We're after tourist business, yes, but we must guard against having the glitter of gold blind our eyes to what lies beyond. . . . Never must we let bigotry creep into our beings. . . . It is imperative that we maintain these priceless gifts which have been given to us in order that we may make the Virgin Islands an oasis of democracy in this troubled world."

It was during Bernard's sophomore year of high school, while he attended a retreat by a visiting Redemptorist priest, that he experienced what he would later describe as "a pivotal moment"—a vivid awareness of the Church as the "mystical body of Christ," the union of all Christians everywhere, living and dead. After the retreat, at his pastor's suggestion, the fifteen-year-old read *Mystici Corpus,* Pope Pius XII's 1943 encyclical that was banned in German-occupied Belgium for containing such subversive lines as "We must recognize as Brothers in Christ . . . those not yet one with us in the Body of Christ." The teaching on the one body with many members made such a deep impression on the youth that he describes it even today as "the dominant teaching of my life." The boy without geographical roots began to feel "very rooted" in the Church.

When the time came to think about college, Bernard sent applications to Harvard (at the suggestion of a teacher who had done her graduate work there); Tufts ("because a girl I liked was going there"); and one Catholic university, Georgetown. In the fall of 1949, he entered Harvard University. For the next four years, he took time nearly every day to write his parents. In these letters, carefully preserved by his mother, one can already hear the voice of the indefatigable evangelist he later became. One evening in his freshman year, he wrote, "There is a discussion going on in our room. We are discussing God, the Trinity, and the afterlife. There are six of us—2 Jews, 2 Catholics, a Baptist, and a poor guy who doesn't know *what* he believes." Two months later, he remarked of a freshman smoker that had included "night club" acts: "It really was incongruous to have this disgustingly base entertainment in a building that at one time served as a Church." He ended the letter by applauding the appointment of a new governor for the U.S. Virgin Islands: "It is a wonderful commentary on the U.S. that a Jewish person has been appointed, and I think that it is a wonderful commentary on President Truman that he did not give this little plum to someone who did more than his share to get him elected."

The years at Harvard seem to have been happy ones, or Bernard an unusually uncomplaining youth, for the tone of his letters is uniformly

Bernard Law, voted "Most Intelligent Boy" by the Charlotte Amalie High School Class of 1949, with classmate Gloria George, "Most Intelligent Girl." The "Class Prophet" predicted Bernard would become a mathematics professor.

upbeat. As he pursued his studies, he thought off and on of becoming a priest, of entering the Foreign Service, and of becoming a psychiatrist. His favorite courses were in the history department. "History," he told his parents, "is without doubt the most tremendous subject. It seems to me the only logical way to understand (or attempt to understand) existing institutions. God, existing outside of time, sees all time at a glance. That is the perfect way, for He is perfect. Therefore in our finite way, approaching perfection entails seeing all we can of time; the future is impossible, under normal conditions, for us to see; ah, but the past! I'm far from caught up, but am enjoying myself." As for the present, Bernard was "caught up" in politics when Adlai Stevenson ran against Dwight Eisenhower in 1952. A gung ho member of the Harvard Democrats, he knocked on Cambridge and Somerville doors to drum up support for the brainy but uncharismatic Democratic candidate. In a letter to his mother (who had surprised him by becoming a Catholic while he was away at college), he attributes his zeal for action to parental examples: "Like it or not, you are both militant crusaders, that's why I'm like I am."

For Bernard Law, as for many Catholic students at Harvard before and since, St. Paul's Church in Cambridge was a spiritual home away from home. He sang in the Men's Schola there, and it was at St. Paul's that his vocation to the priesthood took shape. By graduation day 1953, he had made his decision. His mood that spring seems to have been buoyant. One morning he wrote, "Dear Folks, There's nothing particularly newsy to write about, except that the Blessed Sacrament, the weather and everything else must be in a heavenly conspiracy to make this day bursting with happiness—and it's only just nine o'clock."

As Bernard was not from the Boston area, he was encouraged by the late Bishop Lawrence Riley, with whom he had discussed his call to the priesthood, to give his talents to a part of the Church that was more in need of priests. Accordingly, that fall, Bernard entered St. Joseph Seminary, an apostolate of the Benedictine Order, in St. Benedict, Louisiana. Two years later, he matriculated at the Pontifical College Josephinum in Worthington, Ohio, where he completed his studies. At the age of 29, he was ordained a priest in the diocese of Natchez–Jackson, Mississippi. He was assigned to a parish in the port city of Vicksburg, once the site of a Spanish fort, and later the scene of an important battle in the American Civil War.

The year was 1961. The Church was preparing for the Second Vatican Council that would open the following year; the civil rights movement was gaining momentum in the United States; and the young curate was about to be swept up in currents of change that would alter the face of the Church and the nation. In Vicksburg, he threw himself into parish life, calling on parishioners, teaching religion classes, and ministering to the sick. Memphis lawyer Ray Terry, a Vicksburg native, recalls being struck by how the

"Thou art a priest forever." Bernard Law at his ordination, June 1961, with (L to R) his late father's friend Judge Richard Carter, great aunt Ida Stubblefield Parkinson, mother Helen Law, and aunt Mary Law Collins

new priest in town "went into homes as priests had never done before" and by Father Law's loving attention to those who were suffering—from the town drunk to a young boy dying of brain cancer.

When he learned that his Vicksburg parishioners were curious about the impending Council, Father Law put together a talk on the subject, and soon found himself on the lecture circuit. The newcomer's speaking and writing abilities attracted the attention of Jackson's Bishop Richard Gerow, and in early 1963, Father Law was transferred to the state capital to become the editor of the diocesan weekly, *The Mississippi Register*. His mother, a widow since 1955, moved to Jackson to be near her son.

Another young priest of the Jackson diocese, Father Patrick Farrell, who had just arrived from his native Ireland, recalls that "Father Law's gifts and talents were noticed by everybody—he was extremely bright, engaging, personable, a man who got energized by work rather than tired, and a great gatherer of diverse people." The Irish priest noted, too, that his colleague's racial attitudes were different from those of most white Mississippians. Father Law had kept up with his friends in the Virgin Islands, as he would in later years, inviting them to attend the major events in his life. According to Father Farrell, who presently serves as Rector of the Jackson Cathedral, "He felt passionately about racial justice from the first moment I knew him—it wasn't a mere following of teaching, it came from his heart."

Bishop Gerow had made an inspired choice for the diocesan paper. With Catholics a small minority in Mississippi, and often targeted for persecution by the Ku Klux Klan, the *Register* had been rather timid on racial issues. That changed in June 1963, when the new editor wrote a lead story on the evils of segregation, featuring the U.S. Bishops' 1958 *Statement on Racial Discrimination and the Christian Conscience*. Just one week later, respected NAACP leader Medgar Evers was gunned down by an assassin outside his Jackson home. Father Law attended the wake with Bishop Gerow, and the next issue of the *Register* bore the headline "Everyone is Guilty" over a statement by the Bishop that "We need frankly to admit that the guilt for the murder of Mr. Evers and the other instances of violence in our community tragically must be shared by all of us. . . . Rights which have been given to all men by the Creator cannot be the subject of conferral or refusal by men. . . . Our conscience should compel us all to acknowledge the deep moral implications of this problem and to take some positive steps towards recognizing the legitimate grievances of our Negro population." (Ray Terry, who later became Deputy General Counsel of the Equal Employment Opportunities Commission, believes that the Bishop's statement was mainly crafted by Father Law, remarking that Law "had a way of helping older priests adapt to changing times.") When Bishop Gerow and other local religious leaders were invited by Attorney General Robert Kennedy to the White House to discuss the crisis in Mississippi, Father Law accompanied them and was excited to have the chance to meet President John F. Kennedy.

Later that summer, Father Law editorially chided local public officials for their lack of moral leadership: "Until a politician can dare to speak out in clear defiance of the oppressive policies of the Citizens' Councils, Mississippians will remain a captive people. Freedom in Mississippi is now at an alarmingly low ebb." The next year, his article titled "Legal Segregation is Dying" won the Catholic Press Award for editorial writing. Massachusetts District Judge Gordon Martin, who was a Justice Department attorney in Mississippi at the time, recalled in a *Boston Globe* article that Father Law "did not pull his punches, and the *Register's* editorials and columns provided a sharp contrast with the racist diatribes of virtually all of the state's daily and weekly press."

In "Freedom Summer" 1964, when three civil rights workers were reported missing and suspected murdered, Father Law was a member of the interracial, interfaith group of clergymen who met to discuss the crisis with President Johnson's emissary. After the bodies of the three slain young men were discovered on a Neshoba County farm, Law urged decent citizens to have the courage to stand up to racists. "In Mississippi the next move is up to the white moderate," he wrote. "If he is in the house, let him now come forward." When the local Knights of Columbus protested their national organization's support of freedom riders, Father Law cancelled a speaking engagement with the local group, sending them a stiffly worded letter.

His exposure to virulent racial prejudice in Mississippi heightened his awareness of the need for spiritual leaders to beware of conforming to the prevailing culture. In the wake of the bombing of a Jackson synagogue, he wrote, "In all charity, it must be said that democratic church polity has often led to a shackled pulpit. When the pulpit becomes a sounding board, even indirectly, for the prejudices of a congregation, then that pulpit is dead." Together with a few like-minded leaders of other faiths, he established and became Chairman of an interfaith Mississippi Council on Human Relations. Two members of that group soon paid a high price for their modest step. The home of the treasurer, a rabbi, was bombed, and the secretary, a Unitarian minister, was shot and severely wounded as he was getting out of his car. The FBI advised Father Law to keep them informed of his movements, and Bishop Gerow, fearing for his priest's safety, moved him from a parish on the outskirts of Jackson into the cathedral rectory.

Father Farrell was impressed by his colleague's boundless energy. Father Law pushed the Catholic community to take an interest in the problem of housing for the poor and helped to establish a literacy program for adults. As Vatican II got underway, he participated in founding "Operation Spark," a kind of traveling caravan that presented workshops on the new liturgy and celebrated Masses throughout the state. At the end of a busy day when everyone else was tired, Father Farrell recalls that Father

Law would often set off to the hospitals to spend time with the sick and dying. Bemused that his old friend, once considered a dangerous liberal, is now regarded in some quarters as a conservative, Father Farrell says, "Bernard Law was always a social liberal dedicated to racial integration, social justice, and ecumenism—but he was never a doctrinal or ecclesiastical liberal, he was always faithful to the Magisterium."

In his Mississippi years, Bernard Law took the initiative to reach out, not only across racial lines, but also to the Protestant and Jewish communities. That experience enabled him to be of valuable assistance to Bishop Gerow's successor, Bishop Joseph Brunini, who served on the first National Conference of Catholic Bishops' Committee for Ecumenical and Inter-Religious Affairs. While aiding Bishop Brunini, Father Law had the opportunity to accompany him to the last session of the Vatican Council in 1965. He also became acquainted with Monsignor (now Cardinal) William Baum who was the Ecumenical Committee's Executive Director. As Cardinal Baum recalls his first meeting with the man who became his close friend over the years, he was struck by Father Law's affability and his enthusiasm for work. He was well pleased when, in 1968, the energetic young priest from Jackson was appointed to succeed him at NCCB headquarters in Washington, D.C. In 1971, Law returned to Mississippi to become Bishop Brunini's Vicar-General in the Diocese of Natchez–Jackson.

A new chapter in Bernard Law's life opened on 5 December 1973, when he was installed as the fourth Bishop of Springfield–Cape Girardeau, Missouri, again succeeding William Baum, who left that post to become the Archbishop of Washington, D.C. His longtime mentor Bishop Brunini, from whom he had learned a great deal about episcopal work, presided at the installation. In his homily on that occasion, the new bishop pledged himself to continue to work for unity among Christians and to promote dialogue with the Jewish community and other religious groups. Sounding a theme to which he would often recur, he said that the most valuable contribution the Church can make to ecumenical dialogue is to speak her own faith clearly, completely, and unambiguously.

The diocese of Springfield–Cape Girardeau had been carved relatively recently from the diocese of Kansas City and the archdiocese of St. Louis. Thus a major challenge for Bishop Law was to foster a sense of a local church. The challenge was compounded by the fact that the Catholic population of the diocese was small (about fifty thousand of a total population of a million) but spread over a large geographical area. It took the bishop about five and a half hours to drive without stopping from Springfield to Cape Girardeau.

Not far from Springfield was Fort Chaffee, Arkansas, where a large refugee camp was established in 1975 to hold Vietnamese "boat people" who had fled their native land after the fall of Saigon. Bishop Law's attention was drawn to their situation by the editor of his diocesan paper who urged him to celebrate Mass there for the thousands of Catholics who were awaiting resettlement. The bishop readily agreed, and at Fort Chaffee he learned of the plight of a congregation of nearly two hundred Vietnamese men religious who had been told by U.S. authorities that they could not be resettled together in one place unless they could get a single sponsor for the whole group.

Pondering the situation, the bishop had a brainstorm. He recalled that there was a former minor seminary at Carthage, Missouri, owned by the Oblates of Mary Immaculate. It was vacant except for one elderly Oblate, who was struggling to keep the place from falling into ruin and dreaming of the day when the missionaries would return. Bishop Law placed a call to the Oblates' Provincial in St. Paul, Minnesota, to ascertain whether the order would be willing to rent the facilities for a dollar a year so as to enable the diocese to sponsor the community. When the Provincial said yes, the Bishop solicited the aid of several major superiors of men and women religious to recruit brothers who could help get a farming operation started, and retired sisters who could teach English to the Vietnamese brothers. He then went back to the refugee camp and invited the community to take up residence in the seminary.

Several good-hearted citizens of Carthage, a town of about eight thousand, greeted the first busload of newcomers with a covered dish meal. The men then proceeded to the seminary chapel where Mass was celebrated in Latin, their only common language with their American sponsors. Only the lone remaining Oblate, the Bishop noticed, was sad: "Poor Father John—his prayers were being answered but he didn't realize it."

The Congregation of Mary Co-Redemptrix flourished in Carthage, aided by the contributions of fellow refugees from the Fort Chaffee camp who settled in the region. After a time, at Bishop Law's suggestion, the brothers organized a "homecoming" reunion for former residents of Fort Chaffee who were more widely dispersed throughout the United States. It must have been a strange sight for Carthage's mostly Southern Baptist residents when about three thousand Vietnamese visitors, many in traditional costume, showed up one summer day for a procession that wound through the town behind a float of Our Lady of Fatima and a convertible carrying Cardinal John Carberry of St. Louis while a crop-duster scattered rose petals and the promises of Fatima from the sky. The homecoming culminated in an outdoor Mass where Bishop Law was introduced to the indigenous custom of setting off firecrackers, rather than ringing bells, at the consecration. "It was great," he recalled. "They had a terrific loudspeaker system, and that meant their neighbors were hearing the Mass for the first time!" The Carthaginians apparently took it all in good stride, for a delegation of town leaders appeared the next day to welcome the visitors.

The Carthage "Marian Days" have since become an annual cultural and religious festival—and something of a match-making occasion—attended by as many as fifty thousand Vietnamese from all over the United States. And the Carthage religious congregation has prospered, purchasing its leased property from the Oblates, building an auditorium and retirement home, and expanding its farming operations. The bonds between the Vietnamese community and the bishop who befriended them have endured as well. Cardinal Law made a point of being present on the occasion of Pope John Paul II's canonization of Vietnamese martyrs, the only bishop from the United States to do so. And when the Cardinal's mother died in 1991, several Vietnamese friends drove all night from Carthage to be present at her wake in Boston.

It was in Springfield–Cape Girardeau that Bernard Law developed and deepened his understanding of the ministry of a bishop as teacher, priest, and shepherd. The work of a bishop is far more demanding than that of the head of any secular organization, for it encompasses "teaching" and "sanctifying" as well as "governing." Among those roles, according to the Second Vatican Council's teaching on the episcopate, "preaching the Gospel occupies an eminent place." Moreover, as *Lumen Gentium* makes clear, every bishop has responsibility not only for his local Church, but, in communion with the college of bishops, for the universal Church.

In 1984, Bernard Law was called to live out those responsibilities in a new context as the eighth archbishop of Boston, the fourth largest archdiocese in the country with over two million Catholics. The opening prayer for his initial Mass in Holy Cross Cathedral was, characteristically, one that evoked the theme of the universal Church as a mystery experienced "in the corporate life of a billion men and women scattered throughout the world in dioceses such as our own":

> *God our Father, in all the churches scattered throughout the world you show forth the One, Holy, Catholic and Apostolic Church. Through the Gospel and the Eucharist bring your people together in the Holy Spirit and guide us in your love. Make us a sign of your love for all people and help us to show forth the living presence of Christ in the world.*

The following year, Pope John Paul II made him a Cardinal, with this solemn instruction: "Receive the red biretta, the sign of the dignity of the cardinalate, by which is signified that you must show yourself fearless, even to the shedding of your blood, for the increase of the Christian faith, the peace and tranquility of the people of God, and the freedom and growth of the Holy Roman Church."

The assignment to Boston, with its large Catholic population, ingrained traditions, and secular atmosphere, posed fresh challenges to a man who had mainly served in places where Catholics were in a minority. It is dif-

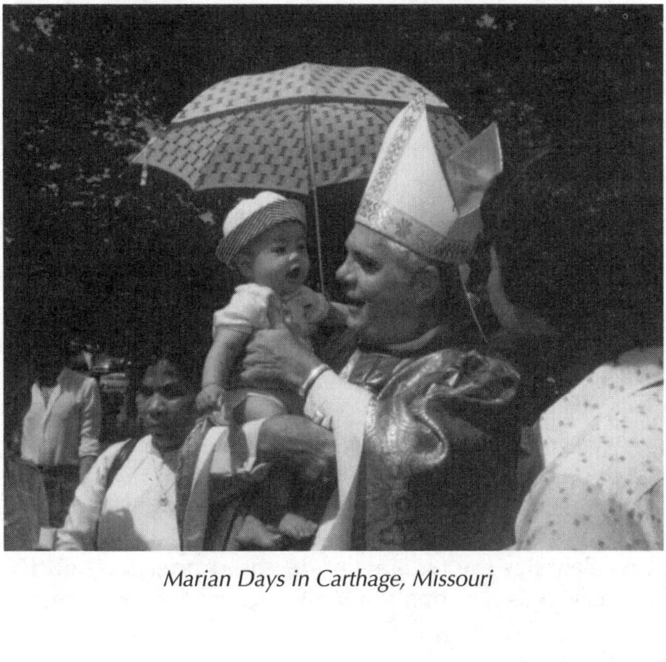

Marian Days in Carthage, Missouri

ficult, as the saying goes, to be a prophet in one's own land. But in Boston, it is difficult to be a prophet, period—and particularly if one is *not* a native son. The new archbishop had to make his way in what was then still a heavily Irish Catholic community, fond of its colorful rogues and historically ambivalent about asserting its Catholic identity.

Yet, once again, Bernard Law's path had brought him to a place where his particular background, strengths and talents would soon be needed. Though few could have foreseen it in 1984, Boston, like other large cities, was about to be caught up in the swift currents of globalization, and its Catholic population would become steadily more diverse with the influx of immigrants from far corners of the earth. The Harvard educated, bilingual outsider with a global outlook set out at once to get to know the city's 404 parishes, visiting two or three each weekend for his first fifteen years.

Today, after some consolidation owing to demographic shifts, the Archdiocese encompasses 368 parishes, with about 700 active diocesan priests, 130 Catholic elementary schools and 35 Catholic high schools. During a typical week, the Cardinal begins each weekday with Mass at 7:30 a.m. That daily Mass, according to members of his household, is the heart and center of his life, the most important part of the day. He tries not to have appointments before ten o'clock, so that he can devote the first part of the day to prayer and quiet work, such as his weekly column for *The Pilot*. Then follows an hour-long meeting with his Vicar-General to go over the day's agenda—which may range from ordinary archdiocesan business to matters arising in connection with the many boards and congregations on which the Cardinal serves (he chairs the U.S. Conference of Catholic Bishops International Policy Committee, the Boards of Trustees of Catholic University and Saint John's Seminary, and serves on many Vatican Congregations and Councils).

Afternoons are ordinarily devoted to meetings and appointments. Once a week, the Cardinal meets with his twelve-member cabinet composed of priests and religious, laymen and laywomen. The cabinet system was established as a result of a study he initiated shortly after his arrival in Boston to determine how he might deal most effectively with the more than eighty Church agencies under his jurisdiction. At the weekly sessions, each department head reports on the principal matters that have arisen in his or her domain (pastoral services, education, health care, social services, development, community relations) since the last meeting. These meetings help to keep the department heads abreast of developments in each other's areas.

Any given day is apt to be punctuated by visits to the grieving or the afflicted, for the Cardinal makes a point of attending the wakes of parents and close relatives of priests, tries to visit his priests when they are in hospitals, and celebrates the funerals of deceased priests. Msgr. Paul McInerny, who served as Cardinal Law's Secretary for several years, recalls

Bernard Cardinal Law with Pope John Paul II.

that "When driving home at night after the last event in a grueling day, he often stopped at a hospital, not out of a sense of obligation, but because he has a real love for his priests."

A major focus of Cardinal Law's ministry in Boston, in fact, has been his effort to foster a collegial atmosphere among the priests, to keep abreast of their concerns, and to counter the loneliness that can sometimes attend the life of a parish priest. His Emmaus program provides opportunities for priests to meet on a regular basis for prayer, reflection, meals and fellowship.

Among Cardinal Law's other innovations, the Archdiocesan Synod he convened in 1988 stands out as a watershed event which brought large numbers of laypeople more fully into the life of the local Church. The purpose of that series of meetings was to conduct an archdiocese-wide self-study and to frame a plan for the future. According to Msgr. McInerny who co-directed the Synod with Sister Mary Ann Doyle, the process was a turning point for the Archdiocese in two major respects: it brought to the fore many lay Catholics who were eager and willing to be more engaged in the work of the Church and, in so doing, it tapped the energies of the area's burgeoning communities of "new" Catholics from the Caribbean, Latin America, and Asia. The Synod thus foreshadowed what the Church in Boston will be like in the twenty-first century.

For the lay women and men involved (most recruited by their pastors), the discussion and drafting of "mission plans" in the Synod's working groups provided our first experience of active participation in Church affairs. Many of us had grown up thinking that the layperson's role was to go to Mass, to put our envelopes in the collection basket, and to try to be good people, while priests and sisters took care of everything else. We had not yet grasped the full extent of the lay vocation that has been so forcefully emphasized by Pope John Paul II. The parish councils established as a result of the Synod assured that such opportunities would continue at the grassroots level. Meanwhile, the Cardinal has kept pushing the process further, encouraging participation by laywomen and men in more facets of Church life, urging his priests to do the same, and establishing programs geared to the desire of many adults for continuing religious education.

Following the practice he established as a parish priest in Mississippi, the Cardinal has been an active citizen of the greater Boston community. He was the moving spirit behind the foundation in 1987 of *Challenge to Leadership*, a group of leaders from business, labor, the academy, government, the nonprofit sector, and religious organizations who support initiatives to address problems in the areas of economic development, education, and juvenile crime. Over the years, he has spoken out and supported initiatives on a broad range of issues—testifying against the return of the death penalty; campaigning for affordable housing; criticizing welfare "reforms" that diminish government's role in helping families to overcome poverty, and joining forces with the *Ten Point Coalition*, a group founded by several African-

American ministers to address the material and spiritual conditions that underlie black-on-black violence in Boston. His highly visible advocacy on behalf of the most vulnerable and marginalized members of the community has made him, in the eyes of many, the moral voice of the Commonwealth.

In May 2000, the entire nation heard that voice when Bernard Law delivered a stirring homily at the funeral of his friend John Cardinal O'Connor. In a packed St. Patrick's cathedral, with the then-President and First Lady of the United States, Bill and Hillary Clinton, and other prominent abortion rights supporters seated before him, the Cardinal spoke truth to power, exclaiming: "What a great legacy he has left us in his constant reminder that the Church must always be unambiguously pro-life!" The faithful responded with prolonged applause, prompting Cardinal Law to remark softly, "I see he hasn't left the pulpit."

Whether at the local, national, or international level, Bernard Law's message to his fellow Catholic citizens has been the same: Catholics must be unambiguously pro-life, pro-family, and pro-poor in the public forum, and wherever else their work and responsibilities place them. They do not seek to *im*-pose their views on anyone, but they must not be denied their right to *pro*-pose their viewpoints like any other citizens in a democratic society. In a 1999 speech, he spelled out what it means to be unconditionally pro-life, pro-family, and pro-poor:

> That means that, unlike Cain who murdered his brother Abel, we understand that we are our brother's and sister's keeper. That means that we live as one human family with God as our common father. That means that the people of Turkey and the Sudan and China are not strangers to our hearts. Our love for everyone, wherever they live, and especially the poor, the weak, the sick, the dying, and our younger sisters and brothers not yet born, must know no bounds. To be unconditionally pro-life means to champion the cause of the unborn and the dying, to make the support of the family of paramount importance, and to be unrelenting in our effective solidarity with the poor. This is who we should be as Catholic citizens, with apologies to no one.

Defying categorization as "liberal" or "conservative," Cardinal Law has been as passionate and eloquent in his pursuit of social justice as in his defense of the value of human life from conception to natural death. In an address celebrating the tenth anniversary of Women Affirming Life in the spring of 2000, he said:

> How do we live the Gospel of Life? We live it by being *with* people—the sick, the dying, the single parent, the homeless, the prisoner, especially at the fragile beginning and ending of life. As a culture, we have become increasingly insensitive to life, to the point where the Holy Father said in *Evangelium Vitae* that we are engaged in a war of the powerful against the weak. The Holy Father is correct. We are in a war. The Church stands with the weak, and we must, too.

Sounding a similar theme in a talk to new members of the U.S. Bishops' International Policy Committee about disparities of wealth and racial and ethnic tensions, he sought to instill in the men and women around the table his own sense of urgency: "The resources of our faith give us a power and a vision not found anywhere else. They find their most eloquent expression in the social teachings of the Church, and no one has contributed to them more richly than Pope John Paul II. If we don't use them, we have failed in our responsibility. We can never give up."

The Cardinal is well known for refusing to give up. During the year 2000, he made debt relief a priority in accordance with the tradition of Jubilee as a time for helping the poor to make a fresh start. On behalf of the Archdiocese of Boston, he forgave $28 million in debts, owed mainly by the thirty poorest parishes, and then turned his attention to the plight of poor countries indebted to the World Bank, the International Monetary Fund, and affluent nations.

The U.S. Congress was not favorably disposed toward contributing to a program to reduce the crushing debt burden on the poorest countries in the world. In the summer of 2000, they were set to appropriate only a small portion of the funds the American government had agreed to supply to a G-7 debt relief program. At that juncture, Cardinal Law wrote an Op-Ed piece in the *Washington Post* explaining the practical consequences of the debt burden as seen through the eyes of Church workers who serve the poorest of the poor in over three hundred thousand hospitals, schools, and relief agencies throughout the world. Debt service, he wrote, was draining the resources needed by the least developed nations for education, health care, and progress toward self-sufficiency. Then, he visited House Majority Leader Richard Armey and Speaker Dennis Hastert to further explain the views of the U.S. bishops. While debt relief was admittedly not a panacea for poverty reduction, he told them, no progress could be made in the poorest countries without it. It was a much-needed first step.

Several weeks later, when debate opened on foreign aid in the House of Representatives, members from both sides of the aisle stood up to press for an increase in funding for debt relief. In the end, the House voted for full funding of the U.S. commitment for debt relief for the year 2001. In reporting that shift of direction, the *New York Times* professed puzzlement. But USCCB Secretary for Social Development and World Peace John Carr is convinced that Cardinal Law's explanation of the idea of Jubilee to Representatives Armey and Hastert played a significant role.

Bernard Law's love for and facility with the Spanish language has served the Church well over the years. Locally, when speaking to an audience that includes a large number of Hispanics, he often addresses a part of his speech to them in their mother tongue. On the national and international stage, he has emerged as a bridge-builder between North and South American bishops, and as the key U.S. figure in the process through which the Church in Cuba prepares for a post-Castro society.

The Cuban connection began with a friendship struck up between Cardinal Law and Jaime Cardinal Ortega at the installation of John O'Connor as archbishop of New York. Since then, at Cardinal Law's instance, Catholic Charities of Boston has become one of the most important nongovernmental organizations in Cuba, working with Caritas Cubana to provide direct aid for social programs, especially those ministering to mothers, children, and AIDS patients. The Boston prelate has been a prominent opponent of the U.S. embargo on trade with Cuba, arguing that the hardship imposed on Cuban citizens, especially where necessary medical supplies are concerned, is not outweighed by any political advantage. In a statement issued in November 2000, he said, "I look forward to the new Congress successfully acting to end a policy that hurts only the poor of Cuba, while providing unmerited propaganda for the regime." All told, he has made about a dozen visits to the island nation (beginning with his first visit at the age of eight, when the United Fruit Company boat carrying him and his mother to Barranquilla docked at Cienfuegos).

Not surprisingly, Cardinal Law was a prominent participant in the 1997 Synod for America where Pope John Paul II encouraged bishops from North and South to think in terms of "America." Asked how he personally sees the idea of "America" unfolding in the Church, the Mexican-born, Carribean-raised Cardinal replied that he has observed impressive progress in annual meetings of the Inter-American Conference which he has attended from time to time since 1968: "The bishops are beginning to recognize the challenge to work together to see America as an entity. Debt relief, migration, and NAFTA are issues that brought us together, and we are planning a very significant meeting on globalization. It's very easy, however, to fall back into 'North' and 'South.' The Holy Father is far ahead of us."

Like Pope John Paul II, the Cardinal takes special delight in being with young men and women. Another prominent American Catholic leader, Mother Mary Quentin Sheridan (past president of the Council of Major Superiors of Women Religious), has observed Cardinal Law in a variety of settings over the years—from board meetings where he sits with business leaders and educators, to the Synod for America attended mainly by high-ranking prelates, to the World Youth Day in Rome in the summer of 2000. At the World Youth Day, Mother Mary Quentin recalls that the Cardinal began by singing with the audience of young people. "He went where they like to be," she says, "with a litany of invocations, calls and responses. They got into it, and then he spoke. He asked them to close their eyes for a few moments while he spoke of vocation and the world's needs, alluding to the threats to human dignity posed by contemporary culture."

Afterwards, in responding to questions, "he was able to become a child in his thinking—he uses every gift he's got to try to reach everybody. He never shuns a question, but leads the questioner. If someone disagrees, he is never contentious, but never compromises. He is a negotiator for God."

What has impressed her most in varied contexts, she says, is "his gift of being a message to whomever is present to him." To illustrate, she tells an anecdote that affords a revealing glimpse of the off-duty Cardinal. While in Rome, Cardinal Law often stayed in the apartment of his old friend Cardinal Baum, who was the Major Penitentiary of the Catholic Church. On one of these occasions, one of Mother Mary Quentin's sisters who works in the apartment was cleaning the floor after a disastrous plumbing mishap. She looked up to see the Boston prelate standing behind her. "May I have an apron?" he asked, as he cheerfully got down on his hands and knees to help mop up.

Cardinal Baum, who has also observed Bernard Law in many contexts, lauds his colleague's kindness and boyish exuberance. The Boston Cardinal, according to the Rome-based Baum, is liked and respected among the world's bishops for his intelligence, energy, and generosity. What stands out for Baum, above all, is Law's "absolute fidelity to Our Lord Jesus Christ and his capacity to proclaim His word with conviction, fervor and eloquence." Msgr. McInerny adds that Cardinal Law "is thoroughly a man of the Church. My impression is that from the time he was a little boy, he loved the Church, and for him that means the universal as well as the local Church. He can't separate the two because the two are inseparable."

Boston, however, is tough on its leaders, and Cardinal Law has not been an uncontroversial figure at his home base. He attracts deep loyalties, owing to his gift for making and nurturing friendships, and when he circulates among his flock it is plain that they enjoy being with him. But in some quarters, he has been castigated as too "soft"—as when he called for a temporary moratorium on clinic protests in the wake of shootings at two Brookline abortion facilities. And in some academic circles, he has been dubbed "Marshall" Law for his fidelity to the Magisterium. His ordinations of priests and deacons have been disrupted at times by angry feminists and homosexual activists.

Bernard Law has held fast, however, to the course he charted in Mississippi in the 1960s. In refusing to conform to the prejudices of the times, he has become a sign of contradiction in one of the most highly secularized cities in America. He has rejected the unspoken rule that would exclude religiously grounded moral viewpoints from the public square; he has challenged the smug relativism of the academic establishment, and he has opposed the fashionable notion that freedom requires independence from all external authority. And on a day like Mother's Day 2001, in a cathedral packed with Catholics of every race and nationality, one senses that rank-and-file Catholics are proud of their Cardinal for his counter-cultural stands. One senses that they are grateful for his encouragement to take pride in their common religious heritage. One senses that they are inspired by a leader who calls them to be the best that they can be. One senses that they admire the way he afflicts the comfortable and comforts the afflicted.

When asked about the memories, good and bad, that stand out most vividly from the Boston years, the Cardinal mentions the phenomenon of clergy sexual abuse as by far the most painful. Those close to him testify to the anguish he feels on behalf of the victims, and to his dismay at the wounds inflicted on the priesthood. He counts among his most treasured recollections his ordinations of priests, his pilgrimages with young people of the archdiocese to World Youth Days—and the outpouring of sympathy he received on the death of his mother in November 1991. Another unforgettable experience was his 1986 journey to Auschwitz where pilgrims from the Archdiocese were accompanied by members of the Jewish community including Holocaust survivor Sonya Weiss, and the late Lenny Zakim with whom the Cardinal had worked closely on Christian-Jewish relations.

As he looks to the future in his eighteenth year as Archbishop of Boston, the Cardinal is increasingly preoccupied with the problem of formation, especially of adults. That concern manifested itself with historic consequences in 1985 when the Cardinal, in the course of an address to an Extraordinary Synod of Bishops in Rome, suggested that the Church needed a fresh articulation of the faith in order to address contemporary minds. Dominican Father (now Cardinal) Christoph Schönborn of Vienna once observed to a Boston audience:

> I believe that Cardinal Law's argument first set out at the 1985 Synod of Bishops remains difficult to refute. "We have to teach faith," he said, "in a world that becomes more and more a global village." And he added, and now I quote from the original Latin text: "Juvenes Bostoniensis, Leningradiensis, et Sancti Jacobi in Chile induti sunt *Blue Jeans* et audiunt et saltant eandem musicam." While the Latin may fall short of Ciceronian standards, the basic point remains clear enough, and what is more important, many other bishops, especially from Africa, shared and still share Cardinal Law's vision.

The American Cardinal's recommendation was warmly received by the Synodal bishops, and the Holy Father responded by establishing the Commission that produced the Catechism of the Catholic Church and naming Bernard Law as a member. During seven years of work, according to Cardinal Baum who also served on that Commission, Cardinal Law's zest for the project never flagged. That service was, in Baum's view, "one of his greatest contributions to the Church." But before the ink was dry on that project, Cardinal Law had already directed his formidable energies to devising ways to implement adult formation—the next step in enabling Catholics to better fulfil the missionary vocation that every Christian receives in baptism.

The love of Church ignited in young Bernard Law by a mission priest in Charlotte Amalie has been a hallmark of his ministry from Mississippi in the 1960s to Boston at the turn of the century. He was just a newly ordained priest when the Fathers of Vatican II charted a course for bishops, but their words in *Lumen Gentium* must have been inspired by the hope that men like Bernard Law would emerge to lead the Church into the Third Millennium. "The duty of a bishop," the Council Fathers wrote, "is to promote and to safeguard the unity of faith and the discipline common to the whole Church, to instruct the faithful to love for the whole mystical body of Christ, especially for its poor and sorrowing members and for those who are suffering persecution for justice's sake, and finally to promote every activity that is of interest to the whole Church, especially that the faith may take increase and the light of full truth appear to all men." Bernard Cardinal Law seems not only to have taken his bearings from that instruction, but to have brought it to life with uncommon energy—gathering peoples, caring for souls, and preaching the Good News from the city on a hill.

I

ADVOCATE FOR THE COMMON GOOD

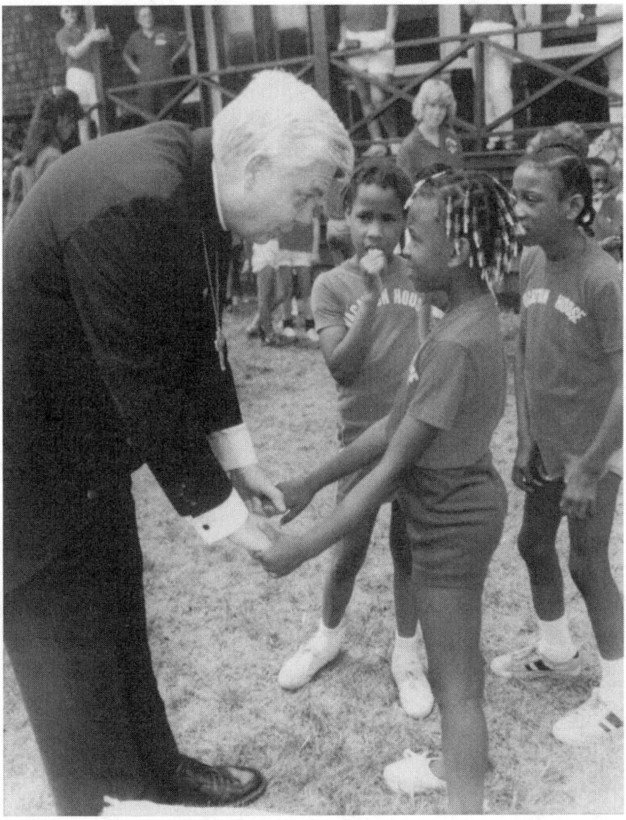

1

Religion in Our Civil Life

At Governor Ashcroft's Prayer Breakfast

Jefferson City, Missouri, 9 January 1992

Thank you so much, Governor Ashcroft, for the favor of your invitation to be with you this morning.

How faithful this prayer breakfast is to the genius and spirit of our nation. There are those who would rewrite the Constitution today—who would alter the meaning of its first amendment. Religion was not thought to be an alien element in our body politic by our nation's forebears. We proclaim God as the source of the unalienable rights of life, liberty and the pursuit of happiness. Our coins proclaim that "In God We Trust." Not only do governors pray, but so do legislators as they begin their labors. These examples could be multiple as illustrative of the way in which the reality of God is woven into the fabric of our civil life. We are a people who have, from our beginning as a nation, heard the Word of God as recorded in 2 Chronicles: "If my people who are called by my name humble themselves, and pray and seek my face, and turn from their wicked ways, then I will hear from heaven, and will forgive their sin and heal their land."

We hear that word today. We seek the face of God. We search out God's way together. We pray for the grace of conversion, of a change of heart, for there is never a time when we can presume to have exhausted the possibility of good, of love in our lives.

What a blessing it is to be here, together, public officials, business leaders, religious leaders to pray together, to seek the face of the Lord together, to ask God to heal our land.

There are those who would read what we do here today as something close to subversive—subversive of their false notion concerning the separation of Church and State. There are those who read the First Amendment as constructing an impenetrable wall of separation between religion and public life. In effect what they would do is precisely what the amendment was intended to protect against: inhibit the free practice of religion and establish an ersatz state religion of secularism.

What we do here today is an authentic reflection of our history and the American spirit, and I am glad to be here.

What is the function of religion in our civil life? It clearly must be more than a ceremonial presence, or else it would soon be rendered meaningless. The role of religion is, I think, the prophetic role. I am reminded of my Mississippi days and the comments attributed to a lay person who was upset by the pastor's sermons because—I suspect—they were too close to the mark. "The preacher," he said, "has done quit preaching and gone to meddling."

The prophetic role is, I think, to meddle. I am not infrequently accused, and erroneously, I would submit, of involving myself in politics when the only thing I'm doing is meddling. As a matter of fact, the preacher who doesn't meddle isn't worth his salt.

Paul says—"Let love be genuine; hate what is evil, hold to what is good." The prophetic voice echoes Paul's words and expresses that *evil* and that *good* in terms of our life together as a society. In doing that today, I am aided by the recent statement of the U.S. Bishops on the family and children.

That *evil* is one infant every second killed by abortion in our world—30 million world-wide, 1.6 *million* in our nation.

That *evil* is that one out of five children in this nation grows up poor. That *evil* is that our infant mortality rate is last among 20 western nations.

That *evil* is that our nation has the highest divorce rate, the highest teenage pregnancy rate, the highest child poverty rate, and the highest abortion rate in the western world.

That *evil* is that an estimated 5.5 million U.S. children under twelve are hungry, and another 6 million are underfed.

That *evil* is that the rate of teenage suicide has tripled in thirty years.

That *evil* is that more teenage boys die of gunshot wounds than from all natural causes combined.

That *evil* is that more than 25 percent of our teenagers nationwide drop out of school, and that SAT scores have declined 70 points since 1963.

That *evil* is that more than 8 million children are in families without health insurance. Here in Missouri, it is estimated that 600,000 persons are without access to health care because they lack health insurance and are not eligible for Medicaid. Many others are under-insured.

That *evil* is that mothers and children make up an increasing proportion of the homeless in our land.

Paul says—"Let love be genuine . . . hold fast to what is good." John says—"If anyone says he loves God, whom he does not see, and does not love his brother whom he does see, then that man is a liar." James says,

"Religion pure and undefiled before God is this, to care for orphans and widows in their affliction" (James 1:27).

We need to heed the words of Sirach: "To the fatherless be as a father, and help their mother as a husband would" (Sirach 4:10).

My sense is that the human heart responds to the plight of children. This Christmas in Boston, where we are experiencing a difficult economic climate, I was struck by the generosity of so many, especially to children.

The problem is that the poor are too often invisible. The problem is that children do not vote; they are not organized. The problem is that we have been focusing so much on the shortcomings of government programs that we have forgotten how essential government programs are if we are to fulfill our responsibilities as a society to the poor.

The good that I believe we must affirm is the right to life of every human person from the first moment of conception to the last moment of natural death. A peri-pregnancy caregiver program which will include the training and certifying of caregivers to assist women experiencing problems around the time of pregnancy so that they can choose continued life for their children would be a incalculable good.

The *good* to which we must hold fast is the child and the family. Our life as a society as well as our government programs must support marriage and family. The child suffers with the break-up of marriage and the breakdown of family.

The good we must affirm are sound and innovative programs which are supportive of the child and family, particularly the poor.

The good we must affirm are tax policies which are equitable, based on the ability to pay, and designed in such a way that families will receive some needed relief. Children do not have the value of livestock in our tax laws.

While it is essential to demand cost effective programs and to continually monitor their effectiveness, it is imperative—if we are to do good and avoid evil—that the poor are not made to pay the greater burden of an economic recession.

The *good* we must affirm is the right of our children to the best education possible. Critical to this is the acknowledgment that parents are the primary educators; society and government are to assist parents, and must not usurp the right of parents as educators. Parental choice should be empowered, not limited. The poor and middle income parent of elementary and high school–aged children should be aided through tuition tax credits or vouchers to make possible for them the kind of choices that rich parents have for their children.

The good we must affirm links education with real reforms, which include removal of bureaucratic overlayers, which stimulate competition for quality and outreach to children at risk.

The good we must affirm looks not only to our own land—but sees in every human person a sister, a brother, sees in every human person the Lord.

Because we who gather here believe in God and seek His face, because we, like those gathered with Solomon, want to turn from our evil ways, I am confident that God's word in Chronicles will be fulfilled in us: "I will hear from heaven, and will forgive their sin and heal their land."

2

+

On Compassion
Homily at Harvard's Memorial Church
23 February 1992

Be *compassionate,* as your Father is compassionate.

In God's self revelation, it is His *compassion* which makes it possible for us to enter into the mystery of Divine love, of God's life.

"Show us the Father and we shall be satisfied," Philip said to Jesus. The response of Jesus to Philip's question is critical to Christian faith: "He who has seen me has seen the Father." Christian faith proclaims with Peter that in Jesus we encounter the Messiah, the Son of God, the revelation of Divine love; we encounter the Father's compassion.

Compassion in its faith usage implies a desire, a will to be with another in his or her life; it implies a sharing in the joys and burdens of another's life. If we understand that God is the unmoved mover, pure being, Infinite Truth, and Beauty, and Good, the notion of the Father's compassion towards us depends on God's self-revelation. For without God's revelation, we could not understand the Father's compassion.

The creation account of *Genesis* unfolds the saving truth of the Father's compassion. The existence of all that is, is rooted in God's word—"Let there be." Our existence, our existence in a universe which sings to us of the goodness and beauty of God, proclaims to the person of faith the compassion of God. "Man and woman he made them," and so in the Garden where lived Adam and Eve we come to understand the compassion of the Father. The world was meant to be a paradise in which all moral choices would be made by man and woman in accordance with God's word.

God wills to be with us, but we can refuse to let Him into our lives. The compassion of the Father does not render us bereft of the ability to choose between good and evil. The choice of evil is the rejection of God, it is the refusal of the Father's compassion. Sin, in the powerful imagery of Genesis, is hiding from God. In His compassion God called out to Adam and Eve, but as a consequence of their refusal to follow God's word—God's life-giving word—they became fearful of God and they hid.

The tragedy of sin is nowhere more poignantly presented than in this image of the human heart rejecting Divine compassion. The consequences of sin are seen not only in alienation from God, but also in alienation from oneself and from one another.

A self-conscious shame resulted from the refusal of Adam and Eve to live in accordance with God's word. Cain was to kill his brother Abel. This fratricide is not simply the expression of a primitive humanity from which we have evolved—unfortunately what has evolved are the myriad ways in which Cain kills Abel again and again. We have not yet learned that we are brothers and sisters one to another, and that the Father's compassion is to be experienced by each of us. The ultimate word of sin is death, and in so many ways what we have come to is a culture of death.

The plan of a compassionate Father for us is a world in which Cain recognizes and loves his brother Abel. In place of the unity willed by God for us, our world reflects, in the words of Pope John Paul II, "the existence of many deep and painful divisions." A casual reading of today's newspapers bring so many to mind: Haiti, the Middle East, Ireland, the poor in our own community and throughout the world, refugees in growing numbers and diminishing hope, to mention but a few examples.

The good news which forms the disciples of the Lord is that those who have seen Him have seen the Father, have known the love of God, the Father's compassion. The Book of Wisdom beautifully foretells the Incarnation:

> When all things were in quiet stillness,
> and the night was in the midst of her course,
> Thy almighty word leapt down from Heaven,
> down from Thy Royal Throne.

John, in the Prologue to his Gospel, writes that:

"The Word became flesh, and dwelt among us."

The Word of God who is life, who is love, who is truth, who is compassion became flesh and dwelt among us. The ancient tradition of addressing Mary as Theotokos is no mystic flight from the Gospel account. It is rather the Council of Ephesus' recognition that the child she bore within her womb was indeed the Word of God incarnate.

Small wonder that from the early centuries of the Church there has arisen the tradition of seeing Mary as the Icon of the Church. Her fiat, her response to the Angel Gabriel: "Be it done to me according to thy Word," is the response of the Church, of every faithful disciple.

Jesus came that we might have life and have it more abundantly. It is our *yes* to Him, in our *yes* to God's revealed Truth that we have freedom and that we have life. The enduring promise of Jesus is that he does not leave us orphans. The compassion of the Father which he incarnates is present to us in Word and in the grace of sacraments. The compassion of the Father also touches the lives of others through us—through what we say and do.

The compassion of the Father is all that David did in mercifully sparing Saul's life and much more. The compassion of the Father finds its ultimate expression in Jesus' death upon the cross. In the scandalous words of Scripture he became sin for us. He bore the iniquities of us all. He suffered and died that we might have forgiveness for our sins and newness of life. He taught us that there is no greater love than to lay down one's life for a friend—and he made us all friends through the blood of His cross.

The compassion of the Father in the Genesis account of the Garden and in the ministry of Jesus clearly teaches us how we are to live our lives. Jesus did not present his teaching in tentative terms, as one option among many for eternal life. When he told his followers, "Unless you eat the flesh of the Son of Man and drink his blood, you shall not have life in you," most of those followers left him because of the difficulty of his saying. His reaction was not to moderate his teaching so that he might better accommodate it to the taste of his listeners. On the contrary. He looked at the few who remained with him and challenged them: "Will you too go away?" Peter responded—"Lord, to whom shall we go? You have the Word of everlasting life."

That word of everlasting life which Jesus gives us today . . .

"Love your enemies"

"Do good to those who hate you"

"Give to all who beg from you"

"Do to others what you would have them do to you"

That word is not an easy word to live. Like those who walked away from him almost two thousand years ago, we too so often say—"This is a hard saying."

What consolation there is for us in the Father's compassion revealed in Jesus. Recall the woman caught in the act of adultery who was brought before him. The Father's compassion touched the hearts of those who had brought the woman to him in the anger of a self-righteous mob. One by one they left when Jesus said, "Let him who is innocent cast the first stone." Finally, there was only the woman and Jesus. He looked at her and said, "does no one condemn thee, woman?" "No one," she answered. "Neither do I condemn thee," he responded. And then he added—"Go, and sin no more."

Our failures to live his life-giving word do not exhaust the Father's compassion. We, like the woman in John's account, can receive forgiveness for our sins, know the freedom that his truth brings, experience the more abundant life that Jesus won for us through the cross.

The Father's compassion bids us speak the truth in love; bids us to see and to love the Lord in others, particularly in the poor, the persecuted, the sick, the imprisoned, the refugee—and all those in any need. The Father's compassion bids us to recognize in ourselves beloved children, fashioned in the image of God, redeemed by the blood of Christ, and destined to live forever in the joy and peace of the heavenly Kingdom.

Be compassionate, as your Father is compassionate.

3

Statement on Political Responsibility

(With the Bishops of Massachusetts)

23 October 1992

On November 3rd, citizens of the United States go to the polls to choose our national and state leaders. Freedom, justice and peace in a democratic society depend on the active participation of its citizens. Every citizen of voting age has a moral obligation to exercise that franchise in an informed and responsible way.

Choosing leaders should involve more than party loyalty or personal preference. Informed voting means knowing the candidates, the positions they espouse and the proposals they offer for building a society in which life is affirmed, in which freedom is protected, and in which justice, based on the equal dignity of every human being, is pursued.

Citizens must examine the candidates and the issues not from a selfish personal perspective but from a commitment to the good of every person, the common good of city, state and nation and the ultimate good of all humankind. Such an outlook says "no" to abortion, to euthanasia, to violence, to injustice, and to those policies that are contrary to sound family life. Such an outlook says "yes" to life, from conception to natural death, to educational choices and reform, to accessible health care, especially for the poor, and to a responsible national economy. With the kind of leadership which builds a nation of sound character, good moral life, and just practices, our country will then be able to make its proper contribution to world peace and help build a better world for the generations to come.

A commitment to truth is incumbent on the candidates, on the media, and on all who have the task of bringing the issues to the people. On the part of the voting public, it is our duty to vote on November 3rd in an informed way. It is our personal responsibility to make our choices based on an appropriate vision of the person and society.

+Bernard Cardinal Law
Archbishop of Boston
+Most Rev. John Marshall
Bishop of Springfield
+Most Rev. Timothy Harrington
Bishop of Worcester
+Most Rev. Sean O'Malley, OSF
Bishop of Fall River

4

Violence Begets Violence

On the Murder of Dr. Gunn in Pensacola, Florida

24 March 1993

The bullets which rang out in Pensacola have wounded us all. There is no isolated violence. Violence begets violence. The murder of Dr. David Gunn is yet another proof of the culture of death which pervades our society.

The murder of Dr. Gunn was the decision of one man, the choice of one individual to take the life of another. The human solidarity to which we are destined and without which we all suffer is destroyed by such choices. The fabric of society is rent when the life of one is at the mercy of the choice of another.

The tragic irony is that this murder presumably was committed in support of the right to life of those unborn human beings threatened by abortion. Elective abortion, as millions of us are certain, is the deliberate choice of one individual to take the life of another. No semantic change, no judicial decree can alter the overwhelming evidence that there is an unbroken continuum, and undeniable unity of human life from the first moment of conception on.

Presumably the murderer of Dr. Gunn was convinced that his act would serve a higher good, namely, the saving of lives which would otherwise end in abortion. Such is also, presumably, the justification given by those who choose or defend abortion; some good is perceived as greater than the life of the unborn child. In either case, the end does not justify the means.

Abortion activists proclaim the righteousness of their cause on the basis of "right of choice" and the "right over one's body." To reduce abortion to the exercise of a "right over one's body" is to ignore the obvious but essential fact that it is no longer one but two, or probably more, bodies. Legal basis is found in a Supreme Court decision. Those of us who oppose abortion recognize that the legitimate choices of individuals should indeed be protected. We also recognize that men as well as women have limited rights over their own bodies. Such a right is not an absolute. When one individual's existence is threatened by the choice of another, however, or when one individual attempts to do critical harm to him- or herself, then freedom of choice or the right over one's body is appropriately limited by society.

The Supreme Court decision in support of the choice for abortion is a formidable obstacle to the right to life. It is a demonstrable fact, however, that decisions of the U.S. Supreme Court have been reversed. The clearest parallel to abortion is the Court's history on slavery. The Dred Scott decision in 1857 upheld the "right" of slavery. In effect, the United States Supreme Court declared that blacks were non-persons. Abolitionists recognized the terrible error of that decision, and eventually the Court corrected itself. One does not lightly question a decision of the Supreme Court. Supported by empirical evidence and the historic revulsion of western civilization to abortion, however, it is more than reasonable to assume that the Court was in error in Roe v. Wade.

For those of us who recognize the right to life of the unborn human being as an inalienable right which society is duty bound to respect, we must concentrate our efforts at supporting women threatened by pressures to choose abortion, and we must try more effectively to present our case to the public. The latter is not easy. Clearly the media is allied with, and, indeed, is leading the charge of the proponents of abortion. Furthermore, polls indicate that the entertainment world is overwhelmingly pro-abortion. Elected officials of both parties have increasingly found it convenient, or presumed it to be politically necessary, to support the right to choose abortion.

Those who support the right to life are often portrayed as right-wing bigots with a singular and exclusive concern for life before birth. The pro-life movement is not infrequently caricatured as a men's movement, although many more women belong to Women Affirming Life than to the National Organization of Women. At times the pro-life movement is likened to a fanatic religious cult.

The reality is that the pro-life cause cuts across the spectrum of belief and non-belief. While many in the movement find added reasons in faith for their position, the pro-life movement does not rely in the public debate on reasons drawn from faith in God or the dogmas of religion. The arguments brought forth in the public debate are drawn from empirical data, from constitutional theory, and from attention to the universal testimony of our history as a people until 1973.

Any thought that the pro-life movement can be lectured or intimidated into silence is a vain hope on the part of those who champion the right to choose abortion. Sooner or later, pro-abortionists will be forced to move beyond the arrogance of power into an open debate on the issue—a debate which must begin with an analysis of the clinical evidence which reveals the reality of abortion for what it really is: the destruction of human life. Once that debate occurs, it will follow as the day the night that the moral conscience of this nation will bring about a reversal in law.

Even then, however, something more is needed, as something more is needed now. What about the mother for whom the birth of her child poses serious problems, the woman caught in a web of poverty, fear, or loneliness? As it is, some in our society would now offer nothing more than the money to rid her of her child. Surely, a humane society can offer more than that. In spite of all that religious agencies and other groups attempt to provide in support of life, the state and much of society hold out only the option of abortion. What is needed is a more compassionate society, a culture of love in place of our culture of death. We need to surround such women with the love and support which makes life the clear option. We need to recognize, as a society, that in many instances adoption can be the best alternative for the child and the child's mother. We need to help young mothers through their pregnancy and beyond, to the point of adoption or to the point where mother and child together are able to face the future with hope. We need to affirm and support both the mother and the child. To do less is to place all life ultimately at risk.

The pro-life movement attempts to do this in many ways. Several weeks ago I met with a representative group of more than fourteen pro-life organizations, and I was profoundly moved by the one-on-one assistance provided to so many mothers and their children. It seems to me that what is needed most of all today from the pro-life movement is that which in fact constitutes the bulk of its efforts: assistance to pregnant women who otherwise are without the material means and human support to bring their children to birth.

What is also needed is prayer. Prayer is needed to maintain peace and compassion in the face of such an enormous evil as abortion. Since Roe v. Wade, twenty-five million abortions in this country have ended lives equal in number to one tenth of our population! Every life is sacred. The murder of one person is an abomination. Have we any idea of the enormity of evil and loss of human potential in twenty-five million abortions? We must pray for ourselves and for the nation.

We must also make the case for our position whenever we can, with clarity and with precision. We cannot assume that those who are pro-abortion have heard our arguments but have dismissed them. It is difficult to hear with the incessant mantra for abortion being chanted by politicians, media stars, newspapers, radio, and TV. The educational establishment, too, is caught up in the mantra. Doctors themselves are victims of this propaganda barrage; witness to this are those doctors who have come to see, in the face of the awful clinical reality, what abortion really is, and have become leaders in the pro-life movement.

In the final analysis, the challenge of the pro-life movement is to change hearts. While there is a legitimate role for political efforts, the real challenge is to bring about a shift in societal attitudes. This cannot be done by the manipulation of judicial and political power, as the proponents of abortion have sought to do. They have failed. Try as they might, they cannot and will not silence the pro-life movement. Power is all the proponents of absorption have on their side: their reasons cannot finally persuade human hearts.

Those who involve themselves in direct action through Operation Rescue constitute a minority in the pro-life movement. Little media attention has been given to the fact that over five million persons recently wrote to their senators and congressional representatives in opposition to FOCA. Thousands of persons in this Archdiocese are regularly involved in prayer and in providing material means for pregnant women needing assistance. Thousands of women belong to Women Affirming Life, which is only one organization of pro-life women.

Those who are pro-abortion often portray the pro-life movement as essentially the effort to block entry to abortion clinics. This is simply not true. At the same time, it does appear that our society has adopted a double standard for those engaged in such acts. Currently in Massachusetts, three participants in Operation Rescue are serving prison sentences. Two of these prisoners are priests. Father Thomas Carlton is serving a two and one-half year sentence at Billerica House of Correction. Father Francis Hagerty, S.J., is serving a one year sentence at the Barnstable House of Correction. Mr. Bill Cotter is into his second year of a two and one-half year sentence at the Worcester House of Correction. One wonders if there would not be public outcry and in-depth investigative reporting of these sentences were it not for the fact that it is politically incorrect to be pro-life.

Those who engage in prophetic acts in support of life, in an effort literally to rescue a child from abortion, have the necessary task of ensuring that their acts are without even the semblance of violence. Leaders and participants in Operation Rescue with whom I have had contact are totally committed to non-violence. While the pro-life movement certainly includes violent activists, the movement is not defined by them, and they remain a minority among the millions in support of the right to life.

A doctor shot dead. One and one-half million abortions each year in our nation. Surely, our society is capable of better than this. Please God, the tragic event in Pensacola will bring us to a self-examination about many things: the value of every human life, the role of physician in society, the evil of violence, the need for gun control, the necessity for a comprehensive response to the needs of pregnant women and their children. We can and we must do better.

5

Racial Discrimination Is a Sin

Remembering Mississippi's Hazel Brannon Smith

22 April 1994

The other night I caught the end of a TV movie based on the life of Hazel Brannon Smith, an uncommonly brave newspaper publisher-editor who was one of the few to tell it like it was in Mississippi in the sixties. She was a good friend, as was her husband, Smitty.

The few minutes of the movie's end brought back many memories of those years. When I was ordained a priest in 1961, Mississippi was a divided society. What made it particularly harsh was that it was a division confirmed by the laws of the state. Restaurants, hotels, mental hospitals, railroad stations, schools, water fountains, and buses were all segregated by the force of law.

When the tremors of change began to move through Mississippi and throughout the old Confederacy, resistance mounted. It took different forms. There was the old method of hooded hoodlums whose blasphemous use of the cross inspired fear. There were unholy alliances with those charged with keeping the peace, an alliance which took the lives of three civil rights workers in Philadelphia, Mississippi. There were bombings and burnings destined to keep things as they were. There were the more sophisticated methods of intimidation used by the White Citizens Councils. These last were particularly menacing to those who might otherwise have sympathized with the necessity to change legal segregation. A father would be warned that a young child would not be safe walking home from school, or a well orchestrated but private boycott would bring economic havoc to the business or profession of someone suspected of supporting integration.

My memories are not theoretical. I was at the wake of Medgar Evers. I saw the smoldering ruins of rural churches. I walked in solidarity with others to atone for the desecration of a synagogue. I felt dismay at the ability of a climate of fear to intimidate good people into silence and inaction. I knew, personally, the fear of the night.

There is another Mississippi, thank God, and thank the likes of Medgar Evers and Hazel Brannon Smith. There are four scenes which stand out in my memory as beacons of hope, as powerful reminders that change is possible.

- When President Kennedy was killed, a memorial Mass was celebrated at St. Peter's Cathedral in Jackson. The church was filled and the congregation was thoroughly integrated. Some in that Cathedral were experiencing integrated worship for the first time. Not too many blocks away, "ushers" were posted outside some other churches lest "trouble makers" attempt to enter. In the grief of the President's tragic death, there was comfort in the Catholic Church's witness to the fact that we are all God's children.
- The first major event in the newly de-segregated hotels of Jackson was the diocesan CYO convention.
- A moment ever vivid in my memory is the concert of Leontyne Price held in the Coliseum in Jackson. The Coliseum and the area around it had served as a temporary jail for freedom riders just a few years before. At that memorable concert, Leontyne Price, a native Mississippian, walked out on stage before an integrated audience of thousands of proud Mississippians. Before she could sing a note, this descendant of slaves received a prolonged, standing ovation.
- Finally, the inauguration of William Winter as governor. By that time I had left Mississippi to become a bishop in Missouri. The governor-elect invited me to be a part of his inauguration. Leontyne Price stayed at the Governor's Mansion and sang the National Anthem. Mississippi had come a long way.

All of this by way of background to the request of a Mississippi-based white supremacist group to peddle its warped ideas in South Boston. If the law demands that every idea, however destructive of the common good, has a right to be expressed, then let the venue for that propaganda be carefully determined, perhaps at City Hall Plaza at six in the morning. South Boston deserves a rest.

It should be perfectly clear to Catholics that racial discrimination is a sin. No Catholic may participate in good conscience in a group which supports the notion of white supremacy, of black supremacy, or of any other racist theory. It is not enough simply to ignore the purveyors of racism. History amply shows how insidious and destructive such notions can be.

Mississippi has moved from where it was in Jim Crow days. There is no need for Massachusetts to adopt Mississippi's discarded laws and customs.

6

✣

The Way Is Development

On the UN's Cairo Conference on Population and Development

Pittsburgh, Pennsylvania, 12 August 1994

As I trust you are aware, there will be a highly significant Conference in Cairo in September of this year. From 5 to 13 September, the United Nations Conference on Population and Development will be held in Egypt, and it will result in a Plan of Action which will be urged upon the nations of the world as they develop policy in these areas. This Cairo Conference is one of a series which began with the 1974 Conference in Bucharest to be followed by the 1984 Conference in Mexico City.

The Church is highly concerned about the Cairo Conference, and that concern is inspired by the Draft Document that has been prepared by those charged with preparing for that Conference.

The issue of concern is *not* the topic of the conference. Indeed—all too little is being done by the nations of the world in the area of development. Furthermore, population trends must be taken into account by the nations of the world. The draft document for this conference, however, does not inspire confidence that this important topic, population and development, will be adequately addressed.

As a matter of fact, in a document of 113 pages, only 7 are dedicated to the issues of development. For the other 106 pages, the issue is primarily population control. Are those who are alarmed at the way the Cairo Conference is being planned simply ignoring, like the ostrich with head in the sand, the fact of imminent world catastrophe from a population growth that is spiraling at an ever faster rate? The truth of the matter is that the rate of growth of the world's population has actually decreased over the past twenty years. Furthermore, it can be effectively argued that development of a nation is the most effective way of reaching a birth rate in the best interest of that nation. Granted the fact that in some areas of the world where the rate of population growth is arguably too high, the most effective way of dealing with that rate—fueled as it is by conditions of extreme poverty—is all but ignored in the planning document for Cairo: that *way* is development.

All of which has led some to suspect that the Cairo Conference is being fueled by ideologues who are minimally interested in development and more interested in a social revolution which flies under the banner of population control.

It is ironic that this Conference meets in Cairo during a year which the United Nations has proclaimed as the Year of the Family. The planning for the Cairo Conference has not exhibited a lively interest in the family. Quite the contrary. It employs ambiguous language about the family, and opts for a vision of society that puts the individual—in a destructive isolation—at center stage. Far from rooting the individual in the family, which is the natural ordering of human relationships, the family is effectively trivialized while the state is accorded an inordinate power over the most intimate of human relationships, and, indeed, over life itself.

What a stark contrast there is between the draft document for the Cairo Conference and the eloquent affirmation of the family contained in the Holy Father's Letter to Families. He states quite clearly:

"Among (the) many paths along which man walks, the family is the first and most important. It is a path common to all, yet one which is particular, unique and unrepeatable, just as every individual is unrepeatable; it is a path from which man cannot withdraw."

The wonderful challenge open to the nations of the world is to build a culture, a civilization of love. Instead, we appear to be mired in a culture of death.

The destructive agenda being pursued in the planning of the Cairo Conference has an active supporter in the United States. When the Cardinals of the Church met in extraordinary consistory in June, we were unanimous in decrying what appears to be a form of cultural imperialism on the part of the powerful and rich nations.

I would urge all here present, those of this country in which we meet or those of other countries, to mobilize an immediate response to the crisis the Cairo Conference poses. First—pray—and pray for the family which is at risk. Second—contact the President, Senators, and others in government. Voice your concern, and suggest a better approach.

The Pro-Life Committee of the NCCB on April 8 of this year issued a statement containing five principles reflective of the Church's thinking on population issues. These should be at the core of our discussion on the Cairo Conference. These are those principles:

1. Decisions regarding population issues must be based on the recognition of the human person.
2. Population policies must support marriage and family life.
3. Population policies and programs must be built on respect for human life.
4. Coercion of any kind, whether of nations, groups, or individual couples, is unacceptable.
5. Population policies must be viewed in proper relation to social and economic development.

We must build, in the words of a U.S. Bishops' Pastoral, "a new covenant between North and South, between rich nations and poor for sustainable global development."

There are efforts to marginalize those who hold our principles. The Boston Globe, in an unusually long editorial on the Cairo Conference, suggested that the Church should "get out of the way."

I urge you to show your resolve not to get out of the way, but to do all you can to let your voice be heard, in union with the Holy Father, in the cause of the family, of human solidarity, of a civilization of love.

Thank you.

7

✣

Overcome Evil with Good

Two Weeks in January 1995

A MATTER OF PRUDENTIAL JUDGMENT: RESPONSE TO ABORTION CLINIC VIOLENCE, 6 JANUARY 1995

We have lived these days in the dark shadow of violence. Our hearts are filled with heavy sorrow as we remember the events of last Friday. May the God of love and mercy bring those who were killed to that place where every tear will be wiped away, and may the compassionate Lord console all those who knew and loved these two young women.

Violence manifests itself early in human history with the story of Cain and Abel. Cain killed his brother, Abel, out of jealousy. When God inquired of Cain the whereabouts of Abel, he answered: "Am I my brother's keeper?"

The rhetorical question was really a repudiation of the counsel of the Prophet Isaiah: "Turn not your back on your own flesh." Cain's fratricide was rooted in that primordial violence, the original sin of our first parents' disobedience. Their willful rupture of their relationship with God set the course of a fallen human nature.

If we are to root ourselves effectively in the way of non-violence, it is essential to recognize that violence has its beginning in a turning from God and a turning from one's neighbor. That vision of human solidarity which flows from Christ's teaching is foreign to the violent heart. Jesus said that we would be known as His disciples by the love we show one another. His teaching is not restricted to a small community of beloved disciples but rather implies a solidarity embracing every human being from the first moment of conception until the last moment of natural death. He taught us that in serving the needs of others we serve Him.

Inspired by this message of universal love, St. Paul wrote in the Letter to the Romans: "Let love be genuine; hate what is evil, hold fast to what is good. . . . Repay no one evil for evil, but take thought for what is noble in the sight of all. . . . Never avenge yourself. . . . Do not be overcome by evil, but overcome evil with good" (Romans 12).

There are few persons who would claim that abortion is a moral good. For most persons who champion the right to an abortion, it is seen as the only way out of a painful and difficult situation. While this is an unacceptable view for those of us who hold all human life as sacred, it does present the possibility of some common action among persons who are not agreed on the question of life.

If abortion is seen by a pregnant woman as the only way out of a difficult situation, then do we not have a responsibility to present alternatives to abortion to that woman and the child she carries?

Is this the only thing society can say to such a woman: "We will help you have an abortion"? Surely we can do better than that. Adoption should be presented as the positive alternative which it is. Existing residential programs for unmarried pregnant women should be more widely known and celebrated. Governmental programs and tax policies should be reviewed as to their impact on unmarried and married mothers and their children. The media could be of inestimable value in helping present realistic and holistic alternatives to abortion.

In calling for a moratorium on pro-life demonstrations outside of abortion clinics, I do not imply that such demonstrations are poorly motivated or that they are not peaceful or that they are illegal. It is, for me, a matter of prudential judgment. Prudence sometimes calls one to refrain from something that is good in itself. That is the case here. I have in mind peaceful, prayerful, legal demonstrations. Any demonstration characterized by violence would, of its very nature, be out of order.

My motive in asking for this moratorium is to avoid, on the side of the pro-life movement, anything which might engender anger or some other form of violence. The pro-life message cannot be heard in the midst of violence, whether that violence be in thought, word, or deed. We need to focus calmly and prayerfully on the pregnant woman and the child she bears. In this calm, perhaps our society will hear more clearly the words of Isaiah: "Turn not your back on your own flesh."

Within the next several weeks I will designate a church in each of the five regions of the Archdiocese where there will be scheduled times of prayer before the Blessed Sacrament for pregnant women and the children they bear. Hopefully, those who have engaged in prayer before abortion clinics will accept this as an appropriate way to heed the advice of St. Paul:

"Rejoice in your hope, be patient in tribulation, be constant in prayer" (Romans 12).

These have been most difficult days in which we have seen the tragic complexity of evil. May we not lose heart as we seek to affirm life and reject all forms of violence.

Bernard Cardinal Law

FURTHER CLARIFICATION IS IN ORDER, 13 JANUARY 1995

Last Monday the first reading at Mass provided me great encouragement in reviewing my appeal for a moratorium on pro-life demonstrations and prayer vigils before abortion clinics. We read that day from Isaiah:

> Here is my servant whom I uphold,
> my chosen one with whom I am pleased,
> Upon whom I have put my spirit;
> he shall bring forth justice to the nations,
> Not crying out, not shouting,
> not making his voice heard in the street.

These stirring words find their fulfillment in Jesus, upon whom the Holy Spirit descended and of whom God the Father said: "You are my beloved Son. On you my favor rests."

In all we do, we seek to be His disciples. We pray that Isaiah's words, fulfilled in Him, will be reflected in our poor efforts as we seek to establish justice on the earth: "A bruised reed he shall not break, and a smoldering wick he shall not quench."

There has been an incredible amount of attention given my statement and last week's column. Some of that comment failed to reflect adequately my thought. Perhaps some further clarification is in order.

The moratorium is suggested to permit a conversation to begin. In the volatile atmosphere of December 30 when first I made my suggestion, it seemed clear to me that any action which might exacerbate tension should be avoided on the part of those of us who are pro-life. On the side of those who support abortion, I asked that they refrain from universalizing blame for the act of one individual. Yesterday, a local official of Planned Parenthood asked that those favoring the choice of abortion refrain from protests in front of clinics. This is a good sign.

In the past week, it has become abundantly more clear to me that there has been no substantive conversation between those of us who are pro-life and society as a whole, at least not in Boston, during the past decade. Routinely, the pro-life message has been either ignored or caricatured. A not-too-thinly-veiled anti-religious and, at times, anti-Catholic rhetoric has fueled the public discussion. The price of admission for entry into the public debate all too routinely has been acceptance in advance of abortion. An advertisement of Planned Parenthood in the January 5 issue of the New York Times is an example of anti-Catholicism and inflammatory rhetoric. I call on the print and electronic media to assure a full and impartial coverage of the pro-life position.

Beyond, then, the desire to calm an emotionally charged atmosphere, my reasons for a moratorium include the hope of establishing a climate in which a conversation can begin among persons not accustomed to speaking to and hearing one another on this issue. That conversation has a very specific purpose: to unite in support of alternatives to abortion for those pregnant women who are considering an abortion.

It should go without saying that this does not imply a change in my judgment about abortion. Any and every abortion is, by definition, the taking of an innocent human life, and this is never permissible. When I first preached as Archbishop of Boston in March of 1984, I said that abortion is the primordial evil of our time. Surely no one fails to see the tragedy of fifteen million abortions in this country during the last decade. Every abortion is also a profound tragedy for the mother.

The conversation which I believe a moratorium makes possible is not about facilitating more abortions. Quite the contrary, it is about providing women in tragic circumstances with alternatives to abortion which are compassionate, loving, and realistic. I believe this conversation is possible because most women and men in our society would prefer the choice of life over abortion.

There obviously is a need also to engage the pro-life issue more fundamentally. There are ways in which this can and should be done. The full array of means provided by a democracy for the development and change of public policy should be used by the pro-life movement. We have done so and will continue to do so.

For those of us who are Catholic, the pro-life position, so clear in terms of science, philosophy, and the fundamental rights enshrined in the Declaration of Independence, becomes ever so much clearer in the light of the Church's teaching. Any suggestion that there is ambiguity in the Church's pro-life teaching or division among the bishops on this issue is patently false.

How best is the pro-life vision advanced? The Church has a proud record of social service which embraces all in need. It has been my privilege as Archbishop of Boston to participate in the development of programs for persons living with AIDS, to enhance our programs which have assisted tens of thousands of pregnant women, and to have established a Fund for the Unborn which has assisted two thousand women and their children in the past ten years. Many parishes and the St. Vincent de Paul Society extend themselves in a loving and personal way to make possible the choice of life. There is no better way to communicate the pro-life message than to reach out in love to those who are alone in their need.

Prayer is essential in all we do. Starting on Saturday, February 4, and continuing every Saturday thereafter, there will be five churches designated in the Archdiocese for special prayer for life, particularly for pregnant women and their children. The time of prayer will be from 8:30 A.M. until 2:45 P.M. It is the inherent power of prayer, not where we pray, that is important. On Sunday evening, January 29, I invite you to join me in prayer at Immaculate Conception Parish, East Weymouth. Mass will celebrated at 7:00 P.M.

To those who have participated in peaceful prayer vigils outside of abortion clinics in an effort to support the right to life, I want to give the assurance that the call for a moratorium does not deny my admiration for your commitment to life. It is, rather, an urgent suggestion that the message you proclaim may be heard more effectively if expressed in another way. I do not ask that less be done in the cause of life. I ask that much more be done, but in other ways. In no way do I suggest that such vigils are illegal, nor do I believe they should be legislated against. All I ask is that my prudential judgment concerning a moratorium be thoughtfully considered. I am most grateful to all who have done so. May this sign of good will lead to a new level of public discourse.

My meeting on Wednesday with Governor Weld was a significant conversation showing how persons who differ on the issue of life can be in agreement on seeking alternatives to abortion. I am hopeful that progress will be made as the points we discussed are pursued.

Bernard Cardinal Law

CONFRONTING A CULTURE OF VIOLENCE: STATEMENT BY THE BISHOPS OF THE BOSTON PROVINCE, 15 JANUARY 1995

As the twenty-second anniversary of Roe v. Wade approaches, we wish to reiterate the Church's constant and unchangeable opposition to any and every abortion as the direct taking of innocent human life. We continue to be committed to working to protect the dignity of every human life. We joined our brother bishops of the United States in a pastoral statement issued last November, entitled "Confronting a Culture of Violence." In that document we stated that "for our part, we oppose both the violence of abortion and the use of violence to oppose abortion."

It is our prudential judgment that at this time a moratorium on public demonstrations and prayer vigils before abortion clinics is in order. This does not imply a negative judgment about the integrity of intention of those who have demonstrated before clinics, nor is it intended to limit the right of every American to free assembly and free speech. We hope that this moratorium might create an atmosphere in which civil discourse between those who oppose abortion and those who favor it might be encouraged to the benefit of women, their children, and our society as a whole.

Surely few, if any, Americans see abortion as a moral good. A common search for alternatives to abortion would be a positive force for good in our society.

We commit ourselves and our dioceses to make ourselves available to join with persons of good will, whatever their personal convictions on these matters, in providing realistic and compassionate alternatives to abortion. We call on others to join us in this new venture.

May Mary, through her powerful intercession, obtain for us the grace to see more clearly the face of her Divine Son in every man, woman, and child and thus learn to love the Lord in all our brothers and sisters.

Bernard Cardinal Law
Archbishop of Boston

Most Rev. Kenneth Angell
Bishop of Burlington

Most Rev. Sean O'Malley OFM, Cap.
Bishop of Fall River

Most Rev. Leo O'Neil
Bishop of Manchester

Most Rev. John Elya
Melkite Bishop of Newton

Most Rev. Joseph Gerry OSB
Bishop of Portland

Most Rev. Thomas Dupre
Administrator, Diocese of Springfield

Most Rev. Daniel Reilly
Bishop of Worcester

8

✢

A Brilliant Synthesis

On Pope John Paul II's *The Gospel of Life* 30 March 1995

Today the Holy Father has made public an Encyclical Letter on the value and inviolability of human life. By custom, this Encyclical Letter will be known by its first two words in the Latin text: *Evangelium Vitae* (the Gospel of Life). This title breathes the confidence of the message and the messenger.

In the face of what the Holy Father has come to call the culture of death, this encyclical is a confident affirmation about the dignity and inviolability of every human person from the first moment of conception until the moment of natural death. In this letter, human life at all its stages is presented as a gift from God, and every human being is acknowledged as reflecting the presence of God in the world.

In the opening chapter, the Holy Father echoes the Church's abiding concern for every human being on the earth, particularly those who suffer. In a particularly moving section of the encyclical, the Holy Father reflects on our times in the light of God's discourse with Cain in the book of Genesis. God questioned Cain, after he killed his brother Abel. The Holy Father says: "The Lord's question: 'What have you done?' which Cain cannot escape, is addressed also to the people of today, to make them realize the extent and gravity of the attacks against life which continue to mark human history; to make them discover what causes these attacks and feeds them; and to make them ponder seriously the consequences which derive from these attacks for the existence of individuals and peoples.

"Some threats come from nature itself but they are made worse by culpable indifference and negligence of those who could in some cases remedy them. Others are the result of situations of violence, hatred, and conflicting interests, which lead people to attack others through murder, war, slaughter, and genocide.

"And how can we fail to consider the violence against life done to millions of human beings, especially children, who are forced into poverty, malnutrition, and hunger because of an unjust distribution of resources between peoples and between social classes? And what of the violence inherent not only in wars as such but in the scandalous arms trade, which spawns the many armed conflicts which stain our world with blood? What of the spreading of death caused by reckless tampering with the world's ecological balance, by the criminal spread of drugs, or by the promotion of certain kinds of sexual activity which, besides being morally unacceptable, also involve grave risks to life? It is impossible to catalog completely the vast array of threats to human life, so many are the forms, whether explicit or hidden, in which they appear today!"

Clearly, it would be impossible for anyone to read this encyclical of the Holy Father and come away with the notion that the Church has a narrow focus when she discusses the issue of life.

Not only does the Holy Father underscore the elements in the culture of death, but he addresses the philosophical roots which undergird this culture. While the encyclical is addressed in the first place to the household of the faith, its pertinence is by no means limited to the Church. The culture of death is a threat to all of us.

The Holy Father's focus on culture is of particular importance in understanding this encyclical. Dominant patterns of contemporary thought, the direction of political theory, and the analysis of contemporary ethical thought underscore the fact that the individual is often the victim of the culture of death. The Holy Father manifests exquisite sensitivity, for example, to women facing the possibility or the reality of abortion. While the teaching of this encyclical is unmistakably clear on the unacceptability of procured abortion under any circumstances, it is nonetheless replete with compassion and with the offer of reconciliation for those who have been responsible for such acts.

I found this encyclical particularly helpful in terms of current discussions on public policy and the situation which we face in this country. It is helpful to have a very clear and authoritative restatement of the Church's opposition to abortion and euthanasia. Here in Massachusetts and elsewhere there is a fascination with capital punishment. This encyclical, like the *Catechism of the Catholic Church* before it, points out clearly that instances where this might be justified are rare indeed.

Those who serve us in political office will find particularly helpful the Holy Father's teaching about the moral responsibility of public officials. Not only does the Holy Father reject the notion that one can be personally opposed but politically supportive of abortion, he also indicates how such a false moral dichotomy undermines the very notion of a democratic society.

The encyclical could not be more timely for us in the Commonwealth of Massachusetts as we deal with the unbelievable assault on human life which is present in the legislature's consideration of physician-assisted suicide. Finally, the public discussion on welfare reform which has gone on at the state and national level will find in the encyclical a rich contribution of thought reminding us that we are, indeed, responsible for one another, particularly for the poor and the most vulnerable.

While the Holy Father portrays very accurately the many dimensions of the culture of death which pervade our society, he nonetheless speaks in a hope born of his faith in God and in a recognition of the many signs that are present of a culture of love which is nourished by the Gospel of life.

In 1991 the Holy Father called an extraordinary Consistory of Cardinals. It was at that consistory that the Cardinals requested of the Holy Father an encyclical on the issue of life. After having consulted the bishops of the world for their input, the Holy Father has now issued this encyclical, the Gospel of Life, as a service to us all.

I commend it to the careful reading and study of all in the Archdiocese, particularly those who are charged with the ministry of teaching. I intend to send copies of the encyclical to my brothers and sisters in leadership positions in other churches, ecclesial communities, and religious bodies. This encyclical serves us as a brilliant synthesis of the Church's teaching on life at a time when the world's greatest threat is a systematic disregard for the sanctity of human life. In so many ways, the sad and tragic rejection of human solidarity captured in Cain's response to God is echoed in our laws, in our institutions, in our political rhetoric, and in our personal choices: "Am I my brother's keeper?" A society that lives as though it is not is a society immersed in a culture of death. It is against this reality that the Holy Father proclaims a Gospel of Life.

9

+

Very Much a Family Event

On Independence Day

30 June 1995

The fact of our nation's existence becomes ever more amazing as we grow older. Those who were responsible for fashioning the independence of the thirteen original colonies could hardly have foreseen what this nation would become. The sheer geographic vastness coupled with the diversities of culture, race, language, and religion might easily have swayed them from their task had they been able to foresee what was ahead.

When we gather this fourth of July weekend to relax with family and friends, it is appropriate that we give thinks to Almighty God for the blessing which is ours in this nation.

This is not to say that all is well in the land. After all, anything short of God is capable of greater perfection. It is an appropriate time, however, to focus on those undergirding principles which insure the greatness of that unfinished experiment which is this nation.

We proclaim ourselves to be one nation under God. It is so important for our future that we not lose sight of the fact that this nation does indeed rest upon a belief in God as the source of inalienable rights.

To proclaim ourselves to be "one" nation is to affirm an amazing achievement. Where else in the world does there exist such a rich diversity of peoples living in relative tranquility and order? This is not to deny the persistent presence of the degrading poverty nor to close one's eyes to the rate of crime, the many forms of violence, the corruption and discrimination which are all too present. At our best, however, we have the means to cope with our shortcomings and failures.

On July 5 there will be time enough to engage in active public debate on a variety of issues on which there is strong difference among us as a people. On the Fourth of July, however, our focus should be on gratitude to God for what has been achieved toward the fulfillment of a dream now over two hundred years old. It is a dream rooted in the conviction that every human being counts, that every human being is endowed with inalienable rights of life, liberty, and the pursuit of happiness.

Our greatness as a nation has come when our laws and policies have been in pursuit of that innate dignity of every human being. Our times of disgrace have come when the individual has been sacrificed to greed or discrimination or some other dehumanizing force.

It is not by accident that our Fourth of July celebration is very much of a family event. The individual cannot be truly honored and respected apart from the family. The fundamental unit of any society including our own is the family. To ignore or to deny this is to rend the fabric of society.

May God bless this nation with a heightened sense of its promise. May God mend our every flaw and help us to be ever more clearly, "one" nation under God.

In other places in the world differences are expressed through the violent acts of terrorism and war. In this nation, our strength is revealed when we deal with our differences in civil discourse. May God grant us the wisdom to handle our differences while yet recognizing that we are, indeed, "one" nation.

10

✢

He Transformed a Racetrack into a Cathedral

On Pope John Paul II's 1995 Visit to the United States

13 October 1995

Being with the Holy Father during this past week was like a spiritual retreat. It would be difficult to imagine how his visit to the United States could have been improved upon.

From the moment that he stepped out of his Alitalia jet at the Newark Airport, and descended down the steps unaided by the cane which was a necessity for him until a short time ago, he captivated the hearts of all who came in contact with him.

Several impressions stand out for me from that visit. First there is his indomitable strength and energy. His schedule was a grueling one even for those of us who simply were present. His was the task to be present to all those around him: those immediately before him, the thousands gathered for worship with him, and the millions joined with him by means of television and radio. He never appeared to lack the energy necessary to make personal contact with everyone.

Supporting this indomitable energy is a rich life of prayer. When he knelt for nearly an hour during the recitation of the rosary at Saint Patrick's Cathedral, I was not very far from him. There was no doubt that he was totally absorbed in prayer. In those moments he was present to God in a profound way.

During the day of his visit to the United Nations, which included the celebration of Mass with thousands of persons in the evening, the Holy Father offered Mass privately very early in the morning.

This quiet prelude in prayer before the start of his schedule reveals the source of his energy.

The Holy Father's ability to communicate transcends age, race, nationality, gender, and religion. He was among us as a man of God with an evident love in his heart for every human being on the face of this earth, and with a profound hope for our future if we but recognize more clearly our own dignity as human beings and the demands of human solidarity. It was this message which he brought so eloquently before the United Nations. He not only spoke affirmingly about the role of the United Nations in our world, but he challenged the United Nations as well to elaborate a declaration on the rights of nations to parallel the declaration on human rights. The events in recent years indicate clearly the necessity for such a focus on the part of the United Nations.

His interaction with the Church in the United States reflected a profound appreciation for us as a people of faith. Again and again he drew attention to the accomplishments of the Church in the United States, particularly in the area of education, social welfare, and health care.

The Holy Father's admiration for our nation and its foundational principles was abundantly evident in his remarks. He called to our mind the inherent greatness in the ongoing experiment of democracy which is the United States of America. He inspired us not to lose heart in those foundational principles, and he urged upon us the importance of leadership in the cause of freedom and the respect of every human being.

Specifically, the Holy Father reminded us as a nation that we will not fulfill our destiny unless we give room in the public debate for those principles which are rooted in the human heart and which are illumined by religious faith. The Holy Father has reminded the Catholic Church in the United States, and indeed, he has reminded all religious bodies of their obligation to be actively engaged in public policy debates.

Most powerfully, the Holy Father's visit reminds us of the importance of the good news of salvation which is celebrated in Word and sacrament. He transformed a racetrack, a football stadium, a baseball stadium, and an outdoor meadow into cathedrals. How beautifully he reminded us, as did his predecessor, St. Peter, that the Church is a temple built of living stones, which we are, with Jesus Christ as the cornerstone.

Please God, we will all be strengthened in our faith by his visit, and encouraged to live our lives in love for everyone, particularly those most in need.

John Paul II, we do indeed love you.

11

Marriage Not Just Another "Life-Style"

On a Domestic Partnership Bill

14 March 1996

Last night's action of the Boston City Council in extending certain benefits to "domestic partners" is both poorly reasoned and harmful to the common good. It is shocking that, reportedly, some councillors who voted for this wrong-headed proposal did not even realize what they were doing! The only hope now is that Mayor Menino will refuse to sign the measure.

Proposals to treat "domestic partners" like married couples for purposes of employment-related and other benefits overlook the basic reason why society has traditionally used marriage as a touchstone for according special benefits and exemptions.

That reason remains as compelling today as when the state first began to accord special treatment to married couples. Society has a special interest in the protection, care, and upbringing of children. Because marriage remains the principal, and the best, framework for the nurture, education, and socialization of children, the state has a special interest in marriage. The state and society do not have a comparable interest in how adults in general organize their lives.

At the present time, moreover, the economic circumstances of child-raising households are deteriorating. Married couples with children are working harder and harder just to make ends meet. Single parent households are in dire distress. Government surely has a constructive role to play in assisting child-raising households, and creative new thinking on how to fulfill that role is urgently needed. Meanwhile, the last thing child-raising families need to hear from the government is that marriage is just another "life-style" of no more or less interest to the state than other ways in which adults organize their households.

Underlying the special treatment of marriage is the recognition that married couples who raise their children well are not just doing something for themselves and their own children, but are rendering a priceless service to the common good. That service merits recognition and reward, and more than justifies the benefits and exemptions that have traditionally been reserved to married people.

I would urge all who reject the City Council's action to communicate their opinion to Mayor Menino and to urge him to veto the measure.

12

✢

A Step Closer to Barbarism

A Letter to President Clinton after His Veto of the Partial-Birth Abortion Ban Act

22 April 1996

The Honorable William J. Clinton
President of the United States
The White House
1600 Pennsylvania Avenue
Washington, D.C. 20500

Dear President Clinton:

We are writing to express our shock and disappointment over your decision to veto H.R. 1833, the Partial-Birth Abortion Ban Act.

This action was indefensible because it completely ignored the obvious inhumanity of the partial-birth procedure, the moral convictions of most Americans and the clear will of Congress. In no way does partially delivering late-term children alive and then stabbing them in the back of the head with scissors represent any kind of medical advance. Your decision to support the continued use of such a brutal procedure brings our society a step closer to barbarism.

At three congressional hearings on this issue, women who said they had undergone a partial-birth abortion and physicians who favor it were invited to testify and answer questions about the need for such a procedure. This fair and open process confirmed that the violent "partial-birth" procedure has no medically accepted use, causes unimaginable pain to children on the verge of being born, and poses serious health risks to women. The twelve physicians on the American Medical Association's Council on Legislation voted unanimously to endorse a ban on partial-birth abortions after reviewing the medical evidence.

In this context, the use of several women brought forward by the abortion lobby to win sympathy for your veto decision was an irresponsible act of political theater. Especially appalling was your suggestion that such abortions are somehow a positive good for families and society, because some of the children killed with this technique had severe illnesses or handicaps. Surely, this is the opposite of the message that our highest public official should be sending to the parents of children with disabilities.

In short, Mr. President, we see this veto ceremony as the low point of your presidency. We fear it is also the harbinger of even worse things to come, as our society accustoms itself to viewing death as a solution to individual and family problems. We and the other bishops of the United States will do everything we can to urge an override of your veto, so that some modicum of respect for defenseless human life is reflected in our nation's laws.

Sincerely yours,

His Eminence, Bernard Cardinal Law
Archbishop of Boston

Most Reverend Kenneth A. Angell
Bishop of Burlington

Most Reverend Daniel A. Reilly
Bishop of Worcester

Most Reverend Leo E. O'Neil
Bishop of Manchester

Most Reverend John A. Elya
Melkite Diocese of Newton

Most Rev. Sean O'Malley, OFM, Cap.
Bishop of Fall River

Most Rev. Joseph Gerry, OSB
Bishop of Portland

Most Reverend Thomas L. Dupre
Bishop of Springfield

13

✣

On Women, Celibacy, Marriage

Viewpoint, the *Boston Sunday Globe*

14 July 1996

On Wednesday, Cardinal Bernard Law talked with editors and reporters at the Globe about a variety of topics. His comments on the vulnerabilities of capitalism got the most attention, but for many people, his reflections on the role of women in the Roman Catholic Church, priestly celibacy and marriage are equally important. Here is an edited text of his comments on those topics.

INTERVIEWER asks Cardinal Law about surveys that suggest many Catholics want the church to ordain women and allow priests to marry.

CARDINAL LAW: Usually the role of women is reduced to the question of the ordination of women to the priesthood. If you would be willing to simply . . . set that aside, for just a moment, as an issue which can be discussed on its own merits and say: Where does the church stand on the role of women?

I would say the church stands for the role of women in the advancement against tremendous inequities that women suffer and have suffered today. In terms of inequity of pay for the same work. In terms of family-friendly legislation which puts a value . . . on the woman who makes the decision that she would like to be at home for a period of time with the children: our legislation doesn't really support that decision and encourage it as far as tax policies go. . . .

The church should be in the vanguard of the promotion of women's rights and women's place in society and women's place in the church and society as a whole. The question—it's a narrow question—of ordination is something that we approach in terms of an understanding of what the sacrament is and how the Lord is the founder of the sacrament. . . .

One can—some do—dispute that line of reasoning, but what I don't think can be disputed is the fact that our position on the ordination does not express a sense of fundamental inferiority. It has all to do with imaging Jesus Christ, who was a male. . . . Now, the issue . . . has created some dissent, and I think a tremendous amount of misunderstanding. . . . If you reduce the issue of the church's position on the role of women to the ordination question and then assume that the church is really not an ally in the promotion of women's rights. I think a terrible resource has been lost and a false battle is engaged.

What is the new feminist? Women themselves discuss that, and I think men have a legitimate ability to discuss it as well. I think it would be very demeaning to assume that all women have a very clear notion of what it means to be a true feminist. Some that I know even don't like the term.

[To say] that the church is not interested in the promotion of the role of women in society and the church, I just deny. But we have not always done, and are not now doing, all that we might to enhance that role. I would accept [that], and say we need to do a better job. . . .

[But to presume that] because of our position on the ordination of women, that there is somehow a second status, inferiority of women, I deny that. . . .

INTERVIEWER asks if the church could reverse itself and allow the ordination of women.

CARDINAL LAW: You can't. You have to understand that that is like saying to me, will the church change its view on the fact that there are two natures in one person. That's not going to change. That isn't something over which the church has control.

. . . Ordination is a matter of the sacraments for us, a divine institution and we don't have the ability to change that. . . . This isn't a new question. There were hereticals since early in the church's life who thought that it was all right to ordain women. . . .

So it's not a question of do I think it can or can't. Obviously, to me, it's a divine institution and it can't be changed.

[Referring back to an earlier topic:] Do I think celibacy could be changed? It can be changed. Do I personally think that it should be changed? No, I don't think so.

INTERVIEWER asks if the requirement that priests be celibate makes sense given the shortage of priests.

CARDINAL LAW: A shortage of priests is again a relative thing. . . .

Will the Holy Father make a decision on this that would open up the possibility of married clergy . . . ? I don't think he would. . . . Certainly, I would accept that decision, but I don't see that in the churches over which I've had pastoral responsibility as a need or as a solution. I have not engaged myself in the kind of in-depth discussion on that issue with bishops of other continents. And I think it would have to be approached that way.

In our society today I believe that what is more important is a calling of clergy and everyone else to holiness of life. And if we live out our commitment fully and unambiguously, I think that [celibacy] could be a very important sign in our society to married people, and to other people. So, I see it as an important sign of value, particularly in our society.

The important thing for us is to live it faithfully and well.

It's always an awesome thing for me to meet [with the deacons] the night before . . . their ordination—as deacons they pledge themselves to lifelong celibacy—and to point out to them that you become celibate only authentically so, only with a very keen sense of a sacrifice that you're making. . . . You're sacrificing one of the greatest blessings on this Earth, which is the blessing of a partner, in marriage, a life and a family of your own. But you're not making this offering, this sacrifice, without love. You're making it in order to be able to love in a very full and unique way those whom you're going to serve.

And unless it's that [kind of sacrifice] it can degenerate into a selfish bachelorhood, which isn't celibacy at all. You can, you know, be biologically celibate, but really not live the gift that that should be in terms of service and yet, it can be lived so beautifully.

Yesterday, I was at St. Patrick's in New York for the funeral of two of Mother Teresa of Calcutta's nuns, sisters who were killed in an automobile accident while driving from Washington, D.C., to Kentucky. And these two had been in Boston just a week before their death and I visited with them and one was a regional superior . . . and these women, both of whom were very highly talented women, gave themselves to what from a human point of view, earthly point of view, is not an easy life. I mean, they've got two salaries, and that's what they have, the Bible and something else and at a moment's notice they might go from Romania to Hong Kong. And yet there is a value to the witness to these women's lives. They speak to us of the value of giving yourself without reserve to the poorest of the poor. And they do that, and they do that with an authenticity; well, celibate clergy should do that.

Do we do it well enough? Well, I'm not going to speak for others, I'm going to speak for myself. No, I don't. No, I need to live that gift more generously, and that's hopefully in prayer, introspection, I can find ways to be more responsive to this tremendous invitation of service that is present in my life through celibacy. But I think that's a valued gift in our society.

I've often puzzled on how Mother Teresa herself so powerfully influences people; even people who may disagree with some of the things she says still cannot help but be moved by the fact that here is someone who genuinely loves and gives herself in love to all. And wants to be available. And I think that's a great thing, that's a great gift in our society.

We need those signs, not to say that married people can't give those signs but . . . obviously a marriage, if it's going to succeed, is going to demand a lot of time given to one another and to one's immediate family, and if marriages are marked by undue intrusion of call and commitment outside the bond, ultimately that bond isn't going to be able to sustain itself. For at best there are going to be two people who have grown strangers to one another, deciding for whatever reason that they will stay together.

You really have to work at making that bond work. That involves time and that needs to be encouraged.

14

✣

The Risk of Solidarity

The Twenty-Ninth Pope John XXIII Lecture

Catholic University of America Law School, Washington, D.C., 20 March 1997

It might be helpful if I acknowledge at the beginning that this presentation is not scholarly, at least in the academic sense. It is not buttressed by research nor is it carefully footnoted. My principal source, more often than not, is an overworked aperceptive mass. These words of St. Patrick from his *Confession* have brought me particular consolation as I searched for a way to begin this presentation. Speaking of his ministry in Ireland, Patrick wrote in about the year 450:

"God showed me how to have faith in him forever, as one who is never to be doubted. He answered my prayer in such a way that in the last days, ignorant though I am, I might be bold enough to take up so holy and so wonderful a talk, and imitate in some degree those whom the Lord had so long ago foretold as heralds of his Gospel, bearing witness to all nations."

These words console me not because I believe delivering this lecture is as holy and wonderful a task as was Patrick's in bringing the faith to Ireland. Nonetheless, I *do* see it as both a holy and a wonderful task to begin a conversation, or—perhaps better—to enter into a conversation on what it should mean to be a law school of the Catholic University of America today. That is what I have set as my task.

I present myself as a participant in what I consider to be an essential, ongoing conversation. My participation is as a layman—if you will. In spite of my name, I am not now nor have I ever been a lawyer, much less a legal scholar. I plead in truth and therefore in humility my ignorance of much that is the daily life of this place. At the same time, it is with confidence in the enduring truth which faith illumines and to which the Church has borne witness for twenty centuries that I make bold to speak.

Yours is an awesome responsibility in this place. Any society, but with a particular intensity our society, is ordered by its laws. The uniqueness of this nation is the way we have self-consciously forged a national unity through a system of law. Citizen and law-abiding are synonymous terms. The cohesion of other nations is often driven by a formative culture. We started as an uprooted people, except for the native Americans who were themselves uprooted by the nation's European founders. Our nation is not finished. We face the new and frightening task of being a world empire far more vast than Rome ever was. The perennial fascination with isolationism simply is not an option anymore. Our influence is global and, I would submit, frightening.

Within this nation our fabric continues to be knit by the enactment of laws and the interpretation of laws. Internationally, new relationships through laws must be established. Law is the question in northern Ireland, Zaire, Rwanda, among Palestinians and Israelis, in the Balkans. Law as it is constitutive of order within and among nations is the place where the law school of the Catholic University of America should focus.

America. What kind of a people do we want to be? What should drive our law in its formulation and interpretation? In what is law rooted? Have we anything to say to those questions as the law school of the Catholic University of America?

Is there a point of meeting between the resources of Catholic faith and the task of a law school in this nation's capital?

The Catholic Church found an unlikely fresh voice in Pope John XXIII, whose name lends honor to this lecture. "An interim Pope," some called him, as he ascended the Chair of Peter almost into his eighth decade. On December 25, Christmas, 1961, he convoked the Second Vatican Council. He said:

"Today the Church is witnessing a crisis underway within society. While humanity is on the edge of a new era, tasks of immense gravity and amplitude await the Church, as in the most tragic periods of its history. It is a question in fact of bringing the modern world into contact with the vivifying and perennial energies of the Gospel, a world which exalts itself with its conquests in the technical and scientific fields but which brings also the consequences of a temporal order which some have wished to reorganize excluding God." In that convoking of the Council, the Pope spoke of a contemporary "weakening in the aspiration towards the values of the spirit."

Quite simply and directly—the Pope set before the Church and the world his hopes for the Second Vatican Council: "In the face of this twofold spectacle—a world which reveals a grave state of spiritual poverty and the Church of Christ, which is still vibrant with vitality—we, from the time we ascended the supreme pontificate, despite our unworthiness and by means of an impulse of Divine Providence, have felt immediately the duty to call our sons (that is, the bishops of the world) together, to give the Church the possibility to contribute more efficaciously to the solution of the problems of the modern age."

In going back to these words after some years, I am struck by the Pope's reference to humanity as on the edge of a new era, and his prophetic words that "tasks of immense gravity and amplitude await the Church, as in the most tragic periods of its history."

We are there. The new era is unfolding. The challenge which the Church faces is immense. I refer not to the perennial challenges of inner conversion for those who are the Church as well as her institutional life, but rather to the unique challenge which this new era presents to the Church in her task of bringing light to the darkness of the world. The Church knows, Pope John XXIII said thirty-six years ago, that "by vivifying the temporal order with the light of Christ it reveals men to themselves; it leads them, therefore, to discover in themselves their own nature, their own dignity, their own end."

There is a myth about Pope John XXIII which can lead to a caricature of the Pope as a cheerleader for the new era that was coming into being. His confidence was not in the world, however. His confidence was rather in the ability of the human person to come, with the light of faith, to a better understanding about the nature, dignity, and end of human beings.

That Council which Pope John XXIII convoked was to say, in fulfillment of its convener's hopes: "Whatever is opposed to life itself, such as any type of murder, genocide, abortion, or euthanasia, or willful self-destruction, whatever violates the integrity of the human person, such as mutilation, torments inflicted on body or mind, attempts to coerce the will itself; whatever insults human dignity, such as sub-human living conditions, arbitrary imprisonment, deportation, slavery, prostitution, the selling of women and children; as well as disgraceful working conditions, where people are treated as mere instruments of gain rather than as free and responsible persons; all these things and others like them are infamies indeed. They poison human society, and they do more harm to those who practice them than to those who suffer from the injury. Moreover, they are a supreme dishonor to the Creator" (*Gaudium et Spes*, 27).

Pope John Paul II has written that "we are facing an enormous and dramatic clash between good and evil, death and life, the 'culture of death' and 'the culture of life.' We find ourselves not only 'faced with' but necessarily 'in the midst of' this conflict: we are all involved and we all share in it, with the inescapable responsibility of choosing to be unconditionally pro-life."

Laws are formulated and laws are being interpreted in our courts by legislators and judges in the grip of this culture of death. The rhetoric of welfare reform and immigration reform, I would submit, is steeped in the culture of death. How can a law school communicate a better vision, how can a law school mediate a culture of life, a civilization of love? That, it seems to me, is the specific task of a Catholic law school. Presuming—which is already a leap in some contemporary circles, that truth, an objective order of truth, exists, and that is attainable by the human mind, and presuming that moral truths bind us to standards of conduct, it is obvious that law should be rooted in truth—truth about the human person, truth about the family, truth about human solidarity. Faith does not invent these truths; it does, however, illumine them.

Let me explain what I mean. When I was a high school student in the Virgin Islands, I was very much at home in a society which was predominantly black. News of race riots on the U.S. mainland was painful and difficult for me to comprehend: most of my friends and teachers, the family physician, the governor of the Islands to whom my father was accountable were all black. My pastor led me to the teaching of Pope Pius XII on the Church as the Mystical Body of Christ. The rich Pauline doctrine was opened up to me. As a teenager, the resources of faith reinforced the conviction borne of my experience that color does not matter, that every human being is sacred as an image of God, and that Christ came that we might be reconciled to God and to one another.

That conviction nurtured my ministry as a priest in Mississippi in the sixties, it nurtured my advocacy for freedom for Vietnamese refugees in camps within Thailand and Hong Kong, it inspired my appeal on the steps of the U.S. Capitol for a ban on partial-birth abortion, it inspired my testimony before a Massachusetts legislative committee against capital punishment and my testimony before a U.S. Congressional committee two weeks ago on physician assisted suicide.

There is a coherent Catholic vision about the dignity and inviolability of the human person, about the fundamental importance of the family for society, and about the implications of human solidarity, particularly with the poor, which is desperately needed today by those who frame our laws and those who interpret them.

The challenges faced by our society are enormous. There is, brooding over all else, the awful reality that our nation is the dominant world power. In so many things, as we go so goes the world. How are we going? Today's legislative focus on partial-birth abortion and the Supreme Court's consideration of the Ninth and Second Circuit Court's decisions on physician assisted suicide present the macabre legal iter of our culture of death. Peter Edelman's recent article on what is euphemistically called welfare reform is a sober exercise in facing the reality of the culture of death in which we find ourselves.

Mary Ann Glendon at Harvard Law School, leader of the Holy See's delegation to Beijing, addressed the topic of Social Justice and Human Rights in a talk at St. John's University, New York, on January 30 of this year.

In that talk she said that "the fact is that, for the past thirty years, the single most consistent champion of human freedom *and* solidarity in international settings has been the Catholic Church. The idea that social justice can and must be harmonized with political and civil liberties has been the touchstone of the Holy See's advocacy in the U.N. and the social encyclicals of John Paul II. Amidst the cacophony of special interest groups and power politics, it has been the Church, and often only the Church, that has stood clearly, consistently, and unmistakably for *all* the freedoms that flow from the common principle of the innate dignity of creatures made in the image and likeness of God." She repeats the question which Pope John Paul II put to the U.N. in a speech marking its fiftieth anniversary. The Pope asked: "Can we not recommit ourselves also to taking the risk of solidarity—and thus the risk of peace?"

The risk of solidarity. That, it seems to me, is the only way to build a more humane society. We must be willing to take that risk. It is a risk which binds us to every human being, particularly the weakest and most vulnerable. It is a risk which binds us to other nations, particularly those who are in greatest need. It is a risk which demands that we redefine national self interest to include the implications of human solidarity. It is a risk which demands that we realize we *are* our brother's, our sister's keeper, it is a risk that demands we heed Isaiah when he says—"turn not your back on your own flesh."

That, it seems to my pastor's heart, is what a law school in the Catholic University of America should be about. It should be helping our society with all the resources of law to take the risk of solidarity.

Let me give three examples.

1. The risk of solidarity in facing physician assisted suicide and euthanasia.

We must begin with the premise of the inherent value of every human life. A human life in itself was sufficient value to call forth our individual and collective respect and support. A human person presents us with the mystery of God's presence. We cannot *control* the life of another, we cannot presume to be the arbiters of life and death. We must be willing simply to acknowledge the mystery that life is in its beginning, in its end, and throughout its course.

I have been moved by the concern of disabled persons with the persistent advocacy for physician assisted suicide. They see this advocacy by a cultural elite as a threat to themselves. Implicit in the move towards physician assisted suicide and euthanasia is the judgment that some lives are not worth living. The chilling devolution of this practice in the Netherlands should provide ample proof of the devastating consequences of this movement. Suffice it to quote the Orwellian words of the Dutch Minister of Health, Else Borst-Eilers: "There are situations in which the best way to heal the patient is to help him die peacefully, and the doctor who in such a situation grants the patient's request acts as the healer *par excellence.*"

There is an *Alice-in-Wonderland* upside-down world if ever there was one! The doctor par excellence is the doctor who kills. In the Netherlands it has already moved to euthanasia of terminally ill, competent patients *without* consent. The request for physician assisted suicide by a patient depressed over the death of family members resulted in the physician's cooperation in her suicide. The case has opened up new killing fields in the Netherlands.

In our courts, the ninth circuit perverts the noble concept of compassion, and the second circuit dismisses distinctions which have long served the medical profession in determining what is and is not acceptable morally and ethically in the care of the terminally ill.

The risk of solidarity with the terminally ill is the call to risk to be with another in loving service as together we wait for the mystery that is death. The loving service must include the transparent expression of respect that is not diminished by the weakness or helplessness that the other might suffer. It includes the control of pain and does not demand that every possible technology must be employed to postpone a death that is medically indicated from the disease.

Above all else—the risk of solidarity demands that we not kill.

2. The risk of solidarity in viewing the poor of our society.

Here, it seems to me, we must re-visit the welfare and immigration reform debates of recent years. Mary Ann Glendon speaks of this as "the challenge of bringing together the two halves of the divided soul of the modern human rights movement: the commitment of the nations to human freedom and their acknowledgment of common responsibility for the poor, the weak, and the vulnerable."

This is not to argue that "reform" is out of order in a moral calculus of welfare and immigration law. It is to say, however, that a blind faith in our economic system's ability to address the immediate needs of the poor is, to say the least, misplaced.

Third and most quickly—the risk of human solidarity with other nations.

What does this mean, for example, with regards to Northern Ireland, Cuba, Iraq, Iran, China, Rwanda, and Zaire? What judgment does this lead us to on economic embargoes? What does it say to the fact that a nation is prohibited from purchasing medicine?

My hope is that the law school in the Catholic University of America would help to clarify what the risk of human solidarity means in legal terms.

Let me close with words which Pope John Paul II addressed to this nation as he departed from Detroit after his U.S. pastoral visit in 1987.

These words, it seems to me, provide a good starting point for the task that is yours:

> For this reason, America, your deepest identity and truest character as a nation are revealed in the position you take toward the human person. *The ultimate test of your greatness is the way you treat every human being, but especially the weakest and most defenseless ones.*
>
> The best traditions of your land presume respect for those who cannot defend themselves. If you want equal justice for all, and true freedom and lasting peace, then, America, defend life! All the great causes that are yours today will have meaning only *to the extent that you guarantee the right to life and protect the human person.*
>
> - Feeding the poor and welcoming refugees;
> - Reinforcing the social fabric of this nation;
> - Promoting the true advancement of women;
> - Securing the rights of minorities;
> - Pursuing disarmament, while guaranteeing legitimate defense:
>
> all this will succeed only if respect for life and its protection by the law is granted to every human being *from conception until natural death.*
>
> Every human person—no matter how vulnerable or helpless, no matter how young or how old, no matter how healthy, handicapped or sick, no matter how useful or productive for society—is a being of inestimable worth created in the image and likeness of God. This is the dignity of America, the reason she exists, the condition for her survival—yes, the ultimate test of her greatness: to respect every human person, especially the weakest and most defenseless ones, those as yet unborn.
>
> With these sentiments of love and hope for America, I now say goodbye in words that I spoke once before: "Today, therefore, my final prayer is this: that God will bless America, so that she may increasingly become—and truly be, and long remain—'One Nation, *under God*, indivisible. With liberty and justice for all' (October 7, 1979).

While I have spoken of the specific mission of a Catholic law school, I am not unmindful that ours is a world of many religions and none. The transcendent value of the human person and the power of God to unify was movingly imaged in a photograph in the *New York Times* last Monday showing King Hussein of Jordan reaching out to the father of Sivan Petihi, one of the Israeli girls killed by a Jordanian soldier. Sivan's mother said to the King "If you would have seen her today, you would have hugged her and kissed her." The King responded: "She will always be alive in our hearts, and I hope you will always consider me a brother." As the King rose to leave, Nisim Petihi, the slain girl's grandfather and an immigrant from Yemen, blessed the King in Arabic.

That is what the risk of solidarity is all about.

15

Remembering Mother Teresa of Calcutta

5 September 1997

MOTHER TERESA, SERVANT OF GOD

Mother Teresa, my temptation is to single out all sorts of folk who are here in this congregation that you should know. But I'm not going to do that, because it would take much too long. However you must realize that within this sanctuary and within this church, and outside, there are men and women, young and old, from parts of Greater Boston and beyond who are here because they recognize in you the presence of God. And that's not bad, is it?

If they were here simply because of you, I'm sure you would be upset. But they are here because they—and I—recognize in you, the presence of God, the love of God. And this, truly, is what our lives are supposed to be, is it not? Jesus makes it very clear: "I tell you, unless your holiness surpasses that of the Scribes and Pharisees, you shall not enter the Kingdom of God."

What, after all, is holiness but following God's will for us? And what is God's will for us? Jesus has expressed it so very simply: we are to love. We are to love our neighbors as we love ourselves. We are, as our opening prayer has said, to go beyond the boundaries which this world sets. And this world sets terrible boundaries to our love: the boundaries of health and wealth, of race and place, of language and age.

But, Jesus says that if we come to the altar to worship the Heavenly Father and, there, remember that our brother has anything against us—

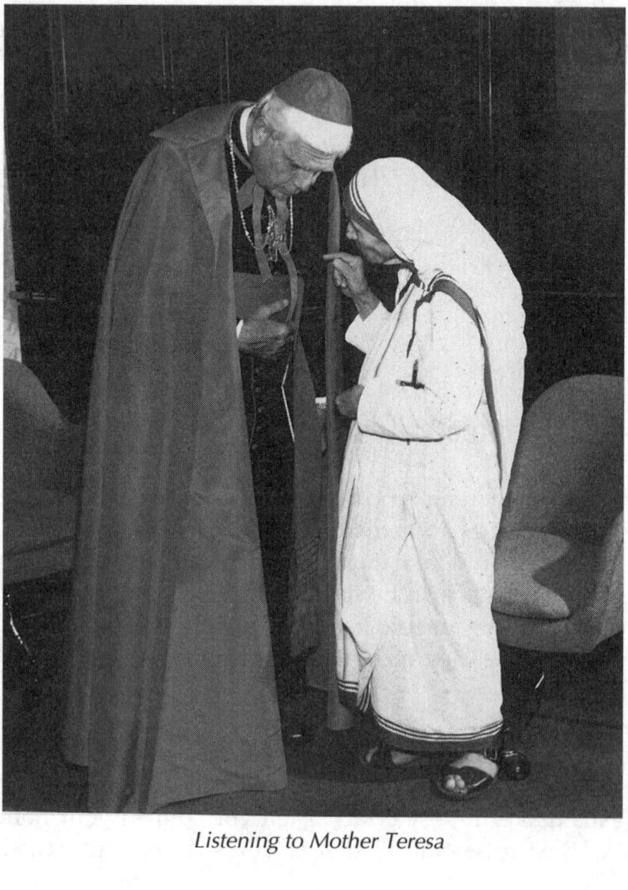

Listening to Mother Teresa

what does that mean? It means, if we have excluded from our love any man, woman, or child, from the first moment of conception until the last moment of natural death—and every moment in between—then God in them is being denied.

What the Lord invites us to do in this Eucharist, and in every Eucharist, is to beg for the grace to erase those artificial boundaries which set limits to our life, *whatever* those limits may be. He invites us to see in every human being the Presence of God, and to live in the love of God.

Paul said, in his letter to the Corinthians: "It is not ourselves we preach." Mother Teresa, you do not preach yourself. That's why you're so authentic! That's why we're all here today. Too many of us preach ourselves and not too many come out to see us. We all want to see the *real thing*—you! You preach Christ Jesus, and through you, we see Him as the Incarnation of Love itself, for He is God and God is Love. "It is not ourselves we preach, but Christ Jesus as Lord and ourselves as your servants for Jesus' sake." How beautifully you, and the four thousand Missionaries of Charity, live that Word of God. How beautifully you are servant to us all for the sake of Jesus—as you are a servant for us in your presence in our midst today.

Paul goes on: "For God Who said: 'let light shine out of darkness,' has shown in our hearts that we, in turn, might make known the glory of God shining on the face of Christ." I have seen you do that in the few short hours that you have been here. I've seen a baby's face light up. I've seen someone almost blind from the ravages of diabetes smile as he has not been able to smile for a long time, because of the touch of your hand and the whisper of your blessing over him. It is the life and love of Jesus that you bring to us.

Friends, Mother has asked me to mention her great hope—she always has a special intention. (I think when she finishes with this world she'll be working on Mars.) She has asked me to tell you that her great desire now is to establish the Missionaries of Charity in China. She asks you to pray with her that this will be realized, and I think I can assure her that we will be united in those prayers.

She had an earlier wish, and the Archdiocese, through the great generosity of someone who left a bequest to assist in missionary work among the poor, is able to provide $70,000 to Mother to assist in the work of the Missionaries of Charity in Vietnam. Another small check, to be used as you decide—even if you'd like to establish another house in Boston or Newton, we'd be delighted with that.

Mother, we look now into our own hearts to acknowledge whatever is an artificial, worldly barrier to the universal love to which we are called. Humbly and honestly, before God, let us acknowledge that that is not the way for us to live. God will give us the grace to make His Love present to all His children on the face of the earth. May it be so.

Mother Teresa, thank you for reminding us so powerfully how we are to live in love.

ON THE DEATH OF MOTHER TERESA

A world without Mother Teresa is a world deprived of a shining light and a moral compass. Few persons have had the ability to touch so many lives as has she. The religious community which she founded, the Missionaries of Charity, ring the globe bringing the simple message of God's love to the most abandoned and forgotten. I count it a singular grace to have known her.

This Archdiocese has had the blessing of her presence in establishing a convent for her sisters, in visiting prisons, and, in her last visit, joining us for Mass and holding in her arms the tiny babies in the neo-natal intensive care unit at Saint Elizabeth's Medical Center.

Deep as is our sorrow at her death, we do not mourn, Saint Paul reminds us, like those who have no hope. The mystery of Christ's death and resurrection was the center of her life, and throws light on her death. The funeral liturgy reminds us that life is changed, not taken away.

May the all-loving God whom she loved so much bring her to the glory and peace of the saints. May her simple message of uncomplicated love take root more firmly in the hearts of all those who mourn her death. In this way, we too will do something beautiful for God.

16

Mission over Business

On the Sale of Jesuit St. Louis University Hospital

9 October 1997

The action of St. Louis University to proceed with a sale of its teaching hospital to a for-profit corporation is distressing news for all who are concerned with Catholic Health Care.

The bottom line of such corporations is profit for the shareholders. The bottom line for Catholic Health Care institutions is the patient. This is a fundamental difference which cannot be glossed over.

St. Louis University's medical school with its teaching hospital has been a leader in the Catholic Church's contribution to health care. This action of the Board of Trustees jeopardizes the commitment of the University to its Catholic identity. Certainly the hospital will cease to be Catholic if this sale is allowed to proceed.

The statement of Archbishop Rigali raises the question of whether the Board of Trustees has canonical authority for the action it has embarked upon. Perhaps the intervention of the Father General of the Society of Jesus and the Holy See can reverse this lamentable action.

What has occurred cannot be seen as an isolated, independent decision. Leaders in Catholic Health Care, as well as the Bishops of the United States are one in our conviction that we should not yield our institutions to for-profit corporations. Business considerations must not take precedence over mission.

17

A Sad Time for Massachusetts

On the Passage of Legislation to Restore Capital Punishment

29 October 1997

This is a sad time for Massachusetts. By the narrowest of margins, our House of Representatives has voted to reinstate capital punishment. It is a pyrrhic victory for the supporters of the death penalty. We are none the safer from violent crimes because of this action. Those who mourn the victims of violent crimes as family and friends will find no lasting consolation in this decision. What we have done these days is engage in a primordial cry to the wind giving vent to our rage and frustration over the unspeakable acts of violence which threaten us as a society.

Our senators and representatives have borne the awful weight of this rage in their deliberations. Now perhaps they and we will be allowed the time to reflect more deeply on the threat to the common good which is posed by the violence that has so permeated our society.

Representatives and senators on both sides of this issue have experienced an ordeal of conscience. Nothing is gained now by making judgments against those with whom we disagree. I do express my gratitude as a citizen for those men and women in the State House who withstood the tide of public opinion and who voted "no." In the end, they will be vindicated.

The task before us now, no matter what our position on capital punishment, is to face more deeply than we have the epidemic of violence which assails us. We can, and please God, we will do better than simply succumb to the cycle of violence.

18

Evangelizing the Dominant Culture

Floyd L. Begin Law Lecture

John Carroll University, Cleveland, Ohio, 28 October 1997

It is a privilege to stand in a distinguished line of speakers beginning in 1987 when the first Floyd L. Begin Law Lecture was given at John Carroll University. I commend the Tribunal of the Diocese of Cleveland for its initiative in this series. Let me say at the outset of my remarks, however, that I am not now nor have I ever been a lawyer. I am neither a civil lawyer nor a canon lawyer. In spite of my name, I am, like the most of humanity, a layman when it comes to the legal profession. It would be presumptuous, therefore, were I to attempt to fulfill the intent of this lecture series with great fidelity. Allow me, therefore, to interpret law in a much more general sense as embracing the truths of faith which are, after all, normative for the life of the Church. My theme will be the interplay of the resources of faith with the wider societies, domestic and international, within which the Church lives.

To contemplate the size of the Catholic Church is necessarily to conclude that it must have some impact on the formulation of domestic and international policy. Worldwide, the Church numbers nearly one billion persons. Within the United States we number over sixty million persons. To render the number of Catholics in the United States a bit more meaningful, it is interesting to note that the number of Episcopalians in the entire United States is just a bit more than the number of Catholics in the Archdiocese of Boston. If one adds together all the Christian denominations in the United States, and includes in that number the Church of Jesus Christ of Latter Day Saints, there is a total of 63.4 million persons. If one excludes the Mormons from this list, then the number of Catholics exceeds all Christian Orthodox and Protestant groups in the United States added together.

Coupled with its size, the Catholic Church as an unparalleled worldwide organizational structure. Father Brian Hehir has frequently commented upon this unique attribute of the Catholic Church.

Within the United States, for reasons in part due to the fact that the Catholic Church encountered a hostile culture in our nation, the Church developed a system of institutions which are unmatched anywhere else in the Catholic world. Our parish structures, our parochial schools, our system of higher education, our system of health care institutions, and our system of social services are unique. The city of Cleveland, for example, has a public school system with approximately 70,000 students. The diocesan school system of Cleveland has 68,500 students. The school comparisons in Boston are similar. There has been national attention given to the excellence of Catholic schools when compared with the public system. The cost of Catholic school education is appreciably less than public education, which also has focused national attention of late.

When one considers social services, the Catholic Church is second to none after the government in the provision of services to the poor and the vulnerable in our society. In the Commonwealth of Massachusetts, the services provided by the Archdiocese of Boston is second only to the services provided by the State itself. This can be replicated in many places across the nation.

Our system of health care institutions is a major player in the national health care environment. Our place in health care is particularly important today, for our presence raises the question whether "for profit" health care systems are beneficial to the national health. Our "not for profit" hospitals have the care of the patient, not profit for the shareholder, as the bottom line.

Given the size and complexity of the Catholic Church as an institution in this nation, and given its close ties with a worldwide organization of nearly one billion people, it is not surprising that the Catholic Church in the United States has been a not insignificant player in the formulation of domestic and international policy. On the international level, no one emerges more clearly as the conscience of the world than does Pope John Paul II. His appearances at the United Nations in 1979 and 1987, following in the footsteps of Pope Paul VI in his visit to the U.N. in 1965, and following the encyclical of Pope John XXIII, *Pacem In Terris,* addressed to all men and women of good will throughout the world, give ample testimony to the Church's commitment to build a world of justice, unity, and peace.

The Holy Father's pastoral visits, more far-flung than all other previous Popes put together, have helped to bring a message of hope, not only to

Catholics, but to all persons of good will. No one can reasonably assess the historic events of 1989 with the fall of Communism and not credit a pivotal role to Pope John Paul II in supporting the hope of freedom in the heart of Poland. The thrilling public movement in support of freedom in the Philippines was a manifestation of the Church in support of justice.

Here in the United States, the Catholic Church, particularly through the Conference of Bishops which is so ably headed by Bishop Anthony Pilla of the Diocese of Cleveland, has addressed such issues as peace and the economy through major pastoral letters, and makes known its position on a wide range of issues through advocacy before the Senate and House of Representatives and before the Administration. No institution in the United States is a more consistent advocate for life, all life, than the Catholic Church.

Beyond her institutional influence, however, there is the far more important influence of lay men and women whose consciences are formed by the teaching of the Church and who attempt to construct here on earth God's kingdom of justice, of unity, and of peace. To the extent that we Catholics are true to the vision of faith, to that extent we are numbered among the peacemakers and among the Good Samaritans of this world.

In moving words which retain their power thirty-two years after they were first proclaimed, the Bishops of the Universal Church said, in the *Pastoral Constitution on the Church in the Modern World, Gaudium et Spes,* of the Second Vatican Council: "The joy and hope, the grief and anguish of the men of our time, especially of those who are poor or afflicted in any way, are the joy and hope, the grief and anguish of the followers of Christ as well. Nothing that is genuinely human fails to find an echo in their hearts." In these words, the Bishops of the world formulated for our time the imperative of the Church to be concerned for others, particularly those most in need.

Jesus came that we might have life and have it more abundantly. When the rich young man in the Gospel approached Jesus to ask what he must do to have eternal life, Jesus pointed to the Ten Commandments. It develops in the story that the rich young man was a good man and lived in accord with the Ten Commandments. Nonetheless, he realized that there was something yet missing in his life, and so he asked the Lord what more he must do. Jesus responded, "If you would be perfect, go sell what you have, give to the poor, and then come follow me." If you would be perfect. In the final analysis, the vocation of every human being is to be a saint. We are called to holiness of life.

Our understanding of the human person is measured by our understanding of Jesus Christ. In that same pastoral constitution, *Gaudium et Spes,* which I quoted a few moments ago, we read in the twenty-second paragraph: "In reality it is only in the mystery of the Word made flesh that the mystery of man truly becomes clear. . . . Christ the Lord, Christ the new

Adam, in the very revelation of the mystery of the Father and of His love, fully reveals man to himself and brings to light his most high calling." This truth is referred to again and again by Pope John Paul II. As a matter of fact, it might be called the hermeneutical key to his pontificate. He focuses our attention on Jesus Christ, so that Jesus Christ might focus our attention more fully on what it means to be human. In revealing to us God the Father, Jesus at the same time reveals to us our own nature.

When Jesus said to the young man, therefore, "if you would be perfect," we must understand this as pointing us to the only way to human fulfillment, to human happiness. That way is the way of Christ, that way is the way of holiness, that way is the way of truth, the way of hope, of justice, the way of love.

The Church, therefore, must not be reduced to a sociological or, much less, a political entity. There is an institutional expression of the Church, to be sure, and we see that at the national and international levels. Nonetheless, the Church is always more than what we perceive in her institutional manifestations. The Church is, in the final analysis, a mystery which brings together Christ and the believer. Perhaps no one has written with more insight into the mystery of the Church than has Paul.

He writes, "I live now, not I, but Christ lives in me." The church proclaims that truth in all her members. St. Augustine, inspired by the writing of Paul, was to exult that, "The Church is Christ, extended in time and space." In our advocacy, therefore, in whatever the Church proclaims on behalf of others in public policy debates on domestic policy or international policy, it is so important that the Church be inspired by that revealed truth that is the gift of faith. It is a revealed truth about who we are as human beings. It is a revealed truth about the innate value of every human being as the image of God. From that beginning flows all that we have to say about and all that we attempt to do to create a more humane society.

Christ says, quite simply, "I am the way, the truth, and the life." Whatever it is that the Church proclaims must be rooted in that threefold proclamation. Christ is the incarnate truth, Christ is the way that we are to live, and Christ is the life we are to live.

It never has been easy for the Church to influence public policy. It certainly is not easy today. In countless ways the question of Pilate reverberates in our society: "Truth, what is truth?" Some years ago the late Cardinal Joseph Bernardin addressed the major issues facing us and he used the image of the seamless garment to show how all of these issues are woven together. There was some misunderstanding about his words, but his use of that image was a powerful one, and serves us well today. Let me give you an example of how I believe that image conveys to us an important truth.

Every so often the bishops of the United States issue a document on public responsibility which catalogs a list of public policy issues upon which the bishops of the United States have taken a position. Some have suggested that the list is too long, others have suggested that it would be better if we would show some priority in our listing. I believe this last point is well made. Let me illustrate why I think this is so.

Using the seamless garment image, all of the issues that face us as a society affecting the life of the human person depend finally on the fundamental right to life. If that right to life is rejected, is violated, is not supported, then that seamless garment begins to unravel. Cardinal Bernardin was not suggesting in the use of that image that the pro-life issue was one among many equally important issues. His words and life amply demonstrated his conviction that the pro-life issue is fundamental, and that if we reject pro-life we run the risk of undercutting every other worthwhile issue in support of a more humane society.

Currently in Massachusetts we are in the midst of a public debate on capital punishment. I had great difficulty last week in writing a column on this issue. It was very difficult to begin the column, because I could not easily find a way to make an appeal to a citizenry with many different points of view. I went to bed without having achieved my task, and the next morning I awoke with the clear insight that my difficulty stemmed from the fact that we live in a society in which the life of the innocent has been rendered frighteningly at risk. The President of the United States vetoes a ban on partial-birth abortion. We mark next year the 25th anniversary of Roe v. Wade which has paved the way for over 35 million abortions in this country. Who knows what medical advances could have been made by some of those aborted children, what beautiful piece of music or poetry might have been composed, what great public leader might have emerged, how many loving mothers and fathers the world might have seen had these abortions not taken place.

If we as a society can make our peace with the death of the innocent, then it is very difficult to argue convincingly against the death of the criminal guilty of the most heinous of crimes. The basis, the fundamental basis for the Church's position on capital punishment is our conviction about the sanctity of every human life. When life is at risk as it is in our society, when we find ourselves enmeshed in what the Holy Father has called a culture of death, it is very difficult indeed to argue convincingly against capital punishment.

There is a problem which is posed by the seamless garment image. The seamless garment image and the thought undergirding it presuppose that the argument from consistency will have force. Cardinal Bernardin sometimes formulated his view in terms of the consistent life ethic. Ours is a society, however, that does not give a hoot about consistency. Ours is a society which does not understand the force of logic. Ours is a society which has denied the existence of a truth independent of an individual's formulation of it. In such a society, civil discourse becomes impossible. In such a society, we are compelled to live the hell of personal choice as the ultimate arbiter of moral value.

There are many wonderful aspects of contemporary society. We have unparalleled abilities to communicate, to gather information, to travel. There is a recognition of human rights as a significant issue by more and more persons around the globe. There are hopeful signs of peace in Northern Ireland as in South Africa. Nonetheless, there is a dominant cultural script which is antithetical to life and which makes it increasingly more difficult for the Church to engage effectively in public discourse. It is not surprising that the Church is systematically marginalized by the elites of the dominant culture. It is recognized that ours is the only integral vision countervailing an individualism run amok, and to a relativism that denies the possibility of truth.

If I sound a bit apocalyptic, perhaps you will forgive me since we are entering a new millennium, and such a millennial change has routinely invited apocalyptic visions. It does seem to me, however, that we have experienced a profound cultural shift in this country. Such a shift has enormous consequences the world over, because the United States is the new Rome. We are the world empire, Bill Clinton is the Emporer, and Hillary is the Empress. The first couple's recent visit to Argentina shows us, I would submit in a frightening way, the power of the empire in its use of the media to purvey a vision that is not consistent with the respect due every human being. The efforts of the United States at the Cairo Conference on Population and Development, and the more subtle efforts at the Beijing Conference on Women amply demonstrate that the empire has a clear agenda of cultural domination. Unfortunately, that agenda is fundamentally flawed in its refusal to acknowledge the right to life of the most innocent among us.

The impressive and in so many ways unique system of institutions which developed in the Catholic Church in the United States was a response to a hostile environment. The dominant culture did not look kindly upon the Catholic presence. One of my predecessors as the Bishop of Boston, Bishop Fenwick, had great difficulty obtaining land for a Catholic cemetery. We were a problem dead as well as alive. To this day, in the older towns of Massachusetts Catholic churches are often found on side streets down by the railroad tracks. The windows of shops in the last century often had signs which indicated that Irish, read Catholic, need not apply. In Charlestown, close to Boston, an Ursuline convent was burned to the ground. While the environment was not always so openly hostile, it was significantly enough so that as the Catholic Church grew, the decision was consciously made to develop institutions which would give expression to Catholic life in a more congenial environment. Those of us who are middle age and beyond will remember what Catholicism was like as it was shaped by those institutions of parish, cultural, educational, and social life.

While it may be overly simplistic to point to one event as a point of change, few would dispute that the election of John F. Kennedy profoundly affected the place of Catholics in U.S. society. We had finally arrived politically. The glass ceiling which had denied Catholics access to the White House was at last shattered. Politically and economically it soon became evident that Catholics were major players.

As the dominant culture became more accepting of Catholics in the political and economic life of the nation, something else began to happen. The moral consensus which had long inspired our national life began to disintegrate. The distrust of all authority which took root during the Vietnam war protests and the subsequent sexual revolution profoundly changed the dominant culture. The Catholic Church, almost alone among the institutions of our nation, has consistently espoused a view of life that embraces the moral consensus which previously held possession in our nation.

Once again the Catholic Church found itself at odds with the dominant culture, but this time with a difference. As Catholics were mainstreamed into the dominant culture, many of them found themselves at odds with the faith-inspired vision which the Church teaches. They have chosen the dominant culture over faith. We are reminded at every turn by the molders of public opinion that Catholics in large numbers of disagree with the Church's teaching on a wide array of issues.

When, therefore, we consider the Catholic Church's role in the development of domestic and international policy, it is important to underscore the fact that today that contribution on the part of the Church is muted because so many Catholics do not speak and act out of the life-giving vision of faith. The prevalence of Catholic politicians, for example, who proclaim themselves to be "personally opposed to abortion, but" have, in effect, lost the compelling vision of faith concerning a more humane society. Our academic institutions have, sadly, traded a confident Catholic identity for an imitation of the secular university. The Catholic theological community in recent decades has generally failed to engage in the task of evangelizing the dominant culture.

Because of all this, it is highly significant that in the middle of November of this year the Holy Father will convene bishops from throughout South, Central, and North America to discuss what he calls "the new evangelization." This will be one in a series of regional Synods of Bishops looking to the new millennium. The first to be held was for the continent of Africa in 1994. Three others yet to follow will bring together the bishops of Asia, Oceania, and Europe. The Holy Father has set three goals for the month-long meeting of the bishops of America:

- To foster a new evangelization on the whole continent as an expression of episcopal communion;
- To increase solidarity among the various particular Churches in different fields of pastoral activity; and

- To shed light on the problems of justice and international economic relations among the nations of America, considering the enormous imbalances among the North, Central, and South of the American continent.

Such a meeting clearly has enormous implications. There is no other institution which could convene a similar meeting that touches so many people in this part of the world. Nonetheless, the meeting is not a day too soon, for the rampant secularization of the dominant culture of this nature poses a great obstacle to the Church's ability to enunciate a life-giving vision. Because the United States is the dominant world power, as our culture goes, so goes the culture of the globe.

The theme of this special assembly for America is most instructive: "Encounter With The Living Jesus Christ; The Way To Conversion, Communion And Solidarity In America."

Encounter with the living Jesus Christ. When we bishops gather in Rome for the month beginning in mid November, our focus will be on that basic activity of the Church: encounter with the living Jesus Christ, who is the way, the truth, and the life. If the Church is to make a significant contribution to the world, she must do so by being true to herself. We will not bring the contribution to public policy debate which only we can bring if we mute that distinctive gift which is ours in the faith of the Church, a faith which proclaims Jesus Christ as Lord, yesterday, today, and forever. The vision of faith speaks to us about God, about the human person, about family, and about human solidarity. These truths are the foundation stones for a more human society.

The Holy Father has called this special assembly for America, this unique Synod of Bishops, to focus on Jesus Christ as the way to conversion. If the Church is to make the most effective contribution possible to the creation of a more humane society, then she will do so by calling her members to a more profound conversion of heart. We need to hear the Lord say to us, individually, "Go, sell what you have, give to the poor, and then come follow me." If we hear those words of the Lord only in terms of a bank balance we have failed to understand what Jesus is saying. What we "possess" might be an inordinate attachment to the dominant, secular culture, to a relativistic concept of truth, to an excessive individualism which, in effect, denies the moral good. Perhaps what we need to give up, to "sell," is a desire to appear indistinguishable from others. Perhaps what we need to sell is the fear of being who we are as Catholics.

The special assembly for America calls the bishops to reflect on the living Jesus Christ as the way to communion. We need to come to a clearer recognition of who we are as the Catholic Church in communion one with the other within and among our local churches, our dioceses, and in community with Peter's successor, the Bishop of Rome. This communion has to be seen in terms of a common profession of faith. When we say, "we believe," as a Church, we define who we are by the truths of faith affirmed.

Given the state of theological discourse in many places in our country, given the unmet challenge of Catholic colleges and universities to affirm confidently and creatively their Catholic identity, it is evident that the challenge of the Synod for us to seek the way to communion is a formidable challenge indeed.

The special assembly for America, the Synod of Bishops which convenes in November, is called to an encounter with the living Jesus Christ as the way to solidarity in America. The way to solidarity in America is not simply a matter of markets, communication networks, and free trade agreements. The way to solidarity in America is the encounter of faith with Jesus Christ as the revelation of God and the revelation of man to himself. In Christ, we are able to see the dignity to which we are called as human beings.

To speak so clearly and unmistakably in religious terms, in Christian terms, in Catholic terms may appear to be dismissive of the fact that we live in a pluralistic society that is made up of people of other Christian denominations, of other faiths, and of no religious belief. A true Catholic vision, however, impels us to view with painstaking respect every human being on the face of this earth whatever his or her beliefs might be. We must, however, be true to who we are as Catholics if we are to make the contribution that only we can make for the common good.

To her glory, the Church in the United States has been unremitting in her advocacy on behalf of the life of the unborn and the life of those who face death from sickness or old age. Our advocacy has been clear and unwavering in support of the poor and the immigrant in the formulation of welfare and immigration reform legislation. The Church in the United States and throughout the world has become ever more clear in her opposition to capital punishment. There is a consistency about our advocacy for domestic and international policy that is rooted in the conviction that every human being is sacred. This, in the finally analysis, is the greatest contribution which we can make in the formulation of this nation or any nation's domestic and international policy.

My hope for the Synod is that it will occasion a profound renewal throughout the Church. This renewal, please God, will ground us ever more deeply in our faith in Jesus Christ as Lord and Saviour, as the way, the truth, and the life, and will then ground us ever more deeply in the heart of that mystery which is the Church. If this occurs, then the new millennium should see a Church in the United States, in Latin America and Central America, in Canada, and throughout the world that is unremitting in her commitment to create here upon earth a more humane society. Our program will be simple. We will be pro-life in our defense of the dignity of every human being. We will be pro-family in our recognition that the family is the fundamental unit for any society. And we will be pro-poor, recognizing that the quality of any people can be measured by the way in which it responds to the poor, to the sick, and to those most vulnerable in its midst.

I have not so much spoken about what the Church has accomplished in the formulation of domestic and international policy. Rather, I have expressed my hope for what the Church might contribute to the common good if she experiences the renewal she so desperately needs.

19

In a Room So Full of Love

On the Twenty-Fifth Anniversaries of Roe v. Wade and of Pregnancy Help

16 January 1998

"Light and shadows." This is the title which the bishops of the United States have given to their statement marking the twenty-fifth anniversary of the Supreme Court's rulings in Roe v. Wade and Doe v. Bolton. Those of us who were charged with preparing the document for consideration by the full body of bishops were anxious that we not focus exclusively on the rulings themselves and the horrible consequences which followed upon these rulings. We wanted also to focus on the light of hope and love that is evident in the response of men and women within the Church, of other Christian denominations of faith, and of no faith who have banded together during these past twenty-five years to affirm the value of human life.

Last Saturday I was privileged to participate in a luncheon marking the twenty-fifth anniversary of Pregnancy Help. This is an agency which began in the wake of these terrible judicial decisions of the Supreme Court. Mrs. Alice Grayson was a founder of Pregnancy Help in 1973. A decade later, Pregnancy Help became associated with the Pro-life Office of the Archdiocese of Boston, and now both the Pro-life Office and Pregnancy Help are integrally joined to Catholic Charities of the Archdiocese of Boston.

Pregnancy Help reflects the light of love and hope provided by hundreds upon hundreds of volunteers. At the luncheon on Saturday, four women spoke their stories of an earlier despair turned to hope through the loving response of Pregnancy Help. To listen to their stories, and to know that they represent thousands more like them, is to realize that the help that can make the difference between death and life is, in many cases, a very little thing. Some spoke of long-term care through pregnancy and beyond. Others spoke of a prompt response to an immediate need to pay a bill. In every case, it was the fact that people cared, that people wanted to be of help, the fact that one was not alone that made the difference.

All too often there is a public caricature of the Pro-life Movement as a movement of intense, fanatic, and angry individuals. That is so far from the reality. When I walked into the hall last Saturday, I stopped to visit with some of the volunteers at a table near the door. One of the volunteers said to me, "Cardinal, isn't it wonderful to be in a room so full of love?" That said it all. It was a room filled with love. As we mark the sad anniversary of Roe v. Wade, we need to remember that what the Pro-life Movement is all about is to call us to a deeper love for the mother and the father and for the child within the mother's womb.

In a wonderful autobiography called *Fighting for Life,* Governor Robert P. Casey reflects on his own commitment to the pro-life cause. In that book he says this: "Surely no two human beings could be more bound together, more natural allies in life and love than a mother and her baby. So infants were always viewed by humanity, especially by women themselves, at most times in most places—until our time, when suddenly we find them driven apart, when the maternal instinct to nurture and protect the child is turned on its head.

"Everything depends on that tie of love. Sever it, and you have not only set in motion countless little tragedies, you put society itself on the short route to chaos." The most disastrous effects of the Supreme Court's action twenty-five years ago, the deepest shadows the Court has cast over our culture, is precisely that. It is the severing of the tie of love between mother and child. Whenever it happens, there is a compounded tragedy. Not only is life lost to the world, but a mother's heart is shattered, a father is deprived of his role rooted in our human nature, and society suffers a terrible mortal wound. The brave women who have been helped by Pregnancy Help bring the light of life to this culture of death. How blessed we are in the Archdiocese with Leslie Collins and all of those who are associated with her in Pregnancy Help. How blessed we are in the many others who, through other agencies and privately reach out in love to pregnant women who are in difficult circumstances.

The commitment of this Archdiocese continues unabated. No woman need choose an abortion because of the lack of emotional and material support. Through Pregnancy Help, through the Cardinal's Fund for the Unborn, through our Pro-life Office and countless other agencies of Catholic Charities, we count it a privilege to serve in love the cause of new life.

20

Irish Boston Changed the Face of City and Nation

On Wreath Laying at the Irish Famine Memorial

28 June 1998

I was unable to be present earlier today at the official dedication of the Irish Famine Memorial because of a long-standing commitment to take part in the Fiesta of Saint Peter and to bless the fisherfolk and fishing fleet of Gloucester.

I have hurried home to Boston this evening because I did not want to let this day go by without being here personally to thank God for the great gift of the Irish people who, fleeing the famine of their homeland, came as another of God's gifts from the sea to the shores of our city. Sadly, many of Erin's daughters and sons did not survive the desperate voyage, but died tragically either on board the "coffin-ships" or at the Deer Island Hospital. We remember them in a particular way today and we commend them to God's bountiful mercy.

Happily, though, many of those who fled the "An Gorta Mor," the Great Hunger, survived and struggled to turn the tragedy of the Old World into the triumph of the New. The thousands of Irish who came to Boston changed the face of our city and of our nation. They blazed a trail for the successive waves of immigrants from other European nations, from Asia, Africa, South and Central America who, over the years, followed in their footsteps. How good it is for us to be here, honoring their memory, this evening.

The site chosen for the Irish Famine Memorial is a particularly meaningful site in the heart of Boston. It is redolent with the atmosphere and the history not only of the Irish immigrants themselves, but also with the Catholic Church that sustained their faith and supported their souls during times that were most difficult.

Standing at this particular point, at the corner of Washington and School Streets, we have only to look around us to capture the flavor of the Irish-Catholic past: Just a few paces up School Street is a marker that records the site of the former Huguenot chapel where a handful of Roman Catholics met just after the American Revolution to form the first congregation. It was here, on Sunday, November 2, 1788, that a French priest celebrated what is recorded as the first public Catholic Mass in Boston.

Across the way is Franklin Street, where on September 25, 1803, the feast of St. Michael the Archangel, Bishop John Carroll of Baltimore dedicated the Church of the Holy Cross, the first Catholic Church in Boston. When Father Jean Cheverus was named the fist Bishop of Boston in 1808, the little church became Boston's first Cathedral.

And all around us, early Roman Catholics lie in historic cemeteries alongside their Puritan neighbors. Before St. Augustine's Chapel was constructed in South Boston in 1818, Boston's Catholics were buried in the Old Granary Burying Ground on Tremont Street, on Copp's Hill in the nearby North End, or in the Central Burying Ground on Boston Common.

Just close by, on what was called Leveret's Lane, just off what is now State Street (just at the end of Washington Street where we are standing) was the little house where Bishop Cheverus and Father Matignon lived—their refinement and their friendship a source of great inspiration to their Boston neighbors.

When he was growing up, another future bishop of Boston, John Bernard Fitzpatrick, lived close to his father's tailor shop in downtown Boston before he entered the Boston Latin School, which was then located just around the corner on School Street. It was Bishop Fitzpatrick who, shortly after becoming the third bishop of Boston, was instrumental in moving consciences to respond to the victims of the Famine.

And it was in this immediate area, too, that Bishop Benedict Fenwick started the publication of "The Boston Pilot" in 1829, as a means of providing the city's new Irish immigrant population with the news of the world, as well as with information concerning the beliefs and values of their religion. "The Pilot" became one of the longest-running newspapers in United States history, and today still operates across the street, on Franklin Street, on the site originally occupied by the first Cathedral of the Holy Cross.

Wherever we look from where we stand this evening, therefore, we can still see tangible evidence of the warm, constant, and affectionate relationship between the Irish people and the leaders of their Church who came with them to the New World, suffered with them in their adversities, and shared with them their steady progress and their magnificent achievements.

Today's dedication of Boston's Irish Famine Memorial poignantly reminds us that we, all of us, have a great deal to learn from history. As Thomas Flatley, Chairman of the Memorial Committee has said:

> Building this memorial has taught us that the famine offers universal truths about the human condition that go beyond the Irish: compassion needs to be constantly replenished in our society. By keeping the memory of the Irish struggle alive, we become more empathetic to the downtrodden people of our time.

As we gaze upon these beautiful pieces by sculptor Robert Shure, let us recognize and celebrate the agony and tragedy of the famine's victims, side by side with the hope and triumph of the survivors. The drama of the famine continues to play out in so many places in our world today. May we, whatever our ethnic heritage, remember that we are all daughters and sons of God. May we, look back and remember what we have learned from the past, so that we may better be able to respond to the needs of the people of God in the future. May we heed the prophet Isaiah as he says: "Turn not your back on your own flesh."

21

✢

We Thought It the Name of an African Cardinal

On the Occasion of Pope John Paul II's Twentieth Anniversary

16 October 1998

On October 16, 1978, I was attending a meeting at Sacred Heart Parish in Springfield, Missouri. Pope Paul VI had died on August 6. During the short pontificate of his successor, Pope John Paul I, I was in Rome with forty other U.S. Bishops for a course in theology. After his sudden death, I immediately returned to Missouri so that I might mark his death among the faithful of the Diocese of Springfield–Cape Girardeau.

There was no expectation that the work of the Conclave would be completed by October 16. The news of white smoke spread quickly, and our meeting adjourned so that we could all gather around a television and learn who would now assume the fisherman's ring. As his name was spoken, I strained to catch it, but it was totally unfamiliar. At first we thought it to be the name of an African Cardinal.

That was twenty years ago. Today, no one is better known throughout the world than is Pope John Paul II. Had I been in Boston rather than in the Midwest, I would have known of Cardinal Karol Wojtyla and the remarkable impression he made as a lecturer at Harvard University.

His pontificate is a great grace for the Church and for the world. He has exercised the ministry of Peter longer than any other Pope in this century. At the time of his election, it was the first time in 456 years that a non-Italian was chosen as pope. The task of Peter and his successors is to confirm the brethren in the faith. With a seemingly inexhaustible apostolic zeal Pope John Paul II has done that.

No other Pope has begun to match the extent or frequency of his pastoral visits. He has fashioned the papacy into a new mode of pastoral presence. His desire to communicate the good news of salvation in Jesus Christ transcends the barriers of age, of culture, and of language. Whether it is with a small group of children living with AIDS, with his would-be assassin, with millions of young people at Manila, or across the desk from a brother bishop, he is able to communicate his intensity of love for God and for every human being.

There is a dominant theme, a leitmotif to his pontificate. In his latest encyclical, *Faith and Reason*, which was released only yesterday, he himself points to this theme by referring to a passage in *Gaudium et Spes* which he says serves as one of the constant reference-points of his teaching. That reference in the *Constitution on the Church in the Modern World* is so revealing of his thought and his pastoral passion. The Council states: "The truth is that only in the mystery of the Incarnate Word does the mystery of man take on light. For Adam, the first man, was a type of him who was to come, Christ the Lord. Christ, the new Adam, in the very revelation of the mystery of the Father and of His love, fully reveals man to himself and brings to light his most high calling" (*Gaudium et Spes*, no. 22).

The mystery of the Incarnate Word of God totally defines his ministry and absorbs his life. Nowhere is this more evident than being present with the Pope when he is at prayer. He helps others by his prayer to come to a deeper appreciation of the Eucharist as a point of communion with the Lord. To be with him at Mass is to be drawn closer to the Lord.

He teaches us by example to trust in God's love. He carries his burden of pastoral responsibility for the whole Church with a serenity that is nothing less than an extraordinary gift of grace. He lives the truth that we minister in the person of Christ. He doesn't take himself too seriously. He knows who he is because he knows that Jesus Christ is Lord.

Last Sunday he canonized a Carmelite nun, Sister Teresa Benedicta of the Cross, who is more widely known as Edith Stein. In his homily he described her as "an eminent daughter of Israel and a faithful daughter of the Church." He pointed out that "because she was Jewish, Edith Stein was deported with her sister Rosa and many other Jews. . . . In celebrating now and later the memory of the new saint, we will be unable not to also remember year after year the Shoah, that savage plan to eliminate a people, which cost millions of our Jewish brothers and sisters their lives."

In a pastorally sensitive way, Pope John Paul II has raised the consciousness of future generations of Catholics to the unspeakable horror of the Holocaust. He has done this through the canonization of a Jewish intellectual who chose to live out her life as a Carmelite nun.

Yesterday the Holy Father published an encyclical addressed to the bishops of the world. While this encyclical will require commentary and explanation in order to reach the general public, it clearly springs from the heart of this philosopher-theologian Pope. It not only provides a key for understanding his writings and his pastoral initiatives, but also serves as a guide for the efforts of theologians and philosophers who work for the good of the whole Church. With great respect and candor it especially addresses philosophers and others involved in forming human culture, offering them the fruit of his own philosophical reflection as well as confirming the two-thousand-year harmony of faith and reason that the Church has fostered.

Next week, the other bishops of New England and I will meet, one on one, with the Holy Father to review the past five years in the lives of the dioceses we are privileged to serve. We will concelebrate the Eucharist with the Holy Father, and we will break bread at his table in a meal marked by familiarity and humor. We will return home strengthened in our faith by this uncommonly good man whom God has given us as the successor of St. Peter.

Pray for Pope John Paul II. Pray that God might grant him to us well into the new millennium.

22

Advancing the Culture of Life in the United States

Address to the Pontifical Council for the Family

Rome, 23 October 1998

It is a privilege to have been asked to address this significant conference. I thank His Eminence, Cardinal Lopez Trujillo for this gracious invitation, and I commend him and his colleagues at the Pontifical Council for the Family for the many initiatives they have taken in the promotion of the right to life.

You who are participating in this meeting are a source of great encouragement to me. Your participation is a sign of your commitment to use your influence to create a civilization of love, to create a culture of life.

My task is to share some thoughts concerning issues involved in defending human life in the United States of America. Let me tell you a bit about myself so that you will be better able to evaluate my observations. Since 1984 I have served as Archbishop of Boston, which has a Catholic population of slightly more than two million persons. The Archdiocese of Boston is one of four dioceses within the State of Massachusetts which, as you know, is one among fifty states comprising the United States of America. The province of Boston includes three other states: New Hampshire, Maine, and Vermont. Each of these states has but one diocese.

Currently, I serve as Chairman of the Pro-Life Activities Committee on the National Conference of Catholic Bishops. My three year term concludes in November of this year.

It is from my perspective as a local bishop and as Chairman of the Pro-Life Activities Committee that I make these observations.

It is always a temptation to make sweeping generalizations about a society. The temptation to apocalyptic rhetoric is always present in assessing my nation's response to the right to life. It is necessary to state, however, that it is difficult to generalize about the situation in my country or any country. When the Holy Father was departing from Detroit, Michigan after one of his pastoral visits to the United States, on September 19, 1987, he spoke to the nation in these words:

> America the beautiful! So you sing in one of your national songs. Yes, America, you are beautiful indeed, and blessed in so many ways:
>
> - In your majestic mountains and fertile plains;
> - In the goodness and sacrifice hidden in your teeming cities and expanding suburbs;
> - In your genius for invention and for splendid progress;
> - In the power that you use for service and in the wealth that you share with others;
> - In what you give to your own, and in what you do for others beyond your borders;
> - In how you serve, and in how you keep alive the flame of hope in many hearts;
> - In your quest for excellence and in your desire to right all wrongs.
>
> Yes, America, all this belongs to you. But your greatest beauty and your richest blessing is found in the human person: in each man, woman and child, every immigrant, in every native-born son and daughter. . . .
>
> The best traditions of your land presume respect for those who cannot defend themselves. If you want equal justice for all, and true freedom and lasting peace, then, America, defend life! All the great causes that are yours today will have meaning only *to the extent that you guarantee the right to life and protect the human person.*
>
> - Feeding the poor and welcoming refugees;
> - Reinforcing the social fabric of this nation;
> - Promoting the true advancement of women;
> - Securing the rights of minorities;
> - Pursuing disarmament, while guaranteeing legitimate defense:
>
> all this will succeed only if respect for life and its protection by the law is granted to every human being *from conception until natural death.*

In these words, the Holy Father acknowledges a very important reality in the United States of America, namely a passion for justice, and a desire to be of help to the downtrodden. Even as he challenged the people of the

United States, he did so in terms of their own principles and history. Again and again in my own archdiocese I see the generous response of the faithful to special collections to assist the needy of the world, and I witness many individuals who give of themselves to work on behalf of the poor and the less fortunate. I think it is necessary to underscore this, because, in the final analysis, it is a source of hope for the future of my country. It is a country that at its best manifests a warm and generous heart to those in need.

The tragedy is, however, that while the people of the United States demonstrate a commendable spirit of generosity, we have introduced into our culture a view of the human person that wrenches the individual out of the matrix of family and society, thus leaving the individual in a miserable isolation. All of this has been done in the name of freedom of choice, in the name of a "right to privacy." It has resulted in the shameful fact that the United States of America has the highest abortion rate among Western democracies, about four thousand abortions a day. Since 1973, thirty seven million abortions have taken place in this nation which calls itself the land of the free.

One of the fifty states, Oregon, has legalized physician assisted suicide. Capital punishment increasingly is carried out in many states. These executions are not rare. In some states there has been a veritable assembly line of executions.

The abortion mentality in the United States has led us to accept infanticide as acceptable, even if the word is not often used. Within the past month and a half the Senate of the United States failed a second time to override President Clinton's veto of a bill which would have banned the procedure known as partial birth abortion. In spite of overwhelming medical testimony supporting the ban, it continues to be opposed. The driving reason for this opposition, I believe, is the fear of any legislative action which might lessen the control of the abortion rights agenda.

Recently, we have had a rash of instances of mothers or parents killing newborns and very young children. There are studies that show that between 1973 and the mid 1980s the rate of children one year of age and under being killed has doubled.

The culture of the nation has become, to an alarming degree, a culture of death. The media, both in terms of major news outlets and in terms of television dramas and movies is at least sympathetic to, if not overtly supportive of, the pro-abortion agenda.

Of particular concern is the fact that very wealthy philanthropists and foundations tend to espouse positions which promote abortion.

How have we come to this? What has been the history of the pro-abortion mentality in the United States? The far longer history of my nation is one in which abortion has been considered as murder, and therefore a moral evil. In the 1960s there were efforts to liberalize state laws, by the inclusion of clauses which would prohibit abortion except when it was deemed necessary to save the life of the mother, or in cases of rape or incest. Several states, for example Colorado, California, and New York, liberalized their abortion laws. With this liberalization of the laws, the population generally became somewhat desensitized. Little by little, what was rendered legal was coming to be accepted as moral.

By 1972 there was a reversal of this liberalization trend. In several states, the citizens had resort to referenda in which they stated their conviction that there should not be the advance of abortion rights. In 1973, with two decisions of the United States Supreme Court, the states were no longer permitted to protect the unborn. The first of these decisions, Roe v. Wade, is the foundation for the legal advances of abortion rights. At this point, political activity in support of life shifted from the fifty states to the federal level.

I must sadly report that once the Supreme Court ruled on this issue, what was declared legal became, in effect, moral. It is a strength of the United States that it is a nation which abides by the law. This national virtue, however, has the danger of leading us to invest more than legal authority upon the Supreme Court. It is a chilling example of how a bad court decision, pressed by a determined elite, can, in a very short while, profoundly alter the culture of the nation.

The Catholic Church's response to this advance of the culture of death has been significant and is continuing. It is important to state, however, that it is not only the Catholic Church which is engaged in the pro-life movement. There are Jewish voices, Moslem voices, and in the Christian community there are Orthodox voices and the voices of conservative evangelicals speaking in favor of the right to life. While there are pro-life movements within all the major religious denominations in the United States, some of the major religious bodies have, unfortunately, a very weak opposition to abortion.

It is very difficult to engage a public debate on pro-life. Those who support abortion rights frame the question in terms of a woman's right to choose and the dominion that she has over her own body. Obviously, those of us in the pro-life movement feel that the fundamental issue is the inviolable right to life of every human being. What I find particularly chilling is that there is a readiness on the part of some abortion rights advocates to admit that abortion is the taking of a human life. The right to choose for them is so absolute that it includes the taking of a human life.

It is not surprising that we have moved from the taking of life at its beginning to the promotion of the taking of life at its end through euthanasia and physician assisted suicide. There are other specific issues that flow from abortion rights as well, and these would include harmful embryo research, fetal tissue transplantation, IVF [in vitro fertilization], the vigorous promotion of contraception, and cloning. I believe a case can be made that the growing acceptance of capital punishment is a consequence of the abortion rights mentality.

It is well known to all that the position of the U.S. Government at the Cairo and Beijing conferences on women was an unadulterated promotion of the abortion rights agenda. While the efforts of the United States to influence the agenda were more subtle at Beijing, they were no less active. Particularly reprehensible are the efforts of some to use foreign aid as a means of imposing population control methods which are morally objectionable.

It has been a particular sadness to the bishops of the United States and to Catholics active in the pro-life movement that so many Catholic politicians have succumbed to the pressures exerted by pro-abortion advocates. Many of these politicians resort to the explanation that they are personally opposed to abortion, but they do not feel that they can impose their own moral judgment upon others. Again and again the bishops of the United States have attempted, both collectively and individually, to disabuse politicians of this false dichotomy. In our plenary meeting in November we will have an opportunity to visit this issue once again.

The two senators from Massachusetts are Catholic. On many issues they reflect Catholic social teaching. On the issue of abortion, however, the position of each is morally unacceptable. I have made, and will continue to make, personal pastoral interventions with these two senators, I have attempted to address them in the context of a group of their constituents, and I have encouraged Archdiocesan wide campaigns which have resulted in hundreds of thousands of pieces of mail going to these senators. All of this has been to no avail. In the last vote to override the President's veto of a partial-birth abortion ban, both these senators voted to sustain the veto, in spite of a personal appeal on my part, and on the part of thousands of their constituents.

This underscores, I believe, the strength in the abortion rights movement. The moral schizophrenia of Catholic politicians is driven to a large degree by a fear that a pro-life vote will appear to be a vote against women. Of course, any knowledge of the pro-life movement will quickly reveal that an overwhelming number of pro-life activists are women. Nonetheless, the issue is framed by the media in terms of women's rights, and therefore those who promote the pro-life agenda are portrayed as being opposed to the rights of women. It seems to me that the success of the pro-life movement depends on the development of a stronger voice of women in support of life.

A group of women in the Archdiocese of Boston several years ago began an organization which is now nationwide and is called Women Affirming Life. This organization includes a large number of professional women. Some of those who have become affiliated with this organization have told me that before they came together in this group, they felt very much alone in their profession or work place. I would not be surprised if this were not a general phenomenon. Hopefully, groups like Women Affirming Life will help a wide spectrum of women find a more effective voice in support of life.

Allow me to presume to address you directly, particularly those of you who exercise or aspire to exercise political responsibility. Our world today is in desperate need of men and women who operate out of a profound respect for the human person, an awareness that the family is the fundamental unit of society, and a wholehearted acceptance of the implications of human solidarity, particularly with the poor.

Catholic politicians who are grounded in a Christian anthropology and who are well schooled in the social doctrine of the Church have an immense advantage in helping to shape a better world. It is impossible to pick and choose from the Church's social doctrine. When this is done, then sooner or later the human person and society suffer. I have seen support for just social programs dissipate as the abortion rights agenda takes center stage. When the right to choose is the dominant right, concern for others easily becomes negotiable.

We need Catholic politicians today who have the strength of conviction of St. Thomas More. What is most important is to be faithful to the truth which alone can make us free. No political victory is worth a rejection of the truth.

The bishops of the United States have been activists in their promotion of life. On January 22 each year, in Washington, D.C., there is a pro-life march to protest the 1973 Supreme Court decision. On the eve of this march, there is a Mass and an all-night vigil at the National Shrine of the Immaculate Conception. Many bishops from throughout the nation participate—for the last several years it has been my privilege to celebrate that Mass and to preach. The Basilica is filled to overflowing, and the congregation is composed, for the most part, of young people who have come from throughout the nation. On the morning of January 22 there is a special Mass for seminarians who have come from throughout the nation. Tens of thousands of people join the march through the streets of the nation's capital. The pro-life movement in the United States, increasingly, is a movement of young people. The bishops are present in the midst of their people, marching. I have joined with my fellow Cardinals and the President of our Conference of Bishops on the steps of the United States Capitol to present hundreds of thousands of petitions requesting a ban on partial birth abortion. I have stood with Cardinal Hickey and other bishops in a prayerful candlelight vigil outside the White House. I and others have appeared before hearings in the United States Congress and in our state capitals in support of pro-life issues.

It is important also to point out that in spite of the fact that we lost the vote to override the partial birth abortion ban just weeks ago, we are determined as a conference of bishops to do all we can to put this and other issues before our elected representatives again and again and again, until finally we begin to change this culture of death into which we have been plunged.

It might be helpful to indicate some of the other things that are being done by the Church, institutionally, in an effort to promote a culture of life. Many dioceses have set up pregnancy aid centers. It is as important that the Church actively support pregnant women who face terrible pressures to choose abortion. There is a network of supporting agencies throughout the country, many of them sponsored by the Church.

We have an organized "respect life program" during the month of October in every diocese in the United States. In 1972 the Conference of Bishops adopted a respect life program which has been implemented throughout the United States.

We have developed what is called Project Rachel, which is an outreach to women and to men who have been involved in abortion. It is an effort to help them come to the reconciling love and forgiveness of God.

As a Conference of Bishops we embarked on a major public education campaign in 1989, and we named abortion as the fundamental human rights issue.

In the Archdiocese of New York, Cardinal O'Connor founded the Sisters of Life in 1991. In 1998, our national pro-life committee unveiled an exhibit called People of Life—A Story of Faith, Hope and Life, which now travels to dioceses throughout the country and presents, in a powerful way, advocacy on behalf of the unborn.

Major Catholic organizations have become involved in pro-life efforts. It is essential for me to mention the Knights of Columbus who have been extraordinary in their generosity and in their involvement in the pro-life effort. In recent years, through the initiative of the Knights of Columbus, memorials to the unborn have been placed in cemeteries and in the appropriate places throughout the nation.

Approximately 75 percent of the dioceses have pro-life offices or some staff working full time or part time on pro-life issues. Approximately 40 percent of the parishes in our nation have their own pro-life committees. While not all are highly developed, some are exceedingly effective.

Thirty-two out of fifty states have state Catholic Conferences. These coordinate public policy related efforts of the Bishops at the state level. They provide advice and leadership on pro-life legislation in the states, and increasingly these conferences provide coordination on a state-wide basis for efforts related to federal legislation.

In Massachusetts, for example, the four dioceses have worked together through our state Catholic Conference in an effort to mobilize Catholics in the partial birth abortion campaign. We have also developed a special emphasis on end-of-life issues. We have developed a state-wide plan which addresses education, pastoral issues, communication, and public policy. The aim of this plan is to coordinate the various commissions and agencies of the four dioceses so that we can speak with one voice in support of the right to life for those who are terminally ill and in opposition to physician assisted suicide and euthanasia.

The bishops of the United States have formed a national committee for a Human Life Amendment, which has as its goal the adoption of a constitutional amendment to overturn Roe v. Wade. While this committee is a separate and distinct organization, there are programs in which our conference can work in tandem with the MCHLA. It is estimated that on the two efforts to override a presidential veto of the partial-birth abortion ban, the MCHLA worked with dioceses to distribute between forty-five and fifty million postcards, over eight million educational flyers, and prepared detailed manuals for parishes and distributed thirty-two thousand copies of these manuals.

These institutional efforts of the Church at the level of the National Conference of Bishops, the level of diocese, of state Catholic conferences and parishes, are augmented by the involvement of thousands of individuals in efforts of prayer, of fasting, of personal witness before abortion clinics, and of efforts to counsel people who consider abortions.

While the pro-life challenge presented itself first in the 1960s in terms of abortion, the issue of euthanasia and physician assisted suicide is very much with us now. The development of high technology has made many fear being over-treated and dying in pain or attached to needless machinery. There is much confusion about the difference between a right to refuse extraordinary means and a "right" to kill oneself.

A utilitarian culture such as dominates much of the west finds it difficult to deal with persons judged to be unproductive, or to care for those we cannot cure. Such a culture more easily accepts physician assisted suicide. But it is, perhaps most of all, the rampant individualism that characterizes our culture which drives us to consider physician assisted suicide. It is interesting that the judges who have tended to favor physician assisted suicide find in the Supreme Court abortion decision of Roe v. Wade the basis for an individual right to assisted suicide. This "right" is derived as a logical consequence from the right of privacy established by the Supreme Court in Roe v. Wade which has found expression in the right to choose an abortion.

In 1997, our Conference of Bishops sponsored an international conference at the law school at the Catholic University of America on physician assisted suicide. The results of this important conference are available through our pro-life office.

It has been significant that in recent years an increasingly large number of physicians have begun to express themselves on behalf of the pro-life cause. This is particularly evident in the partial birth abortion struggle, and it is evident in the euthanasia and physician assisted suicide debate.

I conclude by saying that those of us involved in the pro-life movement have found the witness of the Holy Father an absolutely invaluable source of inspiration and instruction. His Encyclical, *Evangelium Vitae,* is the Magna Carta for the pro-life movement.

In spite of the shadows cast by a culture of death, the Church in the United States is struggling valiantly to promote a culture of life. Pray for us, as I do for you. Thank you.

23

+

God Is Sovereign, *The* Catholic Vision of Life and Death

To Health Care Leaders

4 March 1999

You will note that the definite article introduces the title of my presentation. My topic is not about *a* Catholic vision, it is about *the* Catholic vision. There are certainly points of interaction between the Catholic vision of death, the vision of other Christians, and the Jewish vision. The Twenty-Third Psalm, for example, or the book of Job are frequent sources of solace and inspiration as Catholics face death.

The Church in a very real way, however, creates her own culture, and she certainly does so with regard to death and dying.

The Catholic vision is informed by faith in Jesus Christ. The Catechism of the Catholic Church expresses the faith of the Church in these words: "Because of Christ, Christian death has a positive meaning: 'For me to live is Christ, and to die is gain' (Phil. 1:21). 'The saying is sure: if we have died with him, we will also live with him' (2 Tim. 2:11). What is essentially new about Christian death is this: through baptism, the Christian has already 'died with Christ' sacramentally, in order to live a new life; and if we die in Christ's grace, physical death completes this 'dying with Christ' and so completes our incorporation into him in his redeeming act" (CCC, no. 1010).

Lent illumines the teaching of the Church on death. We began with the imposition of ashes, a clear sign of our mortality. The older formulary accompanying the imposition reminds us that we are dust, and to dust we shall return. This starkly realistic reminder begins our observance of Lent,

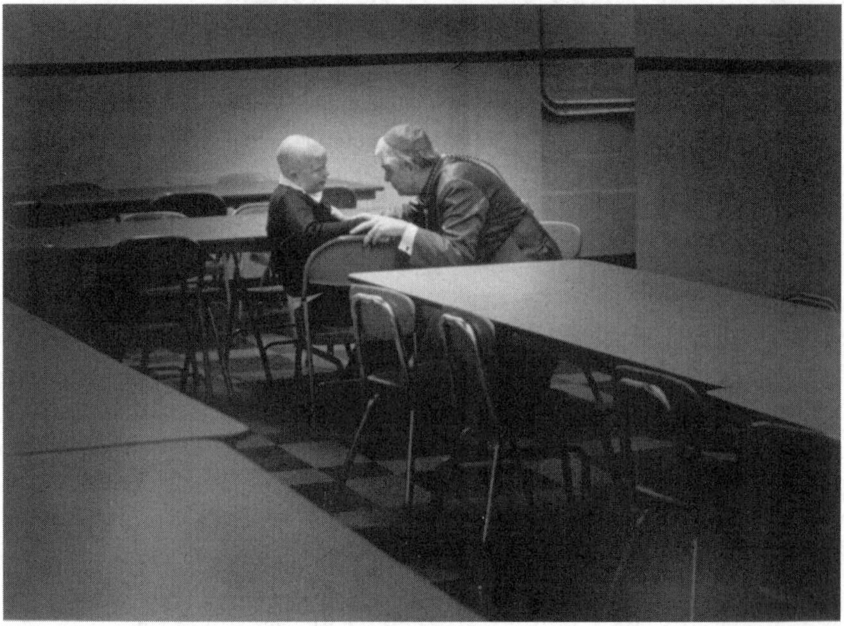

Cardinal with ailing child.

whose meaning is beautifully expressed in the following Sunday's opening prayer at Mass:

> Father,
> through our observance of Lent, help us to understand
> the meaning of your Son's death and resurrection,
> and teach us to reflect it in our lives.

A Catholic's entire life, including dying and death itself, is to be experienced under the cross and in the enduring hope of resurrection.

Because Christian death has been given a positive meaning through the saving death and resurrection of Jesus Christ, we are able to face the reality of death with a serenity that grace affords. Our future does not lie behind us. While the last word of sin is death, Jesus has put to death sin and death itself. With St. Paul we are able to cry out, "Death, where is thy sting, grave, where is thy victory?"

The full funeral rite including the wake vigil, Mass of burial, and burial of the body express the Catholic vision of death. Contemporary efforts to erode the full funeral rite are disturbing because they can easily dim the Catholic vision of death. Whatever separates the experience of death and dying from the mystery of the death and resurrection of Jesus Christ weakens the Catholic vision.

Because the Christian has already died with Christ sacramentally, death itself in the Catholic vision is not seen as the ultimate evil, as the end of life, of hope, of the future. It is not necessary, therefore, to do everything that is technologically possible to sustain life on this earth as long as medicine allows.

The Ethical and Religious Directives for Catholic Health Care Services in nos. 56 and 57 spell out the wisdom of the Catholic vision:

> A person has a moral obligation to use ordinary or proportionate means of preserving his or her life. Proportionate means are those that in the judgment of the patient offer a reasonable hope of benefit and do not entail an excessive burden or impose excessive expense on the family or the community.
>
> A person may forego extraordinary or disproportionate means of preserving life. Disproportionate means are those that in the patient's judgment do not offer a reasonable hope of benefit or entail an excessive burden, or impose excessive expense on the family or the community.

Obviously these directives do not answer every complication that is imaginable. As principles for moral reasoning, however, these and the other directives provide a vision which respects the inviolable right to life of every human person, while at the same time recognizing that death itself is not the ultimate evil to be avoided at all costs.

In the Catholic vision God is sovereign. We are stewards of the great gift of life, ours and that of others. Life itself is of inestimable value because each human being is made in the image and likeness of God. Only God is perfect, however, and we are destined to know that perfection when we see Him as He is in the glory of heaven. Focus on the question of quality of life, therefore, is off the point from a Catholic perspective. Life for us is always the inestimable gift of God; if life on this earth is in any way shaded, we have the sure knowledge that God has destined us for the perpetual light of heaven.

Our Lenten effort to understand the meaning of Christ's death and resurrection and to reflect it in our lives is not only a Lenten effort but should characterize our entire lives. So it is that the burden of one's own sickness, pain, and dying are given meaning through the death and resurrection of Jesus Christ. Suffering is not without meaning for us. Paul's words are both guide and consolation when he says that "we make up the sufferings that are wanting in Christ." Clearly, there is nothing we can bring to render effective the saving death of Christ. His is the all-sufficient sacrifice.

Yet, in a wondrous and loving condescension, God makes it possible for us to join our suffering to that of Jesus on the cross. A common Catholic expression is "to offer up." We offer all that we are, including our suffering, in union with Jesus on the cross.

In all our worthy efforts to care for the sick and dying, it would be tragic if we forgot the rich tradition on suffering that is a part of Catholic culture. I do not speak about morbidity of mind or masochism, but rather a faith-filled transformation of the reality of suffering.

Pain is not a good to be sought for itself. *The Ethical and Religious Directives* state: "Patients should be kept as free of pain as possible so that they may die comfortably and with dignity, and in the place where they wish to die. Since a person has the right to prepare for his or her death while fully conscious, he or she should not be deprived of consciousness without a compelling reason. Medicines capable of alleviating or suppressing pain may be given to a dying person, even if this therapy may indirectly shorten the person's life so long as the intent is not to hasten death" (no. 61).

It is very important that Catholic health care efforts include a competence in pain management. All too often the availability of pain control is not sufficiently known or utilized. Appeal for compassion for the pain-ridden patient is often the most compelling reason why some misguided but well-intentioned people support euthanasia and physician assisted suicide. Pro-life efforts should certainly include a medically sound and morally acceptable treatment of pain.

Compassion, such a rich concept, is set on its head when it is invoked in support of causing death. The word means "to suffer with." Jesus is the perfect model of compassion for us. He has borne our infirmities, our sin, our death. He is Emmanuel which means God-is-with-us. Again and again in the Gospels His compassion finds expression in a look, a touch, a healing word.

We who live in Him are the look, the touch, the word of His compassion for all in need. The concept of compassion is richer yet. Jesus has told us that whatever we do for the hungry, the thirsty, the naked, the stranger, the sick, the imprisoned, we do to him. In showing compassion for the sick and dying we suffer with Christ in our midst. The saints were consumed with the realization that in those most in need they met the Lord.

It is impossible to reflect on this theme without recalling the death and dying of those with whom we walked. Before coming to Logan Airport on Tuesday for the flight to this conference, I visited a retired priest who had just received the news that there is no more treatment for his cancer and death is imminent. He is in the home of his niece and her husband. The children in the house are a precious gift for their great uncle. The home has been lovingly and generously accommodated for him. While other options are available, he and his close-knit family have made the wise choice. We spoke freely, the priest and I, of his death, of his priestly service; we prayed and exchanged blessings. His pain is controlled. He is fully conscious. He is surrounded by love. Yesterday brother priests concelebrated in the house.

More personally, I cannot think of death and dying without the vivid memory of my mother's death on November 24, 1991, the Solemnity of Christ the King. Her memorial card proclaims her

- a faithful disciple of the Lord,
- a vibrant and talented woman,
- a loving wife and mother,
- a loyal friend.

She would have fit into the acceptable category of the purveyors of euthanasia. She had emphysema and congestive heart failure. My prayers had long been that she would be spared the painful death that her illness could imply. Thanks to superb medical and hospital care, and most of all thanks to the grace of God, hers was a beautiful death. Conscious almost to the last moment of earthly life, she and those who loved her most were able to assure one another by the love that bound us together and the love of God revealed in the saving death and resurrection of Jesus. It was my great privilege to be praying with her as she slipped into eternity.

My experiences are the same as those of countless others whose encounter with death and dying are part of the unrecorded glory of the Church's life. Faith is able to transfigure death and dying. With confident hope the Church prays each morning:

> In the tender compassion of our God
> the dawn from on high shall break upon us,
> to shine on those who dwell in darkness
> and the shadow of death,
> and to guide our feet into the way of peace.

Compassion, then, is central to the Catholic vision of death and dying. The Church is present every step along that way from here to eternity. We are in the midst of a revolution in health care and public welfare. The victims of this revolution are the poor, particularly the very young and old, and the sick and dying. A fixation on cost containment has put us in a situation where the most vulnerable are sacrificed for the bottom line. This is not said as an appeal to forego fiscal responsibility. It is a cry, however, for compassion for the most vulnerable in our midst.

The Catholic vision of dying must include advocacy for sufficient public funding for nursing homes, home health care, and hospice programs. Catholic health care institutions, Catholic social service bureaus, and Catholic parishes must work together to ensure that every dying person receives the compassionate care to which every one of God's children is entitled. This care must be extended to all, not only to those of the household of the faith. In every human being we encounter the living God.

Parish-based health care is an initiative which should be promoted. As length of stay in medical institutions continues to be shortened, and as home health care public support is reduced, parishes face a growing challenge to be present with compassionate care to the sick and dying. This calls for the study of existing models and inclusion of this ministry in the ordinary scope of parish life.

A 1998 Gallup survey of 1,200 Americans on spiritual beliefs and the dying process confirm the abiding value of the Catholic vision of death and dying. The survey cites:

- People desire human contact when dying, just having someone close to share their fears and concerns, holding their hand, or touching them.
- People desire spiritual comfort, having the opportunity to pray alone, to have someone pray for them, to have someone help them become spiritually at peace, or to have someone praying with them.
- "The faith communities need to address more and effectively the concerns people have about what happens after death, matters such as guilt and forgiveness."

These and other findings by this Gallup study point to the value of the Catholic approach to death and dying. The pastoral care of the sick which includes communion, anointing, viaticum, commendation of the dying and prayers for the dead responds to the deepest needs of the human heart. The importance of the sacrament of penance and the reconciliation with God and the Church which it affords cannot be overemphasized as a good for the sick and dying. The fear that is often associated with death can often be dispelled by the grace of that sacrament.

How beautifully St. Francis of Assisi points us to seek God's forgiveness in his *Canticle of the Creatures:*

> Praised are you, My Lord, for our sister bodily Death,
> from whom no living man can escape.
> Woe on those who will die in mortal sin!
> Blessed are they who will be found in your most holy will,
> for the second death will not harm them.

It was once said that true philosophy is learning how to die. The French philosopher Albert Camus added that the one ultimate question of philosophy is suicide—what reason do we have for not simply killing ourselves. It is perhaps in facing death, and confronting the question of assisted suicide, that our vision of God's gift of life shines forth most brightly.

This prayer from the Commendation of the Dying beautifully expresses the Catholic vision:

> Go forth, Christian soul, from this world
> in the name of God the almighty Father,
> who created you,
> in the name of Jesus Christ, Son of the living God,
> who suffered for you, in the name of the Holy Spirit,
> who was poured out upon you, go forth faithful Christian.
>
> May you live in peace this day,
> May your home be with God in Zion,
> with Mary, the Virgin Mother of God,
> with Joseph, and all the angels and saints.

24

+

We Speak as Concerned Citizens

Statement at a Hearing on the Death Penalty

22 March 1999

Madam Chairwoman, Mr. Chairman, I am privileged to speak in the name of three other Catholic bishops of Massachusetts, Bishop Daniel Reilly of Worcester, Bishop Sean O'Malley, O.F.M. Cap. of Fall River, and Bishop Thomas Dupré of Springfield. Bishop O'Malley could not be here today, but he is represented by his Vicar General, Monsignor George Coleman.

Last Friday we issued a statement in opposition to capital punishment, and I would ask permission to enter that statement into the record of this hearing.

We speak out of the moral tradition of the Catholic Church, and we speak as concerned citizens. George Washington said in his Farewell Address: "Of all the dispositions and habits which lead to political prosperity, religion and morality are indispensable supports. . . . Let us with caution indulge the supposition that morality can be maintained without religion. Whatever may be conceded to the influence of refined education on minds of peculiar structure, reason and experience both forbid us to expect that national morality can prevail in exclusion of religious principle. It is substantially true that virtue or morality is a necessary spring of popular government."

When Alexis de Tocqueville wrote around 1835 about his impressions of this country as a Frenchman visiting, he observed that the indirect action of religion on politics in the United States is much greater than direct action. He explained, and I quote:

"There is an innumerable multitude of sects in the United States. They are all different in the worship they offer to the Creator, but all agree concerning the duties of men to one another. Each sect worships God in its own fashion, but all preach the same morality in the name of God" (Alexis de Tocqueville, *Democracy in America*, v. 1, p. 290).

The country that de Tocqueville saw over 160 years ago was principally Christian. Today, the religious landscape is much more varied. My brother bishops and I are pleased to be here among representatives of many different religions. We are united in our worship of the one God and our moral conviction concerning the question of capital punishment. Our presence and our voice are in the best traditions of this nation.

The Catholic Church's teaching on this question is authoritatively set forth in *The Catechism of the Catholic Church.* This document was first promulgated by Pope John Paul II on October 11, 1992. On September 8, 1997, the Pope promulgated the definitive Latin language edition of the *Catechism.* In this definitive edition, there are several modifications of the earlier text. I quote the pertinent passage of the definitive text (paragraph 2267):

> Assuming that the guilty party's identity and responsibility have been fully determined, the traditional teaching of the Church does not exclude recourse to the death penalty, if this is the only possible way of effectively defending human lives against the unjust aggressor.
>
> If, however, non-lethal means are sufficient to defend and protect people's safety from the aggressor, authority will limit itself to such means, as these are more in keeping with the concrete conditions of the common good and more in conformity with the dignity of the human person.
>
> Today, in fact, as a consequence of the possibilities which the state has for effectively preventing crime, by rendering one who has committed an offense incapable of doing harm—without definitively taking away from him the possibility of redeeming himself—the cases in which the execution of the offender is an absolute necessity 'are very rare, if not practically non-existent.' (Evangelium vitae 56)

The Holy Father, in his visit to St. Louis a short time ago, spoke to this question in these words: "the dignity of human life must never be taken away even in the case of someone who has done great evil. Modern society has the means of protecting itself, without definitively denying criminals the chance to reform. . . . I renew the appeal . . . to end the death penalty which is both cruel and unnecessary."

The base line of our opposition is the inviolable dignity and right to life of every human person. We are poised on the threshold of a new millennium. We are leaving what could arguably be said to be the most violent of centuries. A day does not pass without some fresh atrocities reported from Borneo, Kosovo, or closer to home. With capital punishment, we all become victims.

We take our stand not because we are unmindful of the monstrous evil that is murder. It is precisely because we recognize that evil that we oppose capital punishment. We do not help those whose lives have been shattered with the murder of a loved one by reinstating capital punishment.

As a society we must not encourage or be motivated by vengeance. This is not the way to a more civil, a more humane society.

Your efforts as legislators are rightly directed to addressing the concern of citizens for safety and freedom from the threat of capital offenders. No person and no family should feel unprotected. All of us have the right to live with a sense of peace and security in our own homes and neighborhoods. We should make any changes necessary in the judicial and penal systems to ensure this, short of taking the life of another person, even a guilty person.

There are many supporting arguments that can be advanced in opposing capital punishment. We have limited ourselves to the innate dignity and worth of every human life, and the negative effects of state sponsored killing on our culture. Violence begets violence. Our hope is for a civilization of love, a culture of life.

25

In a Valley of Darkness

On the Littleton, Colorado, High School Shootings

25 April 1999

Certainly one of the passages of Scripture most often quoted is the Twenty-Third Psalm which begins with the confident proclamation of faith: "The Lord is my shepherd, there is nothing I shall want." The psalmist goes on to say in his prayer: "If I should walk in the valley of darkness, no evil would I fear. You are there with your crook and your staff; with these you give me comfort."

This Sunday we find ourselves in a valley of darkness. Violence hangs over us like a dark, heavy cloud. As though dropping bombs on Serbia and driving Kosovar Albanians from their ancestral home were not enough, our minds and hearts have been riveted once again on a high school—Columbine High School in Littleton, Colorado. How important it is that as we walk through this and every other valley of darkness, we find our strength, our consolation, our light, and our way by following the Lord who is our Good Shepherd.

Jesus—the Lord—is our *light* and our salvation. The darkness which he has overcome in his resurrection is the darkness of sin and death. To walk in the light, it is essential that we *name* the darkness. The heart-wrenching tragedy that struck Littleton is not something new in human history. It is as old as human history itself, and is prefigured in the murder of Abel by his brother Cain. The availability of guns—altogether too accessible and acceptable in our society—is not the answer to what happened. The lack of acceptance, the failure of supervision are not the answers, whatever their influence in the course of events. Ultimately the answer is in the awful choice to end the life of another human being. After Cain had murdered his brother, Abel, God asked him where Abel was. Cain's disdainful and chilling answer reverberated in every shot fired in Littleton last week: "Am I my brother's keeper?" That question contains the answer to the evil of violence: it is the failure to see in one another the image of God, the failure to accept the burden of God's law—which is to love God and to love our neighbor.

We are coming to the end of the most violent of centuries, and we do so immersed in a culture of death. Our families are plagued with domestic violence, our entertainment celebrates violence, our laws condone death. Our challenge is to create a new culture—a culture of life, a civilization of love.

This is not primarily nor exclusively the task of schools. Educators are already overburdened with impossible expectations to compensate for a cultural crisis. Government cannot effect the necessary cultural change. Churches and synagogues through their institutional expressions cannot alone transform the culture. What is essential is for every person to take inventory of his or her own life, to determine the extent to which violence is a part of that life, and to resolve to make whatever changes are necessary to help create a new culture—a culture of life, a civilization of love.

Last Sunday, a seventeen year old Littleton, Colorado high school student, Cassie Bernall, wrote these words:

> Now I have given up
> on everything else—
> I have found it to be
> the only way to really know Christ
> and to experience the mighty power
> that brought him back to life again,
> and to find out what it means
> to suffer and die with him.
> So, whatever it takes I will be
> one who lives in the
> fresh newness of life of those
> who are alive from the dead.

A few days later—she was confronted by another Cain. He asked her if she believed in God. She answered "Yes, I believe in God." The gunman laughed, asked mockingly, "Why," and then shot her.

The last word of sin is always death. Cassie Bernall believed in God because she knew his love in the saving death and resurrection of Jesus Christ.

May we find our way more easily through this dark valley by the light of her faith, and may we live that same faith in love.

26

✢

Statement on the Deaths of John F. Kennedy, Jr., Carolyn Bessette Kennedy, and Lauren Bessette

19 July 1999

In the darkness of night death came swiftly and unannounced for young John F. Kennedy, Jr., his lovely wife, Carolyn, and her sister, Lauren Bessette.

Although no human life is more precious than another to God, the world stopped for a moment, held its breath, and whispered, "No, not again."

A joyous family wedding suddenly became a painful vigil while hundreds of men and woman scoured the sea in search for three young lives full of so much promise.

To Caroline Kennedy Schlossberg, now without parents or sibling, I extend my prayerful condolences.

I offer the same to the parents of Carolyn and Lauren Bessette, who must now fulfill nature's cruelest demand of burying their children.

To Senator Kennedy and the Kennedy family, who once more bear the burden of grief in the face of unexpected tragedy, I offer my sincere sympathy and assurance of prayerful support.

To all who mourn the deaths of John, Carolyn, and Lauren, I offer the one lasting hope without which we would despair.

We all die enfolded in the promise of eternal life given us by the Lord who conquered death and insisted that "I am the resurrection and the life; whoever believes in me, even if he dies, will live, and everyone who lives and believes in me will never die."

27

+

Forgiving Debts of the Poor

Op-Ed, Within the Beltway, the *Washington Post*

20 September 2000

For many religious believers, the year 2000 is a Jubilee Year, a time not just to celebrate the millennium but to make new beginnings and to right old wrongs. In the Old Testament, Jubilee called in particular for a fresh start for the poor, for reestablishing justice and equity. In the spirit of the Jubilee, the Archdiocese of Boston recently forgave $28 million of debts, owed mostly by the 30 poorest parishes. This step is similar to actions by other dioceses and is linked to Pope John Paul II's urgent call for debt relief for poor countries during this year.

More than 30 very poor countries owe well over $100 billion, most to other governments and international organizations such as the World Bank and the International Monetary Fund. Like the Holy Father and other religious leaders, many governments, including our own, many prominent economists and policymakers and key members of Congress have called on the wealthiest nations to reduce this crushing debt burden of the poorest.

In the next few weeks, Congress will decide whether the United States will do its small share. This is the last chance to make the year 2000 a time of hope for millions of the world's poorest people. It will take $435 million. This is an amount large enough to make an important difference to many of the poorest countries, but a tiny three-hundredths of one percent of the federal budget. This small amount would fund two years of the U.S. commitment to the debt relief program approved by the G-7 leaders last year at Cologne, Germany. It is an amount that would encourage other countries holding much more debt than the United States to come forward with their much larger share of the cost of the program.

Unfortunately, it is also an amount that Congress so far has been unwilling to provide.

I find it very difficult to explain to Catholic bishops, missionaries and relief workers in Africa and Latin America why the United States, blessed with such wonderful resources and such a powerful economy, is reluctant to commit such a relatively small amount. They know our budget has a surplus projected to reach trillions of dollars over the next decade. Nor do I have an answer to the pope's appeal. He asked many months ago: [Why is] progress in resolving the debt problem . . . still so slow? Why so many hesitations? Why the difficulty in providing the funds needed even for already-agreed initiatives? It is the poor who pay the cost of indecision and delay."

A U.S. failure to fulfill its Cologne pledge would be devastating. If the United States walks away from its commitment, others will surely follow, thus jeopardizing the whole program. Already major debt relief for Bolivia and Honduras is being held up for lack of U.S. funding. The possibility that this initiative will fail is something that our church partners in Africa and Latin America dread to contemplate. Through a host of church institutions, from relief and development programs to hospitals and schools, they are with the poorest of the poor and see every day in countless ways the practical consequences of debt.

They know the debt relief is not a panacea. It alone will not end poverty. Poverty is much too complex and deep-seated for that. They know that it must be tackled first by their own governments and people working together on a variety of fronts for the common good. Yet their people are too poor to do it alone. Unless the debt burden is sharply reduced, it will continue to drain resources needed for education, health and other essential investments, and make the task of poverty reduction immensely more difficult.

A few weeks ago, the Senate and the House were set to approve only very small amounts for poor-country debt relief. Then something most heartening occurred during the House floor debate on the foreign aid bill. Members from both sides of the aisle stood up to press for much more substantial relief.

Rep. John Kasich, chairman of the Budget Committee, argued that, with our "unprecedented economic power, it does not make any sense to not share some of the bounty that we have with those that have little." Rep. Spencer Bachus, the Alabama Republican, explained: "[I]t is not a total solution to poverty, to hunger, to disease; but it is the first step. It is a necessary step. It is where the journey should begin to free these countries of the burden of debt, the chains of poverty, the shackles of despair."

In the end the House voted to triple funding for debt relief, but this is still only about half what is needed. I hope, nevertheless, that the momentum generated by the signs of substantial bipartisan support for generous funding will translate into the full appropriation of $435 million. With the crowded agenda and the rush to adjourn, funding for debt relief could get pushed aside. I hope that this does not happen. My fervent prayer is that, when Congress adjourns, we will be able to say to the people of Africa and Latin America: "Yes, our country, which has been blessed with so much, will act, in the spirit of Jubilee, to allow a fresh start for the poorest of the poor in your country."

II

A MORAL VOICE IN THE MODERN WORLD

Cardinal Law and Fidel Castro at a meeting that lasted five hours. At the Cardinal's right is Jaime Cardinal Ortega of Havana and to his right is Roberto Gonzales, then on the Cardinal's staff, now Archbishop of San Juan.

28

One Can Witness through a Way of Life

To Carmelite Nuns in Poland

18 August 1986

PRAISED BE JESUS CHRIST

1. Our pilgrimage to Poland would not be complete without this visit to you, dear Sisters. We have come to Poland to praise Our Lord for the abundant graces he has showered upon the Church in this nation throughout its noble but tormented history. He has supported you by allowing Polish Catholics to see their sufferings as a sharing in His own for the growth of God's Kingdom. We have come to learn from this history, especially from the way the Church in Poland has responded to the drama of life in this most deadly of centuries. We have come to learn how to strengthen our own life as Church as we encounter at home what many consider to be an opposition between the worship of God and human fulfillment.

2. We have come to you, dear Sisters, because your way of life discloses more than any other that this opposition is a lie. You have dedicated your lives entirely to God's worship, to the contemplation of His glory. As some would say, you have "left the world," rejected what it has to offer. You therefore pose a great challenge to those who consider your way of life an irresponsible refusal to join in the efforts to make this world more human. This certainly would be a Marxist evaluation of your vocation. Moreover, it is not only Marxists who think this way. This is the view of some in our

culture in the United States. We have come to Poland to learn from your response to this criticism.

3. You incarnate in a striking way the choice facing all women and men from the beginning of our history. We have to decide whether life in accordance with God's loving will of creation and redemption is an obstacle to our liberty and development, or whether it is the only way to reach the goal for which we were created and thus experience the full potential of our nature as persons. You live in our midst as a clear, explicit, unambiguous sign that to seek first and above all the Kingdom of God will indeed bring us everything we need for perfect fulfillment and happiness.

4. In the words of the incomparable St. Teresa de Jesus, Teresa of Avila: *¡Solo Dios basta*! God alone is enough. To say this in Poland today requires from you a great courage and a strong faith. But in a certain sense, such witness is not less difficult in other parts of the world. Marxism is not the only materialistic humanism which considers that the contemplation of God's glory and His worship *no basta,* is not enough, that it is alienating, that it distracts us from the real needs of men and women. We hope to take back to our Archdiocese and country a vivid memory of the way you reject this denial of God's absolute sovereignty in an officially atheistic country, so that we will be inspired to do likewise where a kind of practical atheism proposes the same rejection of the primacy of God's will.

5. On the feast of the Transfiguration I announced the beginning on September 14, feast of the Triumph of the Cross, of a two-year period for a synod of the Archdiocese of Boston. I recalled in that letter the words of Pope Paul VI at the end of the Second Vatican Council about the special need to strengthen our belief in the primacy of contemplation in a world where so many are simply afraid of God, fearing total dedication to Him as alienating, stifling. Pope Paul VI said that one of the purposes of the Second Vatican Council was to learn how to effectively and powerfully proclaim to the modern world that: "God is—and more, He is real. He lives, a personal provident God, infinitely good. And not only good in Himself, but also immeasurably good to us. He will be recognized as our Creator, our truth, our happiness—so much so that the effort to look on Him, and to center our heart in Him, which we call contemplation, is the highest, the most perfect act of the spirit, the act that must be at the apex of all human activity" (December 7, 1965).

6. Today I ask your prayers, dear Sisters, that the Holy Spirit might empower us to see how we in the Archdiocese of Boston might live and proclaim to all in our culture, subject to the different forms in which materialism tempts us, that contemplation must indeed be "at the apex of all human activity" (December 7, 1965).

7. I have had the privilege and honor of being close to your Carmelite tradition since my youth. My aunt, Sister John of the Cross, was a Discalced Carmelite. She prayed for and advised me of my vocation to the

priesthood before I considered it as a possibility. In your midst I want to thank her, now in eternity, for what she stood for and did for me.

8. Poland has given to the universal Church our chief pastor who tirelessly and zealously, again and again, proclaims to the world the superiority of Spirit over matter, just as Pope Paul VI insisted. We know how your Carmelite spiritual tradition inspired, nourished, and sustained Pope John Paul II. Teresa de Jesus and John of the Cross speak to us through him of the primacy of the spiritual. In your midst, with you, I thank Our Lord for the gift of Pope John Paul II to all the Church. I beg that through the intercession of the Blessed Virgin Mary, Our Lady of Czestochowa, we might return home even more dedicated to join him in proclaiming to our tormented world the only path to authentic liberation, fulfillment, and peace: *Solo Dios Basta*! Praised be Jesus Christ!

29

✛

Racism Is a Sin

On the Rodney King Case

1 May 1992

In a moment of profound national tragedy such as this, it is important to turn to God in prayer. I ask that at all Masses in the Archdiocese on this weekend prayers be included for an end to violence, for justice, and for peace.

Whatever the ultimate disposition of the Rodney King case will be, the controverted film clip certainly evokes revulsion as an apparently brutal use of force. It is appropriate that the U.S. Department of Justice is reviewing the case.

The ensuing outbreak of violence with its devastating toll in human life and injury, as well as looting and destruction of property bears out the sad truth that violence begets violence. There are no winners.

Critical to the well-being of any society is a respect for every human person. The haunting specter of racism hangs over the current crisis. Racism is a sin. Whenever a human person is denied his or her identity and is perceived by another simply in terms of racial or ethnic characteristics, and when such stereotyping is negative, there is present the sin of racism.

May God grant us the wisdom to understand that every human being is sacred, and may we be granted the grace to live this truth in all our endeavors: personal, business, civic, and religious.

30

An Appeal on Behalf of Haitian Refugees

A Letter to President George Bush

22 May 1992

George Bush
President of the United States
The White House
1600 Pennsylvania Avenue
Washington, DC 20500

Dear Mr. President:

I have read with profound alarm the report that Haitians attempting to flee their country will be urged, at sea, to return to their homeland. This is being done, as I understand it, because the facilities at Guantanamo Bay are already being overly taxed. While the effort will be made to encourage Haitians attempting to flee to return to their homeland, it is reasonably presumed that a number will continue on their perilous voyage to Florida.

Mr. President, I understand that this is an issue made even more complex by the political conditions within Haiti, the economic blockade imposed by the Organization of American States, and the budgetary implications.

I urgently plead with you on pressing humanitarian grounds, however, to cut through the legal and political Gordian knot and make provision for persons fleeing Haiti to be received aboard U.S. vessels and brought to a processing center either in this country or in some Caribbean country. The sad memory of Jews being refused entry before World War II should teach us that never again should we turn our back on a human being pleading for our help and hospitality.

In the name of all that is decent, we cannot turn our backs on poor Haitians willing to take heroic measures in order to escape a hopeless situation which is made worse by a failure of resolve on the part of the international community.

As our government and other governments strive, and I would hope with greater effect, to help resolve the political crisis within Haiti and to harness international cooperation in the rebuilding of the economy of that land, it is imperative that we do what we are well able to do, and that is extend a welcome to children, men, and women who are proving themselves willing to make a heroic effort to achieve a better life in a free society.

There is no doubt in my mind that you share my overall concern for the people of Haiti. I plead with you, Mr. President, to act resolutely and quickly to come to the assistance of those Haitians who are at risk on the sea even as this is being written. I would also urge an expansion of the in-country refugee processing in Port au Prince.

With warm personal regards and asking God to bless you and Barbara, I am

Sincerely yours in Christ,
Bernard Cardinal Law

31

+

Winter Rescue

An Interfaith Appeal on Behalf of Balkan Refugees

6 October 1992

The world is painfully aware of the frightening humanitarian crisis in the Balkans. But the world may be less aware of the real possibility that war and winter will combine to turn an already frightful situation into a hideous spectacle of death and desolation that we thought could never occur again in Europe.

In July, a Bishops' Conference delegation, led by Archbishop Theodore E. McCarrick of Newark, saw first-hand the pressure on those who could not flee the violence due to closed borders. The delegation also saw the extraordinary work of voluntary and governmental relief agencies with these and other refugees from Bosnia-Herzegovina. But, despite all that is being done, it is clear that more urgent action is needed:

- The displacement of people by means of so-called "ethnic cleansing" must stop;
- Safe passage must be afforded relief convoys so that aid can reach isolated and vulnerable communities, especially in Bosnia-Herzegovina;
- Refugees inside and outside Bosnia-Herzegovina must be protected against the upcoming winter;
- Nations must open their doors to allow temporary refuge for the millions of refugees, who have placed an unbearable burden on Croatia, Serbia, and surrounding countries.

Our Bishops' Conference has sought to address this situation over the past fifteen months by providing more than $1.3 million in humanitarian aid, and by issuing numerous appeals for more urgent action on the part of our government and the international community.

Our individual programs and appeals are not enough, however. As a Roman Catholic Bishop—and in the name of Archbishop Daniel E. Pilarczyk, president of the Bishops' Conference—I stand here as one with other religious leaders to appeal for the protection of the fundamental human rights of each and every victim of this war; and to appeal, with one voice, to the international community to respond more effectively to avert a disaster of potentially monumental proportions.

The human misery in the Balkans is not an accident or an aberration but is the work of human hands; it is the result of what Pope John Paul has called "an absurd and cruel war," driven by the "glaring anachronism" of intolerant nationalism. "This enormous tragedy," the Pope urges, "requires an immediate response and the deepest charity. Christ himself is suffering in these brothers and sisters."

Every dead child, every homeless woman, every mistreated prisoner, every starving refugee, every "cleansed" town makes ever more distant the day that the diverse peoples of the former Yugoslavia will live together in peace and harmony. Because a continuing cycle of hatred and violence is tearing so many people from their homes, today in the Balkans time is not on the side of justice, peace, or tolerance.

That is why Roman Catholic Cardinal Franjo Kuharic and Serbian Orthodox Patriarch Pavle came together again recently to condemn the continuing atrocities in Bosnia-Herzegovina and to appeal for an immediate and unconditional halt to hostilities. That is why there must be vastly greater contributions from individuals, and especially from governments, for relief efforts. And that is why the world community must act now, in this and other ways recommended by our appeal, to do more to help millions of suffering people in the Balkans and to avert even greater suffering in the coming months.

In the words of the recent Vatican document on refugees (*Refugees: A Challenge to Solidarity*), "Human solidarity, as witnessed by any community that welcomes refugees and by the commitment of national and international organizations that care for them, is a source of hope for the real possibility of living together in fraternity and peace."

32

Election of a New President in 1992

Words to William Jefferson Clinton

6 November 1992

What a blessing it is to live in a nation where leadership can pass from one person and one party to another with the peace and tranquility which we have come to take for granted as a nation.

President-elect Clinton deserves the prayers, the best wishes, the best and most creative suggestions, and the willing hands of all as he prepares to assume the presidency of this nation. The election of a President of the United States is not simply a domestic affair; President-elect Clinton will be a major player on the international scene as the world passes through a most challenging period.

As the President-elect prepares to take office, I hope there will be a clear indication of his determination to maintain the strong interest and a consistent involvement of this nation in the peace process in the Middle East. It is so important that momentum not be lost as one side or the other calculates the possibility of gaining new advantages.

As the nation awaits the policies of our new president, I hope we will be sufficiently patient with him as the high rhetoric of a political campaign is translated to realistic goals, particularly with regard to the domestic economy. Our economy is complex and has a direct impact, not only on our lives in this nation, but on the lives of people in every nation. It is unfortunate, but true, that we were not poised as a nation for the revolution of 1989. Our economy had been geared to the cold war, and it simply is going to take time to redirect it.

One of the new problems presented by the revolution of 1989 which our nation has not yet adequately solved is how to respond effectively in the cause of justice and peace when civil strife takes heavy toll in various parts of the world. How, for example, should our nation or any nation respond to the crisis in the Balkans or in parts of the former Soviet Union? How should our nation and how should the international community respond to the ongoing crisis in the Sudan, and in Liberia?

The tragic murder of five religious sisters from the United States and several Liberian young women who were aspirants in their community has brought a focus which one hopes will not be momentary, on a problem which has been ongoing. Liberia is torn by a civil war that has taken thousands upon thousands of lives. The regional peace-keeping force which is in place has evidently not been able to stop this and restore civil peace in Liberia. What is the United Nations to do in such a situation? What should be the policy of our nation? Can we really pretend that situations like this are none of our concern?

And what of the refugees? Each day the net total of refugees in this world is increased by five thousand children, women, and men. The immediate problem and the long-range problem posed by the refugees throughout the world is a major world problem.

Closer to home, there is the continuing problem of Haiti, and there is the intolerable situation which exists in Cuba.

Finally, as political rhetoric fades into the distance and reality sets in, I would hope that the President-elect would take a close look at the matter of the right to life of the unborn and choice in education. To match his eloquent statement of concern for many life issues, such as the plight of the poor, the unemployed, and the sick, I would hope that the logic of that concern will lead him to recognize also the right to life of the unborn.

In the two and a half months before the inauguration, it would be a great thing for the nation if President-elect Clinton and President Bush and their staffs would do more than simply work out the mechanics of transition. It would serve the common good if they would engage their minds and the best minds available in a collaborative effort to look at issues facing this nation.

1989 is one of those rare historical markers. The revolution that year changed the face of the globe. In the final analysis, there is probably nothing more important for President-elect Clinton than to have some very clear ideas as to what leadership he will bring to a world changed by 1989.

The President-elect deserves not only the best wishes but the prayers of us all as he prepares to take the oath of office next January.

33

✣

Peace Cannot Be Achieved without Justice

On Violence in Burundi, Bosnia, and Northern Ireland

28 October 1993

At a time in history when it would seem universal peace could be a reality, armed conflict and senseless violence are spread like an epidemic throughout the world. The little nation of Burundi has been subjected to an unbelievable reign of violence this past week. In recent days unspeakable atrocities committed in Bosnia have come to light. We hold up in prayer in this Mass the victims of violence everywhere, we remember their families, and we pray for their nations. We remember in a special way the victims of violence in Northern Ireland, remembering particularly the Protestant victims of the bombing on the Shankhill Road and the Catholics killed in the current wave of random shootings.

The Roman Catholic Archbishop of Armagh, Cardinal Cahal Daly, has said of this bombing that "it is one of the worst atrocities of a quarter century which has already seen so many horrors. . . . Any statements attempting to 'explain' it or make it seem less inexcusable only compound its evil and only serve to expose the twisted and the perverse logic of those who issue the statements."

We are gathered on the feast of St. Simon and St. Jude, Apostles. We know little about these two men beyond the fact that they were chosen by the Lord to be Apostles—to preach to all the Good News of salvation, to preach a kingdom of justice, of love, of peace. We know they were faithful to that call—faithful unto the death of martyrdom. They were victims of violence in their efforts to bring the teachings of the Prince of Peace to others.

That message of peace is no less valid because of the martyrs it has claimed. The Book of Wisdom tells us that "God did not make death." Our Christian faith proclaims that Jesus came that we might have life and have it more abundantly. Jesus has summarized the teachings of all the law and the prophets in two commandments: "You must love the Lord your God with all your heart, with all your soul, and with all your mind. This is the greatest and the first commandment. The second resembles it: You must love your neighbor as yourself." It is this teaching which has prompted this special Mass.

The troubles in Ireland are a very special cause of concern for us. Ireland and Boston have so many strong bonds. Only last Saturday I witnessed the marriage of a Boston couple who are now in Ireland to experience together their ancestral roots as they begin their married life. On a clear day, it is as if we could see Ireland from Castle Island. Ours must be more than an intermittent nostalgia for an island nation wrapped in a romantic mist, however. If we love Ireland, then we must work for peace in that land. We must press upon our nation's leaders those policies which will further the cause of peace.

The truth must be faced. There is injustice in Northern Ireland. It is a fact that the Catholic minority suffers greater economic hardship and is subject to discrimination. Catholics are too often strangers and aliens in their own land. The terrible cycle of violence over these past twenty-five years has taken more Catholic lives than Protestant. One such life taken is one too many. The public perception, however, sometimes yields the impression that the violence is a one-way street.

It must also be acknowledged that peace cannot be achieved without justice. Justice demands that the men and women of Northern Ireland who have nationalist hopes be accorded an equal place in that society. The fact is that Northern Ireland is populated by persons holding different views concerning her future: some are unionists, some are nationalists. Both views must be acknowledged as legitimate, and the accommodation of both views must be achieved within a constitutional framework.

The governments of both Ireland and Great Britain must be active parties in developing a constitutional solution to the problem of Northern Ireland. Nationalists and Unionists in Northern Ireland must be, equally, participants in the process seeking a constitutional solution. To the greatest extent possible the process must be inclusive of groups within Northern Ireland. An absolute condition for participation in the political process, however, must be the cessation of violence. This is so for groups that are loyalists as well as nationalists.

Our own nation's policy must be a manifest, active interest in furthering the cause of justice in Northern Ireland. Without that, there will be no peace.

There would be no better way to thwart the chance for peace than to allow violence to derail the efforts of those seeking a constitutional solution. The tragic bombing on the Shankhill Road was preceded by and has been followed by the random killing of Catholics. Any efforts to bring together the various elements in Northern Ireland in search of a peace built on justice must be supported. Violence must not be allowed to hold peace captive.

Cardinal Daly said last Sunday in Northern Ireland: "Our Christian convictions must not be confined to our times spent in Church and to periods of worship and prayer. Concern for justice for all must influence our political decisions, our voting patterns, our discussions about current affairs, our contacts and communications with political representatives."

It is no exaggeration to say that if we in Boston were to take the Cardinal's words to heart, we could help the process of peace in Ireland by the influence we could exert on our own nation's policy. May we be so moved.

34

+

Reclaiming Our Children's Future

To the "Ten-Point Coalition" of Christians, Jews, and Muslims

15 May 1994

Thank you very much. I would say to you and to your brothers and sisters who are actively participating in the ten-point coalition, you have been to all of us in this city a sign of light and of hope and we're so grateful for what all of you are doing in that ten-point coalition, and we of the Archdiocese of Boston are proud to stand with you. Congratulations.

I notice in that time when you were given the task of getting some refreshments, I hope you all made it, that there was a member of the civic community, and we spoke for a little bit, and I was reminded in that conversation of the wonderful story of that young woman who was missing in the western part of the state and all sorts of folk were mobilized in searching for her and hoping, very often against hope, that they would find her. The beautiful part of that story, which speaks volumes, I think, to all of us in this room across many difference lines, is that when she was found she was praying. What a beautiful gift that young woman is. What a beautiful gift her tradition is that has brought her to that awareness of God and how proud we are to be in this room as Jews, as Christians, as Muslims, united in the cause of our children, that young girl and all of our children, because we know that the future of this society and indeed the future of any society, lies within the hearts and the future lives of the very youngest of us.

We who gather in this room, at least many of us, are not complacent

about what we see going on around us. We see some things that disturb us, we see some things that, we think, need to be changed, and it is my hope and prayer that you in this room and others like you throughout the Commonwealth will take heart and realize that you don't stand alone, and take hope that if we stand and move together, change can come, and change will come.

At times in our society it seems that there is a cacophony of conflicting opinions in which the loudest is heard first and the only way to resolve conflict is presumed to be by a libertarian velocity that is agnostic about the truth. That seems to be the way, the only way, that some believe that conflict can be legitimately resolved in a society as diverse as are we. We gather here in this room as quite a diverse group of human beings. I'm certain that I could, without too much difficulty, think of three of four theological issues upon which we might disagree a little bit—and of any other issues that we might disagree with as well. But I think that what binds us together and makes us feel very comfortable in one another's company, is that we believe that there is such a thing as truth. We believe that there is such a thing as right and wrong, and we believe that that truth and that right and that wrong is not determined by a plurality of votes or the popularity of the cause. But that truth is truth and we see it in the very nature of things, and right is right and wrong is wrong, and the rightness and the wrongness of choices and the rightness and the wrongness of pattern relationships are revealed within the human heart. I believe we are one in mind. Are we?

There is also a lot of confusion about what the role of the state is. What is the role of government, and we may differ, some of us, on exactly what that role is. The state does have a role. In going about my own social tradition, social teaching, let me indicate the way I think we should expect the state to act. The state is to serve the human person and society. The state is to *serve* the human person and society. The state is to serve the family which is the very basis of any human society. And so the measure of whether or not a state government or city government or national government is doing what it ought to be doing is whether or not it is serving the human person, whether or not it is serving the family's welfare, whether or not it is serving society. The state and society are not the same things. The state is to serve society, but society is greater than the state. And to every person the state owes respect for innate human rights and dignity. For every person, for *every* person. And the state further has the task secondly of setting the conditions so that reasonable men and women can live together in harmony, so that the members of the society will have a freedom and security to pursue goals for the good of the person and his/her family.

Thirdly, the state must fulfill its obligations to the society as a whole, as well as to the members by providing for those goods that advance the common good. Clearly, police and fire, sanitation, maintenance of society. But among these also is the crucial element of education. The state does have an obligation to serve society, to serve the family in the matter of education. Not to take over the role of the family, but to assist the family, the parents, the child. Furthermore, the state has the obligation and responsibility to further the cultural values and ideals that make up the identity of a society. I think that's a point where many of us have grave concern. There seems to be a lack of clarity about those cultural values and ideals which give identity to this wonderfully diverse society we are about, which is still America's experiment in process. At its best, the state fosters and helps those ideals flourish. And our political experiment has expressed the American ideal very well when it speaks of life, liberty, and the pursuit of happiness.

Within that context of the state's role one sees the role of law and the role of civil servants and the role of politicians. Law must reflect truth. It doesn't make it hard. It's not a vote of the legislature which determines what is true and what is false. Law must be grounded in truth. Law must reflect truth and codify it, not all the moral responsibilities that we have before God, but rather to codify those strictures which will bring about that tranquility of order which is peace, fully respectful of the freedom, dignity of persons and groups within the society. Politicians and civic leaders serve the common good. They serve the *common* good, the good of us all, and must acknowledge and respect the truths by which lives are ordered and have meaning, and a society can attain that tranquility of order which alone will bring it peace.

The crisis that we are facing has to do with a breakdown of consensus in our society about what is true and what is false, what is right and what is wrong. And this breakdown has been accelerated by being linked to another strong strain in American life which is individual liberty, which is a wonderful and beautiful thing. And that liberty brought about great things for this country as one of its distinguishing cultural marks. However, if you let it, that principle of individual liberty to a broken consensus on what is right and what is wrong and what is true, leaves the society and hence the state with no bearings and no reference points for the cities. Thus, the pressure of groups and lobbyists for individualistic entitlements increases day by day and wins the day. In the long run, the common sense of good life-minded persons who are the majority, will, I think, win the day.

I believe that there is much more consensus than we may suspect. The consensus is submerged, the consensus doesn't carry the day where decisions are made. And if that reading of reality is correct, then that is the significance of occasions such as this, when persons who do believe that it is possible for us to have a consensus about what is right and wrong. It is possible for us to say what marriage is and what it is not. It is possible for us to define what family is without prejudice to any who suffer the difficulty of broken family or single parenthood. It is possible for us to define what the family is in the ideal and what the family is fundamentally and basically in our nature and what it is that will best serve the child in the future as a working definition of family. Do you think that's possible?

It is possible to say that human sexuality education which has its place in appropriate form and appropriate ways, needs to bring a young person to recognize the great gift that is human sexuality, to recognize the intrinsic purpose of human sexuality and to realize that this is a purpose to be realized within the commitment of love, which is an enduring commitment open to new life and to its sustenance. And to be given the impression that it's perfectly alright at the age of eleven, twelve, or thirteen to anticipate the pleasures without any of the obligations of what human sexuality is all about, is to give a false picture and is to give a sure recipe for human disaster. Are we agreed on this?

Men and women simply don't want a society where promiscuous relations are the order of the day. Citizens know instinctively that laws are to be obeyed. Truth and honesty are right for human relationships—*all* human relationship. Cheating and fraud are wrong wherever they occur. Selfishness that exploits others in any way is to be rejected. However, over the short run it's very easy for us to become confused and diverted and stampeded by self interest groups who undermine common sense reasoning, usually by scare tactics. This can be done in a variety of ways and it's done in ways with disastrous results. Within the last several days I prayed with and comforted the parents and the in-laws of a young woman dying of AIDS who had buried her husband less than two months before. I have two other colleagues, one lay and one priest, dying of AIDS.

The Archdiocese, thanks to the generous response of many people, and the cooperation of the state in an appropriate way, is able to provide housing and care for homeless persons with AIDS, for mothers who are HIV positive and their children. No one needs to convince me of the terrible scourge and the human tragedy that is AIDS. I have seen it and I have felt it. But I would say that one of the amazing things to me is how that tragedy has at times, I think, been used to advance other agendas that make absolutely no sense.

I think that the challenge to a group like this is to be confident, humbly confident before the truth. To look at all truths that are self evident and to realize that they have enduring value and to celebrate those truths in the men and women that you know, young and old, who in faithful marriage and loving family life and devoted service to others, are the ones who construct the good society, who give us that tranquility of order which is peace. And we need to find new ways to express old truths that might tap into the imagination of those who realize that what is being served out as the way to go is nothing but a way to disaster. Because the family and the education of children are the most immediately endangered realities in our society today, we are correct to focus on them. However, it is important to see these for what they are and to see how they relate to a whole host of other issues, especially the fundamental respect for human life that is being attacked at the beginning and end of life today.

This vision of seeing how interconnected are the issues which bring us together is not something that is a challenge to us in terms of our own nation, our own state, our own cities. We can't afford defending morally justified any form of xenophobia or any limitation of our moral compass to the latitude and the longitude of the United States. The answer to the question which God put to Cain is "yes, I am my brother's keeper, my sister's keeper." And we have to realize that, and we have to realize that as a nation, Haiti, Bosnia, Ruanda, the Sudan, China, Vietnam, Cuba, Sri Lanka, are all parts of the whole. They are our brothers and our sisters. The value of the young children massacred at Ruanda are just as precious in God's sight as the children you hold and call your own.

There are right sightings, there are bright sides. The Middle East and South Africa are examples of how persistent committed work toward a better reality can ultimately pay off. We need to pray mightily for peace in the Middle East and for the strengthening of this new reality which is South Africa. There are many opportunities today. There are equally many risks. Today is universally the day of the family. It's nice that we meet on that day. One clear opportunity for us is to see our effort in the context of the International Year of the Family. The Catholic Church has embraced this initiative of the United Nations with great enthusiasm. The Holy Father's Letter to Families is available to you today. In it, the Holy Father points out that the way of society, the way of the Church, is the way of the family. In other words, if the family isn't what it ought to be, then every other expression of social living falters.

The U.S. Bishops have also written on the subject and I have directed the agencies of this Archdiocese to include the theme of the family as part of this year's ongoing programs and projects. The four Catholic Dioceses of Massachusetts for the past several years have determined that the way we will judge all social issues before the legislature is on whether or not this issue thus framed is supportive of the family.

This particular moment in the history of the world, as we focus on the family, is a good time to remind ourselves that the family is the basic cell of society and to urge all with responsibility to use that responsibility to foster and defend family life. I wish that our government at the national level were doing that. They are not. The Cairo Conference on population and development will take place in September. The draft document is the subject of a preparatory meeting of nations in New York in April. The pressure groups from this country might draft this text through the United States delegation. The Holy See and its allies fought back, seeing that a good opportunity has been put at risk by the U.S. in its ideological partners. The result is that we have been falsely reported in the press and unfairly attacked on the floor of the U.N. The Holy Father and the Catholic Church are not going to back down. We will seek out allies and continue to fight for the family, for marriage, for children, for truth and light at Cairo and beyond.

In conclusion, this is a great beginning. Is that a contradiction in terms? In conclusion, this is a great beginning. But it is just that, a beginning. There are distortions. Powerful forces in our society will continue their own propaganda campaigns, well financed and narrowly focused on specific dire sound of words that convey good meanings that are being misused. The stakes are literally our own life as a society, I believe, and our children's future. The Lord whom I hold dear, with many of you, told us that what we do to the least among us, to the little children, is how we will be judged. He is harsh in His judgment against those who cause scandal or harm to a child. He is generous with His divine love to those who welcome a child in His name. Can we do anything less?

35

✣

A Delicate Plant

On the IRA's Declaration of Intent to Renounce Violence

31 August 1994

The good news of the IRA's declared intent to end its violent activity gives us cause to hope. And although this hope for peace and justice remains a delicate plant, it has at last begun to bloom.

It is important to remember that the IRA was not alone in its tactic of violence. Catholics have been the frequent victims of Unionist paramilitary groups. Undoubtedly there will be those on both sides of the conflict who will do all they can to thwart this chance for peace.

It is to the credit of the vast majority of Nationalists and Unionists in Northern Ireland, of Catholic and Protestant Church leaders, particularly Cardinal Cahal Daly, of political leaders in Ireland, England, and the United States, and, most of all, to the constant prayers of the faithful that peace and justice for Northern Ireland seem now more than a dream.

Our prayers and our support for the cause of peace and justice are needed more than ever before.

36

✣

Compassion Fatigue as a Form of Violence

Conference on Urban Violence

Southwest Missouri State University, Springfield, Missouri, 20 March 1995

Mine is a fairly straightforward topic. In the next few minutes my task is to answer the question: "Why is there so much violence in American life." It is a question we put to ourselves, consciously or unconsciously, every time we read a newspaper or watch the evening news. The *fact* of violence is generally conceded.

The homicide rate among 18- to 24-year-olds has increased 61 percent since 1985. Murder is now committed at a much younger age. The murder rate among children 14 to 17 has increased 133 percent since 1985. Currently in the United States, two thousand homicides are committed each year by teenagers. It is sobering to consider the fact that by 2005 the number of teenagers in the United States will increase by 23 percent!

In our Pastoral Message on Violence issued last November, the Catholic Bishops of the United States pointed out that

> the most violent place in America is not in our streets, but in our homes. More than 50 percent of the women murdered in the United States are killed by their partner or ex-partner. Millions of children are victims of family violence.
>
> The number of guns has also quadrupled from 54 million in 1950 to 201 million in 1990. Between 1979 and 1991, nearly 50,000 American children and teenagers were killed by guns, matching the number of Americans who died

> in battle in Vietnam. It is now estimated that 13 Americans die every day from guns. . . .
>
> Our entertainment media too often exaggerate and even celebrate violence. Children see 8,000 murders and 100,000 other acts of violence before they leave elementary school.

The Bishops continue:

"We must never forget that the violence of abortion has destroyed more than 30 million unborn children (in the United States) since 1972."

Each one of us can document our own experience of violence. Less than a week ago I was at the wake of a young woman, barely out of her teens, who was killed by her jealous ex-boyfriend, who then took his own life.

Friday afternoon, St. Patrick's Day, I was in Armagh in Northern Ireland. I visited with two widows, one with four children, the other with five. One, Mrs. Hamill, a Protestant, the other, Mrs. Gray, a Catholic, both victims of the violence which claimed the lives of their husbands and fathers of their children. The motive for the killings of the two men was simply the fact that Mr. Hamill was Protestant and Mr. Gray was Catholic. While we can be grateful that we do not have such extreme religiously motivated violence here, we know that bigotry comes in many forms and easily slips into violence.

Each day's news is replete with the horror of violence. Our entertainment is saturated with violence. And for the moment the nation seems obsessed with the sordid violence in the unending saga of the O. J. Simpson murder trial.

In the eleven years that I have been Archbishop of Boston, I have had again and again the sad experience of ministering to the families of teenagers and younger children who were victims of street violence.

This quick sketch of violence does not touch on the pervasive violence in speech. We are a nation at risk of losing its capacity for civil discourse. Confrontation and protest have all too often replaced public debate.

There is another phenomenon that has taken root in our life as a nation which is a type of violence. It is what I have come to call "compassion fatigue." As a people we appear to be more and more fatigued with caring for others, whether the "others" be sick old people, newly emerging democracies, the poor, unborn and unwanted children, or refugees.

So much for the existence of violence. Is there a coherent answer to the why of this many-faceted phenomenon? Is there a common causal thread running through these various species of violence?

You will not be surprised if I suggest that the answer is sin. Adam and Eve chose their own will over God's will, and in that choice chose death in place of life. The original harmony in their relationship with one another and with God was shattered. When God called to them in the garden, Genesis records perhaps the saddest verse in Scripture: "They hid from God."

The pattern of self-will over God's will repeated itself in the tragic story of Cain and Abel. After Cain killed his brother Abel, he attempted to mask his guilt in his reply to God's query about Abel when he said: "Am I my brother's keeper?"

Powerfully does Isaiah the prophet echo God's clear answer to violence: "Do not turn your back on your own flesh."

Jesus' teaching is clear: we are to love God and love our neighbor, described by Jesus as those in particular need: the hungry, the thirsty, the homeless, the prisoner, the sick person. John, the Beloved Disciple, honed in his moral conscience by the Law, the Prophets, and the life and teaching of Jesus, writes that "If any one says, 'I love God,' and hates his brother, he is a liar; for he who does not love his brother whom he has seen, cannot love God whom he has not seen" (1 Jn 4:20).

A nation's greatness can be measured by the protection afforded to the most vulnerable, to those most in need. What is a nation, however, if it is not the work, the life, the choices of its citizens. The health of a nation can be gauged, therefore, by the choices of its citizens.

The level of violence tells us that all is not well. The danger in such a situation is that we seek a systemic cure in the treatment of symptoms. More prisons, more social programs, more money for education will not, obviously, touch the deeper source of violence.

That source, I believe, lies in a good idea run amok. This nation prides itself in individual freedom. This freedom is assured through a system of checks and balances in rights and concomitant responsibilities. As Professor Mary Ann Glendon has argued in *Rights Talk,* we have tended to so inflate individual rights that an appreciation of the common good has been lost sight of. The individual is seen more and more in splendid, or rather miserable isolation in the choices she or he makes. The measure of the good is drawn more from the desire of the individual rather than from any moral norm independent of the person. Good becomes whatever I choose as good for me, and I become the measure of the universe and of God. It is the Genesis script of Adam and Eve all over again.

Moral relativism is certainly the undisputed choice of our cultural elites today. One has only to watch television, read columnists, survey various academic disciplines to realize that anything is acceptable except a conviction that there are moral absolutes and that there is such a thing as truth. To hold out for moral absolutes and for truth is to run the risk of being branded intolerant or worse.

How can we possibly expect to deal, at its roots, with violence from a perspective of moral relativism? Already we have, as a society, "legalized" abortion. We have effectively taught our children that this form of fatal violence is acceptable on the justification of an individual's choice. How convincing can we be, therefore, in saying to a child that his choice of a pair of sneakers over the life of another child is not justified? Have we not already written the script for violence in our exaggerated emphasis on individual rights?

Few would fail to cite the breakdown of the family as having some causal relationship to violence. Even those who have championed and celebrated the erosion of the nuclear family realize the alarming consequences of teenage pregnancy. I believe this breakdown is the fundamental cause of violence.

A commentator from England, where the cultural challenges are not unlike our own, has made a compelling analysis. These are the words of the Chief Rabbi of the United Hebrew Congregation of the Commonwealth, Jonathan Sacks. They were written in his book, *Faith in the Future.* The Rabbi says:

> The battle against the family has been conducted in terms of rights—the rights of men to have relationships unencumbered by lasting duties, the rights of women to be free of men, the rights of each of us to plot our private paths to happiness undistracted by the claims of others, willing to pay our taxes in order to be able to delegate our responsibilities to the state and otherwise to be left alone. . . . Assisted by birth control, abortion, new work patterns and the liberalization of all laws and constraints touching on relationships, we have divorced sex from love, love from commitment, marriage from having children, and having children from responsibility for their care.
>
> That extraordinary institution, marriage, which brought together sexuality, emotional kinship, and the creation of new life and wove them into a moral partnership suffused by love, has been exploded as effectively as if someone had planted a bomb in the center of our moral life.

These words of the Rabbi, it seems to me, bring us to a sober but realistic assessment of why we have so much violence today.

Recently in Boston, I have been involved in similar events such as this gathering at SMSU. Since 1987 I have participated in something called *The Challenge to Leadership*. It is a forum which brings together leaders of Greater Boston from business, academic, labor, religion, the not-for-profits, and government. We have focused on economic development, education, and juvenile violence. Our aim is to indicate initiatives which can be undertaken by self-selected individuals, institutions, or coalitions. There is a reporting mechanism back to the total membership.

More recently, the Archdiocese of Boston has joined forces with the Ten Point Coalition, an initiative of Black Protestant ministers for citywide Church mobilization to combat the material and spiritual sources of Black on Black violence. What the Rabbi has written would receive a resounding endorsement by the Ten Point Coalition.

Growing out of these two experiences, I have been involved with a smaller but very representative group to discuss in greater depth the crisis of family in our culture, and what might be done. I was struck by the words of a public high school teacher, Linda Thayer, a member of that group, speaking out of twenty-five years of experience in an inner-city high school. After the meeting had gone for over an hour she said, quite simply, "If we do not get the father back into the family, we are going to disintegrate as a society."

I think she is correct. That is our task. In the book *Fatherless America, Confronting Our Most Urgent Social Problem,* David Blankenhorn writes:

> Because men do not volunteer for fatherhood as much as they are conscripted into it by the surrounding culture, only a authoritative cultural story of fatherhood can fuse biological and social paternity into a coherent male identity.
>
> For exactly this reason, Margaret Mead and others have observed that the supreme test of any civilization is whether it can socialize men by teaching them to be fathers. (p. 3)

The thesis of Blankenhorn's thought-provoking book is found in these words:

> The most urgent domestic challenge facing the United States at the close of the twentieth century is the re-creation of fatherhood as a vital social role for men. At stake is nothing less than the success of the American experiment. For unless we reverse the trend of fatherlessness, no other set of accomplishments, not economic growth or prison construction or welfare reform or better schools, will succeed in arresting the decline of child well-being and the spread of male violence. To tolerate the trend of fatherlessness is to accept the inevitability of continued societal recession. (p. 222)

Blankenhorn states that "the essence of the fatherhood idea is simple. A father for every child" (p. 223).

He says what is needed is a fundamental shift in cultural values and in parental behavior. He writes,

> To recover the fatherhood idea, we must fashion a new cultural story of fatherhood. The moral of today's story is that fatherhood is superfluous. The moral of the new story must be that fatherhood is essential. . . . The star of the new script must be the Good Family Man. . . .
>
> At the intellectual center of the new story, defining and sustaining the fatherhood idea, must be two propositions about men. The first is that marriage constitutes an irreplaceable life-support system for effective fatherhood. The second is that being a real man means being a good father. The first proposition aims to reconnect fathers and mothers. The second aims to reconnect fatherhood and "masculinity." Both of these propositions carry profound societal implications. Each will powerfully shape the plot and characters of an invigorated cultural story.

These could be unsettling words, particularly for those who would hear them as calling us back to the way things were. To be sure, what is called for is to recover a continuity with our past. This is not a call for restoration, however. It *is* a call for organic development. What we are experiencing at the moment, and violence is its bitter result, is a discontinuity with our past.

My task is only to say how we have come to be so violent. It is the next speaker's task to indicate how we can become less violent.

In a real sense, however, no one can come and tell you what to do. You who are here, and others like you, are the ones who will shape the future of Springfield. If you take responsibility for that future, and resolutely refuse to have your future molded by the cultural elites of this nation, then there is still hope. The culture can be reclaimed and redirected, but only person by person, family by family, congregation by congregation, community by community. What we need is another cultural revolution, except this time it should start at the grass roots.

37

+

Cowardly Terrorism

On Reports of Church Burnings in the South

14 June 1996

A fire is always a dreadful thing. Strangers are often brought together as neighbors in the aftermath of a fire's destruction. The fact that thirty or more churches have been burned in a short period of time is reason enough to galvanize a national response.

That these churches have all been home to predominately black congregations raises suspicion that racism might be implicated in this rash of fires. Unfortunately, there is precedent lending credence to this suspicion.

In Mississippi, within one year in the sixties, thirty rural churches were burned to the ground. Almost all were home to black congregations. These acts of cowardly terrorism galvanized what came to be the Committee of Concern, a group of clergy both interreligious and interracial. We gave ourselves to the task of raising funds to rebuild those churches.

We did more than build with bricks and stones, however. We forged new and enduring relationships which helped to shape a healthier society.

I am pleased to join in an effort to assist in rebuilding the recently burned churches. This statement is being sent to all the pastors of the Archdiocese, inviting them to provide an opportunity to their parishioners to contribute to this cause. At the same time, I would urge all to join me in the prayer that out of the smouldering ashes we might come to recognize that there is no place for racism in our society, and that we are meant to live together as brothers and sisters.

38

Faith Illumines What Human Reason Knows

Celebrating Twenty-Five Years of the Pope John XXIII Center

Dallas, Texas, 3 February 1997

Mine will not be a heavy presentation. I am conscious of the fact that many of us arrive at this point with a certain degree of fatigue. Some of us are looking forward to a very important meeting which will take place later in a more relaxed atmosphere. I hope, however, that these few remarks will serve as a reminder of this center's history for those of us who have been around for a while, and that for those of you who are newcomers, it may provide a helpful introduction. These remarks are cast in three parts:

First, I will give a schematic history of the Pope John Center.[1]

Second, I will highlight some of the recurring themes in the bishops' workshops.

Third, I will invite a consideration of the center's future.

I. THE CENTER'S HISTORY

At the April 19, 1971, meeting of the Board of Trustees of the Catholic Health Association, the Chairman of the Board, Monsignor Edward Michelin, a diocesan priest from Jackson, Mississippi, expressed the need for a research center to address issues arising from rapid advances in science and technology. The center would reflect upon the implications, moral and human, of these advances. It would be pro-active rather than merely being reactive. It would exist to identify developing issues, do serious scholarly research on these issues so as to provide bishops with research as the bishops developed their teaching on the issues. It would assist Catholic hospitals as they prepared institutional mission statements and policies. It would establish as its primary norm fidelity to the Magisterium of the Church.

I knew Monsignor Michelin. We served together as diocesan priests in Mississippi. His own interest and involvement in Catholic health care institutions reflected the commitment of our bishop, the late Bishop Joseph B. Brunini. It is interesting that this center grew out of a suggestion made by a priest in a missionary diocese of this country. Less than 2 percent of the population in Mississippi was Catholic in 1971.

Prior to its incorporation on December 22, 1971, as the Pope John XXIII Medical-Moral Research and Education Center, the center's study committees considered options. Would the center be a department of the Catholic Hospital Association? Would it be an agency of the United States Catholic Conference? Would it be a chair at a Catholic college or university? Would it be a free-standing, self-supporting institute? The study committee chose the last option: a free-standing, self-funding institute.

Above all others, one person was the prime mover in the establishment of the center. Sistery Mary Maurita Sengelaub, R.S.M., President of the Catholic Hospital Association, pressed for its founding. Due to her quiet advocacy, the CHA Board of Trustees voted a one-time loan of over $168,000 as start-up money. In 1978, the CHA Board indicated that it would be unable to provide additional support beyond making available space and its support services.

The Center had as its first president Father Albert Moraczewski, O.P. Father Albert did an extraordinary job of keeping the Center on track in its early years. His own background in science and philosophy provided the necessary context for the Center's work.

It became clear to the Center's board, however, that it was understaffed and underfunded. On November 10, 1978, the Center convened an interdisciplinary consultation at Notre Dame University. There were over sixty bishops, priests, religious, and laity in attendance. It was an interdisciplinary group representing health care professionals, theologians, philosophers, scientists, ethicists, business leaders, and academics. The group included Catholics, Protestants, and Jews. The question put to the consultation was this: Should the Center continue to exist or should it be folded within some other group? If the consensus was that the Center should continue to exist, the consultation was asked how the Center might relate to the various disciplines. How it might be funded? What needed to happen to strengthen it?

The overwhelming view was that the center should indeed continue to exist in accord with its self-definition, that a strategy for financial support should be developed, and that a president should be recruited whose duties would be administrative, separating out the research and study function which had previously been included in the role of president under Father Albert.

The board accepted the consultation's recommendation and set about the business of recruiting a new president. That role was ultimately assumed by Father William Gallagher, a priest of the Diocese of Providence. In a self-definition which rates as the understatement of the century, Father Gallagher presented himself as a "simple, country pastor." He proved to be an extraordinarily efficient administrator who reversed the deficit financial situation of the Center, establishing a new source of income through the dioceses of the United States. Father Gallagher, Father Albert Moraczewski, Sister Maurita Sengelaub, and Monsignor Edward Michelin deserve to be mentioned always when the history of this Center is recalled.

The consultation was a defining moment in the history of the Center. There was another defining moment. It was the decision of the board to initiate conferences for bishops. The first workshop was held in 1980, and we gather here in Dallas as the sixteenth workshop for bishops. I remember well the particular meeting of our board where these workshops were launched. We were in a small room in St. Louis in the old headquarters of the Catholic Health Association. The idea of this workshop had emerged in our discussion. The perennial question of funding had to be answered. I excused myself from the room and went to a telephone. Those of you who know me well will not be surprised by that. In a call to Virgil Dechant, I described to him the idea, and asked if he thought the Knights of Columbus might possibly be interested in assisting.

While the Supreme Knight was unable to commit to the funding without taking the matter to the supreme board, he nonetheless was encouraging. That was enough for me, and it was enough for the board to move forward with the project. The rest is history. These workshops could never have existed without the support of the Knights of Columbus. Virgil Dechant is the fifth person who must always be listed in recalling the history of the Pope John XXIII Center. All of us are in profound debt to the Knights of Columbus for this and for so many other good works that they do.

Over the years Pope John Center has published its monthly newsletter, *Ethics & Medics*, sent to some thirty thousand parish priests, bishops, and various professionals throughout the world. It has published thirty major studies treating issues such as bioethics, philosophy, theology, and health care issues. It has presented workshops for dioceses, religious orders, hospitals, and other professional groups. It has provided consultation services to individual bishops, Catholic hospitals, and several Dicastries of the Holy See.

In 1985 the Center moved from St. Louis to Braintree, Massachusetts. The move enabled it to tap into the vast medical and educational resources of that area.

During these later years, the Center has provided intern training for those interested in the field of bioethics. It has maintained linkage with other research and education institutes, both at home and abroad.

II. THE BISHOPS' WORKSHOPS

The first Bishops' Workshop was held in Dallas in 1980. We chose Dallas because we wanted accessibility, and we wanted a place that would provide a warm respite from the winter cold of the North. That first Dallas workshop began in the midst of a severe ice storm!

I am indebted to Dr. Peter J. Cataldo for providing me a summary of the keynote addresses and papal messages of the Dallas Bishops' Workshops. To date there have been fifteen workshops between 1980 and 1996. We did not hold workshops in 1982 or 1986. With the exception of 1981, the Holy Father has sent a message to every other workshop.

In his first message, the Holy Father pointed out that the workshop is "at the service of truth and at the service of the human person." Quoting from *Redemptor Hominis,* he stated that there must be a "proportional development of morals and ethics" to the development of technology. The Pope also stated that by their presence at the workshop the bishops show their awareness that to fulfill their pastoral responsibilities to the Christian in the modern world, they must "understand the new opportunities and the new threats that are posed to the human person by ever-developing technologies."

This message of the Holy Father provides the recurring theme of all his messages and, indeed, it underscores the very intent of these workshops. In 1983, the Holy Father quoted again from *Redemptor Hominis,* telling us on that occasion: "Dominion of man over the visible world, which the Creator himself gave man for his task, consists in the priority of ethics over technology, in the primacy of the person over things, and the superiority of spirit over matter."

In 1987, when our workshop addressed the issue of scarce medical resources, the Holy Father addressed the responsibilities of individuals, institutions, and governments regarding what he called "the inequitable distribution of the burdens and benefits of health care," and the widening gap between the accessibility of the best medical technology to some groups, and the "rudimentary and clearly inadequate health care" of others. He stated that this problem must be seen within the context of basic human rights. He said in that message: "As an inherent part of her fidelity to Christ, she (the Church) seeks to continue his healing activity in the world, and to bear witness to him as the Savior of the whole person, body and soul."

Speaking in 1989 directly to the mission of Catholic health care institutions the Holy Father said: "The moral character of all human activity is more clearly identified in the light of our Christian faith, which must permeate and animate the corporate identity of all Catholic institutions. This is particularly true of the Catholic hospital."

In 1990, the Pope reflected on the three major themes of the workshop drawn from the conciliar teaching of Vatican II: the dignity of the human person, the objective moral law, and the relationship between the Church and the world. He pointed out that the dignity of man "is safeguarded and affirmed through loving obedience to God's law. To the extent that the Christian faithful uphold man's dignity and act according to the moral law, the Gospel will enrich the world."

The dignity of the human person;
the objective moral law;
the relationship between the Church and the world.

The Holy Father lifts up these three themes, and certainly they characterize the leitmotif of all our conferences. In one way or another, every one of our workshops has focused on these themes. Again, in 1990 the Holy Father said to us: "As man develops an ever greater knowledge and control of the world around him, he is often increasingly less able to understand himself and the purpose of his life. Your people look to the Church for wise and truthful guidance that will help them discover their human and Christian vocation and respond to it with confidence."

The forward thrust of this Center's purpose is captured in the Holy Father's words to us in 1992: "I pray that your deliberations will contribute effectively to the Church's mission on behalf of man and his dignity, and to that new evangelization of society which will promote the whole human being."

III. SOME THOUGHTS ABOUT THE FUTURE

There is no doubt in my mind that the vision of Monsignor Edward Michelin and Sister Maurita Sengelaub in 1971 was a prophetic vision. What they saw as a necessity for their day is an even greater necessity for our own. The purpose of the Pope John XXIII Center need not change as we move forward.

The society in which we live has changed, however. In 1972, Roe v. Wade had not yet come down as a death sentence through abortion for over thirty million babies in this country. The Supreme Court had not yet taken up a review of two circuit court decisions in favor of physician assisted suicide. Medical technologies which were only schematically foreseen are now before us presenting difficult moral challenges. The delivery of health care in this nation is in the process of revolutionary change.

During the intervening years, bishops have moved from the periphery to a more central role in the health care mission of the Church in the United States. How best can this Center fulfill its founding ideals as we move forward to the new millennium?

1. I believe the Center needs to strengthen the relationship between Catholic health-care institutions, their sponsors, and the bishops. It is imperative that the Church be united as she seeks to incarnate the healing mission of Jesus.

   Competition is the rule of the game in the for-profit corporate world. Cooperation and collaboration, however, should characterize relationships within the Church. The Center needs to be the point of meeting, as it was in its beginning, between the Catholic health-care association and the bishops.
2. The Center should strengthen its consultation capabilities for health-care facilities and bishops.
3. The Center should improve the marketing of its materials. For example, the Center published an extraordinarily important work by Father Benedict Ashley, O.P., *Theologies of the Body: Humanist and Christian*. This book needs to be disseminated as broadly as possible. We need to develop an awareness of this book which could be a rich resource not only within the Church but in the wider community as well.
4. Professor Ralph M. McInerny, speaking at the 1988 workshop in Dallas, said: "We see increasingly clearly that, if the Church were not the custodian of natural morality as well as revealed morality, that natural morality would have no spokesman in the world." What Professor McInerny does is point us to our responsibility as Church to be a light unto the nations, to be a leaven in society. The fact is that the light of faith illumines the truth which human reason knows. The Center must find ways to relate itself to other specialized centers and academic institutions.
5. Finally, these workshops have provided a model for hemispheric interchange. While a great deal has been accomplished at the level of social interaction, I do not believe that we have begun to realize the potential of our geographic representation in the way we grapple with the issues.

> I understand that the Center is rooted in the United States' experience, and that these workshops will necessarily have that context as a primary focus. Nonetheless, I believe there are ways in which this workshop, and the Center in all of its efforts, can reflect more fully the hemispheric dimension of our common interests.

The future is in good hands under the leadership of Dr. John Haas. He builds on the rich legacy of Father Albert Moraczewski, Father William Gallagher, Monsignor Roy Klister, and Father Russell Smith. May the Lord grant him wisdom, prudence, and hope for the task ahead.

NOTE

1. The Pope John XXIII Center has since been renamed the National Catholic Bioethics Center.

39

+

Make the Talks Truly Inclusive

A Plea for Northern Ireland

17 March 1997

On his deathbed in 597, Saint Columbkille turned to his brothers and said "I commend to you, my children, these last words of mine, that you keep among you unfeigned love and peace." There can be no better or more needed prayer for Ireland than that heartfelt one of the great sixth-century saint, numbered among the patrons of Ireland.

There are many, indeed the majority of Irish women and men, who fulfill that prayer in their own daily lives. In the North of Ireland today, there is a broad consensus in favor of peace, a shared commitment by Catholic and Protestant that violence is not the way to go and a desire that lives in the hearts of almost everyone to live in tranquillity with mutual concern for one another. This is perhaps the most significant truth we can observe today: the people of the North are committed to peace, and harmony. They want to go forward to build a society of stable peace, with justice, freedom, and security for all.

This conviction is supported and extended by the new forms of political cooperation that have been developed recently. However slow starting it may seem, however clumsy or unwieldy some may think it, there is growing political cooperation that brings together the British and the Irish governments along with the nine principal political parties that represent the viewpoints of the citizens of Northern Ireland. The talks that one hopes are only temporarily suspended are to be applauded and encouraged. They should be reconvened as soon as possible because much more needs to be done and greater confidence by officials must be placed in their potential.

But it is important to note that they are to go on. It is my hope, shared by many others, that increasingly these political exchanges will lead to real progress with an ever deeper cooperation toward solving the challenges that face Northern Ireland today. To that end I want particularly to acknowledge the younger people, particularly the women who, despite the last twenty-five years of bloodshed and violence, have not become disillusioned by politics and in fact are creating a new generation of potential political leaders for the next millennium.

The glaring exception to all this is, of course, the IRA. It seems that the IRA is being increasingly marginalized by a nationalist community that knows that the way of violence is wrong. The IRA has still not joined the civil community of men and women committed to resolving differences through non-violence. Once again I appeal to the IRA: lay down your arms; give up violence; commit yourselves to the Mitchell Principles and declare a cease-fire which will make you eligible to sit at the table of peace with all your fellow citizens of Ireland.

So long as the IRA continues to keep itself separate from the rest of the community, they will have a negative impact on the atmosphere of civil discourse and peaceful progress. The rest of the community, however, should not let themselves fall back into destructive and harmful patterns. I am thinking of the recent and unwelcome development in Hallyville where loyalist extremists have been harassing Catholics on their way to Mass. I am thinking as well of recent rumors of boycotts and counter-boycotts of businesses by persons in both communities. Do not let momentary setbacks entice the communities into new polarizations and further intransigence.

Instead, everyone should re-dedicate themselves to addressing the real problems that remain in the society today. The fact is that despite the great progress of recent years through the Fair Employment Practice Act, an adult Catholic male in the North is still twice as likely to be without a job than an adult Protestant male. The fact is that unemployment stands at 30 percent, and even more, in certain parts of the North, both Catholic and Protestant. This points to the obvious need to continue developing the economy with new investments from within the island and from overseas. There simply must be new jobs for all, male and female, Protestant and Catholic.

Housing too must receive renewed attention. While there has been significant progress by the government and others in the past decade, there still is too much housing stock that is substandard. Efforts to create new housing will be worthwhile especially in places like the Protestant Shankill Road where much of the housing is clearly not adequate.

During this past year the Marches have cast a long shadow over all of Irish life. The memory of what happened at Drumcree last year remains strong. The North Commission Report has many helpful recommendations. Unfortunately the impression seems correct that the British government has put them on the back burner. The North Commission Report should be implemented without delay and structures be set up that will avert confrontations, respect the civil rights of everyone, and see to it that the legitimate aims of the Loyal Orders and the equally legitimate rights of the nationalist communities are respected.

To that end, everything should be done to encourage dialogue between the Loyal Orders and local residents. Church leaders and community leaders can be most helpful in furthering such dialogue so that this year's "marching season" will not be another time of conflict, fear, violence, and recrimination.

Confidence building is an ongoing task in every society but especially those with a long history of conflict and strife. Those who hold responsibility must be extraordinarily sensitive to this role and do all possible to eliminate causes of friction and engage in actions that will inspire confidence. One example of this is the treatment of Irish prisoners, especially those detained in English prisons. I am thinking particularly of Roisin McAliskey now in an advanced stage of pregnancy, in prison and not yet tried for any offense. Another desirable development would be a fresh look by the British government at the gap between it and the Sinn Fein "conditions" for an IRA cease-fire. All that is legitimately possible to narrow that gap should be done for the sake of getting Sinn Fein admitted to the table and thus make the talks truly inclusive.

One hundred fifty years ago, the great Irish famine brought thousands upon thousands of Irish to these shores, many thousands here to Boston. Our own country has been shaped and strengthened, enriched and blessed by the Irish. It is my hope that our own government will continue to play an active role of encouraging and supporting every effort for peace in Northern Ireland. It is my expectation that all of us who love Ireland will continue to do all we can toward that elusive, but always possible goal. There is "unfeigned love" in our hearts for Ireland and for all the Irish people as we pray with St. Columbkille that our unfeigned love will one day help bring about the peace he prayed for at his death 1,400 years ago.

40

No Moral Justification for the Embargo on Cuba

American Academy of Arts and Sciences, Harvard University, 13 March 1998

In preparing these remarks, I reviewed my correspondence file from persons who accompanied me to Cuba for the Pope's visit. Our direct flight from Boston to Havana might have established a record in itself! Every letter expressed appreciation for the opportunity to participate in a historic and profoundly moving event. Almost to a person there was the expressed desire to be of assistance to the Church in Cuba and to the Cuban people.

These pilgrims to Cuba included bishops, priests and sisters, and Catholic laity as well as Protestants and Jews. There were business leaders, bankers, doctors, and a Health Care System President. There were heads of social service agencies and representatives of foundations, there were lawyers and judges, congressmen, presidents of colleges, a law school dean and a university professor, and the editor of a national magazine. We were a wondrously diverse group, but we found unity in our conviction that the time is now for a change in U.S. policy towards Cuba.

Since returning from the papal visit, I have often been asked if I thought that change might now come to Cuba. The question misses the point that change has already come. An earlier barometer of change focused on the departure of Fidel Castro as the threshold for any substantive change. The events of the past year clearly demonstrate that that barometer simply does not work. The toothpaste is out of the tube, and Fidel Castro squeezed the tube.

Any blueprint for a change in policy which demands a change in leadership in another country is too rigid a starting point and depending on the means willing to be used to achieve that departure, could lack a moral claim. This is not to condone a dismal record on human rights. Religious freedom is certainly not yet fully developed in Cuba. The fact remains, however, that dramatic change has occurred within the past twelve months in the area of religious liberty. These changes could not have occurred without the active approval of President Castro. He has been a promoter, not an obstacle to what is now happening in Cuba.

It is not the visit alone, stunning though it was, which chronicles change. Events leading up to the visit must also be acknowledged. Some in Cuba with whom I have spoken place great emphasis on the private audience accorded Fidel Castro by Pope John Paul II. One must also note the mixed commission of government and Church to plan for the papal visit which marks a sea change in that relationship. The Church was able to engage in a door to door nationwide mission in preparation for the Pope's visit. Religious processions were allowed, as were some outside religious celebrations. The exclusion of the Church from the use of public media was, at least in a modest way but nonetheless establishing a precedent, lifted with the pre-visit nationally televised address by the Archbishop of Havana, Jaime Cardinal Ortega.

Quite before the time of planning for the visit, the Church was allowed a new expression of social services through Caritas Cuba. While its work is still narrowly circumscribed, a principle of public, organized social service by the Catholic Church has been recognized. The backlog of visa requests by foreign clergy, religious, and other Church workers has been broken as the number of visas has dramatically increased.

Change cannot be rooted in a precise paradigm for the future. If we are to measure change realistically, it must be measured against the past. The past that I know in terms of the Church in Cuba begins in 1984. Before then, there were confiscations of Church property, the closing of Catholic schools and other institutional works, the departure, and some would argue the forced exile, of hundreds of Church personnel. There were the labor camps which number among their alumni the present Cardinal Archbishop of Havana. Pervading and justifying all this was an official version of history, employing a method with which we have become all too sadly accustomed in some current trends in the U.S. academy. It is the application of deconstruction to the study of the past in a way which serves an ideological end.

In an earlier visit to Cuba, I objected to President Castro concerning the severe intimidation of the omnipresent Committees of the Revolution. These watchdogs of Marxist orthodoxy saw as dangerously subversive the baptism of a child or the visit of a priest or the regular attendance at Mass. Castro's response, replete with Church history according to Marx, made the claim that the state did allow for religious freedom. The state was powerless, in his explanation, to counter the strong anti-Church sentiment of the people born of what he described as the Church's oppressive and sinful past.

For the past fourteen years, I have been in continual contact with the Church in Cuba. I was present in the Nunciature in Havana the first time Castro met with Cuban bishops. There were no more than three substantive encounters of this kind before the Pope's visit. During the past fourteen years there have been sporadic efforts on the part of the Cuban government to marginalize the Church by suggesting that the bishops were "counter revolutionary," which in our terms would mean unpatriotic and subversive.

Against that all-too-schematic background, focus on Havana, Sunday, January 25, 1998. The Plaza of the Revolution has a new face: a heroic-sized painting on the facade of the national library portrays Jesus in the familiar style of the Sacred Heart. One million Cubans, with a sprinkling of foreign pilgrims, are ranged in front of the altar. Fidel Castro, in a business suit, is in the front row.

For me, one among the many moving moments stands out in a particularly vivid way. During the Havana Mass, the Holy Father commissioned representatives from various dioceses to go forth and present the message of the Church. He presented each with a Bible. The last person to approach the Pope was an older woman, quite frail, who was helped up the stairs by two young men. When she approached the Holy Father, she threw her arms around him. There they were, aging and frail, this elderly woman and the Pope, with their common witness to fidelity in the face of Communist oppression. As she was helped down the stairs, she was accompanied by the thunderous applause of thousands of Cubans.

I wondered what she thought. Must it not have been for her the unfolding of a miracle? What had it been for her these past years in a land governed by Marxism? What must have been her joy in this sea of Cubans, so many young and ecstatic in their celebration of faith? I could only think of Anna in the incident recorded by St. Luke. Anna was an old woman, a widow, who spent her days in prayer and fasting in the Temple. When Mary and Joseph brought the infant Jesus to present him to God in the Temple, Anna came to the scene at that moment. St. Luke says "she gave thanks to God and talked about the child to all who looked forward to the deliverance of Jerusalem."

It must be said that the Cuban government could not have been more obliging and welcoming. The Masses of the Holy Father were televised live nationally.

As the Holy Father left Jose Marti Airport on January 25, he said that in our day

> no nation can live in isolation. The Cuban people therefore cannot be denied the contacts with other peoples necessary for economic, social and cultural

> development, especially when the imposed isolation strikes the population indiscriminately, making it ever more difficult for the weakest to enjoy the bare essentials of decent living, things such as food, health, and education. All can and should take practical steps to bring about changes in this regard.

These are important words of the Pope which have meaning not only for the Catholic faithful but for all women and men of good will, including those who exercise leadership in government. Current U.S. policy towards Cuba was set during the missile crisis. A few things have happened since then, however, including the tearing down of the Berlin Wall and the unraveling of Communist hegemony in Eastern Europe. The visit of the Holy Father to Cuba in January of this year is one of those defining events. A policy driven by events of an earlier time does not meet the challenge of new possibilities which the Holy Father's visit opens up.

One of the strongest impediments to new policy initiatives is the pressure of partisan politics. Is it but the musings of an unrealistic cleric to suggest that an earlier pattern of a bipartisan foreign policy could serve us well again? To that end, I propose the establishment of a bipartisan National Commission on U.S./Cuban relations. Such a commission, perhaps presidential or conceivably organized by a non-governmental body, would have as its charge the development of policy initiatives which could build on the changes already perceived in Cuba since the Pope's visit. The work of this commission should be completed within three to six months. It should not take longer than this because the commission's work would be essentially a simple and straightforward task.

The commission might be co-chaired by President Carter and President Bush or President Ford. It ought to include Senator Lugar; Representative Hamilton; a U.S. bishop; Elizabeth Dole, head of the American Red Cross; two corporate CEOs; two prominent Cuban-Americans; someone from the field of medicine; and someone representing the concerns of the media.

Since the Holy Father's visit, there has been the release of more than four hundred prisoners. While one political prisoner is one too many, this direct response to the Holy Father's visit cannot be dismissed. So very much more needs to be done to broaden the scope of human rights in Cuba. However, I am convinced that the best way to do this is to move the starting point of U.S. policy from the missile crisis to the Papal visit. The Holy Father has amply demonstrated that a policy of positive engagement can achieve far more change within Cuba than can the embargo.

Cardinal Ortega has commented on the so-called Helms-Burton Act that "any economic measure that aims to isolate a country and thus eliminates the possibility of development, thus threatening the survival of people is unacceptable."

It is impossible to reasonably support the embargo against Cuba while at the same time granting most favored nation status to the People's

Republic of China, and while moving into closer relations with Vietnam. Both of these nations have a deplorable record on human rights in general and on religious liberty specifically. If openness is thought to further freedom in those nations where change is not so evident, how is that a different standard is applied to Cuba where there is evident change?

We should not wait for the report of a bipartisan commission to introduce some measures which would ameliorate human suffering in Cuba; which would foster cultural, religious, and other interchanges; and which would therefore encourage the new attitude of openness and change within Cuba. It is time for the U.S. to respond positively to the change that is occurring in Cuba.

There is no moral justification for the current embargo. In terms of effectiveness as an agent of change it has proven to be a complete failure. The most egregious aspects of the embargo, namely the prohibition of sale of food and medicine, must be lifted immediately. The two bills currently in Congress which would do this should be immediately passed. What is needed in Cuba is the ability to purchase food and medicine in the U.S. A singular focus on facilitating charitable donations of food and medicine is patently inadequate.

There are certain things that can be done tomorrow by the President of the United States.

- The president should agree to license direct humanitarian flights to Cuba.
- The President could take immediate action to ease remittance restrictions, increase visiting privileges, and expand opportunities for U.S. citizens, particularly Cuban Americans, to visit Cuba by restoring direct flights. The right to travel is a constitutional right. It should not be violated for outdated political reasons.
- The President could restate that he will continue suspending the international trade bans of Helms-Burton indefinitely. This would help the people of Cuba and it would ease the concerns of our closest allies and trading partners.
- The President should give serious critical attention to the legal opinion that concludes that the Executive Branch has the legal and constitutional right to grant a general license for medicines and for food. Such an action on the part of the President would, of course, effectively end the food and medicine embargo immediately.

The foreign policy initiatives of a president can be decisive. President Nixon went to China. President Carter brought Begin and Sadat to Camp David. President Reagan met Gorbachev in Iceland to ease nuclear tensions and President Bush followed up by reducing our nuclear weapons. President Clinton has the possibility of charting a new relationship between the United States and Cuba.

Let me end by recounting an incident during the Pope's visit. One of the pilgrims traveling with us took a walk along the waterfront. He was alone, it was raining, and the pavement was slippery. He stumbled and fell, with a resultant large cut in the head. Some passerby stopped their car and took him to the emergency room of the nearest hospital. The care he received was both professionally competent and compassionate. However, he was struck by the fact that the only medicine he could observe on the shelf in the treatment room was some alcohol. When the doctor arrived to stitch his wound, he first reached into a pocket of his white coat, removed a light bulb, and screwed it into the empty socket so that he could see more easily. It is not just a bulb that is missing. There is often a lack of power with devastating consequences, especially in surgery. The lack of medicines more quickly and cheaply attainable from the U.S. severely restricts the treatment that can be provided. Even more basically, the effects of the lack of sufficient food threaten the most vulnerable members of the population, the old and the young.

I would submit that the people of Cuba deserve better than that from us. I would submit that it adds no honor to our country to deprive a people of those necessities which should never be used as bargaining chips.

Change is occurring in Cuba. The question is, do *we* have the political will and moral courage to change?

41

We Can Forget That Tragedy Has a Human Face

On the "Peace Agreement for Northern Ireland"

11 April 1998

"Blessed are the peacemakers." These words of Jesus take on special significance for us as we rejoice in the Peace Agreement for Northern Ireland which was reached yesterday, Good Friday. Jesus died on the cross that we might live reconciled with God and with one another. What better way to observe his death than by an effort to bring peace and reconciliation to a people so long and tragically divided.

All the parties to this agreement are to be congratulated and thanked. Without the active support of the British and Irish governments, this agreement could not have been reached. It is gratifying to know that our own government has been an active participant in the person of Senator George Mitchell. President Clinton has rightly made the cause of peace in Northern Ireland a consistent part of his administration's foreign policy.

This agreement is not the end of the road to peace. There remain significant steps before its provisions are assured. Already voices have been heard which vow to oppose this agreement. In the weeks ahead there will be two referenda: one in the south and one in the north.

In the Republic of Ireland, the people will vote on a change in the constitution which would drop the nation's claim to the six northern counties, and acknowledge that such a union could only occur with the approval of the people of those counties. In the North, the people will vote on the framework within which nationalists and unionists can live in cooperation and mutual respect.

The way ahead is fraught with the obstacles of old animosities, political opportunism and cynicism. The way ahead is made easier, however, by the example of so many women and men who have struggled for peace in Northern Ireland. The vote in Northern Ireland is, in many ways, a referendum on that struggle.

When I addressed the issue of Northern Ireland last month on St. Patrick's Day, I said:

> All too often, conflicts are depersonalized; we deal with "issues" or "claims" rather than with persons. For me this year, the situation in the North is epitomized by two persons, two faces: the faces of two lifelong friends, Damien Trainor, a Catholic and Philip Allen, a Presbyterian. Both were shot down in their home town of Poyntzpass, County Armagh, while sharing a pint in a local pub. Sometimes in the press of political events, we can forget that tragedy has a human face, an all too human face. Men and women, children and youth, neighbors: these are the real victims of the divisions and hatreds that for too long have held Ireland captive. So, too, are they the heroes who point to a better future. When we look on the faces of these two life-long friends, so wrongfully slain, we see the face of Ireland and we weep for its past, even as we pray with renewed hope for its future.

Here in the Boston area, throughout New England and throughout our nation we have special ties to the people of Ireland. It behooves us, therefore, to be participants in the ongoing peace process, first, by our prayers, then by active support of those efforts directed towards implementing the peace agreement, and, finally, by providing no forum for those who show themselves to be enemies of this effort which is a reasonable and fair formula for peace.

To repeat again my words on St. Patrick's Day: "May the examples of Damien Trainor and Philip Allen not be lost. Through the intercession of St. Patrick, may their friendship become a prototype for every Irish man and woman and may Poyntzpass become a model for every Irish village and town."

42

Where the Story Is Told, People Respond

A Plea for Victims of Caribbean Hurricanes

6 November 1998

The devastation wrought by recent hurricanes in the Caribbean and Central America has profoundly moved us all. In response to a request for assistance from Cardinal Obando Bravo of Managua, Nicaragua, I visited both Honduras and Nicaragua on November 5 and 6. My purpose was to be in solidarity with Bishop Oscar Rodriguez Maradiaga, S.D.B., of Tegucigalpa, Honduras as well as Cardinal Obando Bravo, Managua, and to be able to use the experience of the trip to tell the story to others.

I was accompanied by those responsible for Health Affairs and Social Services from the Archdiocese of Boston so that they might more competently assess how we might be of help. The quick trip was facilitated by the donated use of a corporate jet.

In concentrating on Honduras and Nicaragua—the countries most severely affected by Hurricane Mitch, it is important not to lose sight of the fact that other countries in Central America sustained damage, and that the effects of Hurricane Georges are still profound in Puerto Rico, Haiti, the Dominican Republic, and to a lesser extent, in Cuba.

The magnitude of destruction in Honduras and Nicaragua is overwhelming. Honduras has a population of 6 million people. Of these 6 million, 1.9 million people have been displaced, which is to say they are homeless or otherwise severely affected. As of Sunday, November 14, the U.S. Embassy in Honduras reported that there are 6,500 people confirmed dead, and there are 10,000 people still missing. Approximately one hundred bridges have been destroyed throughout the country.

In Nicaragua, with a population of four million, there are as of yesterday three thousand confirmed dead. Approximately eight hundred thousand people are homeless or displaced.

Seventy-two bridges remain down. Two have been repaired, including one on the outskirts of Managua which opens up passage to the North. Many roads remain impassible or at least partially obstructed. There is concern for some isolated communities which have not yet been reached.

Both President Aleman of Nicaragua and President Flores of Honduras have turned to the bishops of their countries to be the responsible agents on behalf of their governments for the distribution of aid. This added national burden to the pastoral concern of the Church in unbelievably difficult circumstances calls for our prayers and our material support. Everything is needed: medicine, food, clothes, building materials, and money.

There is a real risk of major health problems because of the shortage of water and the destruction of sanitation systems. CRS is actively present in both countries, and Bishop Ricard will have more to say about this commendable work.

In my short visit I was able to meet Church personnel, our ambassadors in both nations, the presidents of each nation, to survey the damage by helicopter in Honduras, and to visit relief sites, including a tent city for refugees established by the Archdiocese of Managua. I appeal in a special way for Church-to-Church aid. The people of Boston, like those of so many other areas of this country, are responding with extraordinary generosity. Where the story is told, people respond. In solidarity with our brother bishops in those countries, we must help to tell the story. It cannot be sufficiently stressed that the degree of devastation in Honduras and Nicaragua will demand decades of rebuilding. Infrastructures are destroyed.

Several images stand out in my mind. Perhaps they can best convey the story. There was the anguished concern of an elderly woman who told me that of all the possessions she lost in the destruction of her home, the loss of her sewing machine was the most critical. It was the source of her livelihood. A small child in excruciating pain in a hospital in Honduras, all for the lack of a simple medicine unavailable at the hospital and unable to be purchased by a family without material resources. Endless lines of people waiting for water. Over three hundred vehicles in a line waiting for a chance at a gas pump. The overwhelmed physicians at a makeshift clinic at a tent city. A lifeless, muddy expanse where once a settlement of houses stood.

Three specific areas of advocacy on the part of our conference suggest themselves:

1. The cessation of deportations to the countries most affected, and if at all possible, the extension of green cards to those here illegally.
2. The commitment of long term reconstruction funds by the U.S.
3. Advocacy before international monetary and banking institutions in support of forgiveness of debt, or restructuring debt, and extending favorable terms for credit.

Our own country holds approximately $94 million of Nicaragua's outstanding foreign debt. We hold $150 million of Honduras' foreign debt. We should take the lead by example to other nations and the World Bank by forgiving this debt. Cuba has recently forgiven all of the $50 million debt of Nicaragua which it held.

I plead in the name of the Church and the people of Honduras, Nicaragua, and all the affected nations of the region that we commit ourselves as dioceses and as a conference to come to the short-term and long-term needs of our brothers and sisters.

43

+

God, Giver of All Good Gifts

Thanksgiving Day Reflections

26 November 1998

I write this a few days before Thanksgiving. What a beautiful tradition it is for a nation to recognize God, the giver of all good gifts. It is easy enough to point to our shortcomings as a nation, but these very shortcomings reflect the nobility of this ongoing American experiment. A greatness flows from the inspiration found in the Declaration of Independence and in the Constitution.

Last week I participated in the ninetieth anniversary of the founding of the Federal Bureau of Investigation. Looking out on the many men and women who were assembled, representing today's FBI, one could not but be moved by the selfless dedication to duty which these agents express in their professional lives. It was my privilege to bless a memorial wall within the headquarters which commemorates those FBI agents who gave their lives in the line of duty.

On my recent trip to Central America, it was impressive to encounter representatives of the U.S. government in both Honduras and Nicaragua, not only the embassy personnel who serve the nation with great distinction, but also the men and women of our armed forces who were present to assist in relief efforts. I learned that in recent days there has been a movement of engineers, Seabees and others who will assist in the immediate task of reconstructing roads and bridges. As I give thanks to God for the many blessings of this nation, I will remember in a special way the men and women who represent their fellow citizens around the world, and do so in an effort to serve others.

Yesterday I celebrated Mass at the Cathedral of the Holy Cross which was attended by many teachers of our Catholic Schools. It was the second of two Masses allowing me an opportunity to be with all the Catholic school teachers within the Archdiocese. What a tremendous gift they are to the mission of the Church.

After Mass, the principal of St. Matthew's Parish School in Dorchester approached me with a package. The package contained letters written in Spanish to the children of Honduras from the students at St. Matthew's School. There was also a check for $400 representing gifts made by the kindergarten class at St. Matthew's. I heard yesterday that many of the children of St. Theresa's School in West Roxbury gave their allowance to assist in the relief effort. I give thanks for these wonderful children.

As of this morning, the Archdiocese has collected $1,127,702.13 that will assist in relief efforts in Central America. This is a remarkable response, and it fills me with gratitude to be able to serve as Archbishop of such a generous people. Besides the money which continues to come in, we have collected more than 160,000 pounds of food, material, medicine, and clothing. It is our hope to have this flown to Honduras in the first flight next Monday.

One of the gifts we have as citizens of this country is our ability to live out our faith without undue restraint. To be sure, parents of children in Catholic schools do not have the tax benefits to which they are rightly entitled, but we have the opportunity as citizens to seek constitutional remedy for this injustice. We have a task before us as a nation to recognize the inalienable right to life which is flagrantly disregarded through legal abortion. Here too, however, we have the right as citizens to seek legislative relief from this legal abomination.

The greatness of our nation flows from our founding documents and is furthered by an existence of a network of voluntary organizations, not the least among which are the religious bodies of the nation. As long as America keeps focusing on God as the giver of all good gifts, we will continue to be a beacon of hope among the nations of the world.

May God continue to bless America, and give us the grace to live out the ideals which undergird our national identity.

44

+

Los Ojos de la Fe

Reflexión Teológica previa al Congreso Eucarístico

La Habana, Cuba, 1 December 1998

1. Qué agradecido estoy a Dios, bueno y generoso, por permitirme compartir con ustedes este tiempo de reflexión teológica en preparación para el Congreso Eucarístico. Qué apropiado es que sea la Eucaristía el tema unificador de nuestro estudio como Obispos y Teólogos. Cuánto nos enseña el que reconozcamos nuestra unidad en y a través de la Eucaristía. En el Señor, somos uno solo: el Arzobispo de Boston y el Arzobispo de La Habana, la Iglesia en los Estados Unidos y la Iglesia en Cuba. Las palabras de S. Pablo vienen a la mente: "Todos vosotros, que habéis sido bautizados en Cristo, habéis sido revestidos de Él mismo. Ya no existe entre vosotros judío o griego, esclavo o libre, hombre o mujer. Todos sois uno en Cristo Jesús."[1] Esta unidad en la fe, esta comunión que compartimos a través de la Eucaristía, es un milagro de la gracia que trasciende las barreras de la división creadas por la condición pecadora del hombre.

2. Algunos de ustedes son teólogos en el sentido más exacto del término. Otros, sacerdotes dedicados especialmente al oficio de transmitir la Fe, catequistas e instructores. Todos los aquí reunidos estamos comprometidos en la proclamación de la fe. El Catecismo de la Iglesia Católica afirma: "Los Obispos con los presbíteros, sus colaboradores, tienen como su primer deber el anunciar a todos el Evangelio de Dios, según la orden del Señor (Cfr. Mc 16, 15). Son los predicadores del Evangelio que llevan

1. *Gálatas* 3, 27–28

nuevos discípulos a Cristo. Son también los maestros auténticos por estar dotados de la autoridad de Cristo (LG 5)."[2]

3. Nos es útil repetir esa primera tarea de las obispos: "anunciar a todos el Evangelio de Dios, según la orden del Señor." Su mensaje no proviene, pues, de ellos mismos. No son sus propios conocimientos, su sabiduría adquirida a través de la interacción de su inteligencia y su experiencia, lo que deben dar a los demás. Con claridad el Catecismo afirma que los obispos son:

- predicadores de la fe
- que atraen nuevos discípulos a Cristo
- maestros auténticos de la fe transmitida por los apóstoles
- dotados de la autoridad de Cristo.

4. Como obispo, soy muy consciente de la necesidad de colaboradores en mi deber de proclamar el Evangelio, de ser predicador de la fe. En primer lugar, mis colaboradores son los sacerdotes y diáconos. En números cada vez crecientes, también laicos, hombres y mujeres, han tomado su lugar junto a los religiosis, como colaboradores. En la Arquidiócesis de Boston hay dieciséis mil catequistas, la mayor parte de ellos, laicos.

5. Hoy, sin embargo, quiero centrarme principalmente en los teólogos y obispos. De acuerdo con *la Instrucción sobre la Vocación Eclesial del Teólogo,* publicada por la Congregación para la Doctrina de la Fe el 24 de mayo de 1990, con la aprobación del Papa Juan Pablo II, el teólogo tiene la función especial de lograr una comprensión cada vez más profunda de la Palabra de Dios, contenida en la Escritura inspirada y transmitida por la Tradición viva de la Iglesia. Hace esto en comunión con el Magisterio, que tiene el oficio de conservar el depósito de la fe.[3]

6. La misma Instrucción apunta que por su naturaleza, le fe llama a la razón porque ésta revela al hombre la verdad de su destino y el camino para alcanzarlo . . . La ciencia teológica responde a la invitación de la verdad, al buscar entender la fe . . . "La teología, que indaga la 'razón de la fe' y la ofrece como respuesta a quienes la buscan, constituye parte integral de la obediencia a este mandato de Cristo porque los hombres no pueden llegar a ser discípulos si no se les presenta la verdad contenida en la palabra de la fe."[4]

7. En una lúcida afirmación que define bellamente la relación entre la Teología y el Magisterio, la Instrucción declara: "El Magisterio vivo de la Iglesia y la teologío, aun con funciones diversas, tienen en definitiva el mismo fin: conservar al Pueblo de Dios en la verdad que hace libres y hace de él la "luz de las naciones." Este servicio a la comunidad eclesial pone en

2. *Catecismo de la Iglesia Católica,* n.888
3. Cfr. *Instrucción* nn.6 y16
4. Cfr. *Instrucción* n.7

relación recíproca al teólogo con el Magisterio. Este último enseña auténticamente la doctrina de los Apóstoles y, sacando provecho del trabajo teológico, rechaza las objeciones y las deformaciones de la fe, proponiendo además con la autoridad recibida de Jesucristo nuevas profundizaciones, explicitaciones y aplicaciones de la doctrina revelada. La teología, en cambio, adquiere, de modo reflejo, una comprensión siempre más profunda de la Palabra de Dios, contenida en la Escritura y transmitida fielmente por la Tradición viva de la Iglesia bajo la guía del Magisterio, se esfuerza por aclarar esta enseñanza de la Revelación frente a las instancias de la razón y, en fin, le da una forma orgánica y sistemática."[5]

8. ¡Qué trágica ha sido la polarización que ha caracterizado la relación entre los teólogos y los obispos en algunos lugares en tiempos recientes! Por poner un ejemplo, algunos apropiándose de *Ex Corde Ecclesiae,* parecen situar al obispo *fuera* de la universidad Católica. El *mandatum,* más que como signo de comunión eclesial, lo ven como una extraña imposición para el teólogo. A la vista de las tendencias de algunas expresiones organizadas de la comunidad teológica, se comprenderá, que se pueda hablar de lo que aparece como una metodología del disenso. Más que con un resonante "credo," empiezan con la negación, la duda o, al menos, la suspensión del asentamiento de la fe.

9. Contrastemos ese vacío que caracteriza algunas teologías contemporáneas, con estas palabras del Cardenal Ratzinger: "La Iglesia y sus dogmas deben ser considerados como una estruendosa y poderosa fuerza para la teología, no como algo encadenante. Es, de hecho, la estruendosa fuerza que puede abrir la teología hacia sus más grandes horizontes."[6]

En esa misma conferencia, que les recomiendo para su estudio, el Card. Ratzinger dice: "la fe es parte de la teología, y la razón es parte de la teología. Se tambalearía sin una o sin la otra. Esto significa que la teología presupone un nuevo inicio del pensamiento, que no es generado por nuestras propias reflexiones, sino que viene del encuentro con una palabra que siempre nos precede. A este nuevo inicio lo llamamos conversión."[7]

10. Para S. Pablo, como explica el Card. Ratzinger, "el fiel cristiano es una persona que ha sido convertida a, conquistado por, el Señor Jesús. Esto sucede en y a través de la Iglesia que es el mismo Cuerpo de Cristo en el mundo.

A través de sus sacramentos, especialmente del Bautismo y de la Eucaristía, la Iglesia nos hace posible enraizarnos en Cristo . . . Cuando aplicamos esto a la teología, uno puede ver inmediatamente que el teólogo, que suponemos creyente, es verdaderamente teólogo, sólo en y a través de

5. *Instrucción* n.21, citando a Pablo VI, *Discurso a los participantes al Congreso internacional sobre la Teología del Concilio Vaticano II,* 1° octubre 1966.
6. Ratzinger, Card. Joseph, "The Church and the Theologian," *Origins.* May 8, 1986; Vol. 15, n.47, p.768.
7. Ratzinger, "Church and the Theologian," p.766.

la Iglesia. Si esto no es así, si el teólogo no vive y respira a Cristo a través de la Iglesia, su Cuerpo, pensaría que no estamos en absoluto tratando con un teólogo, sino con un simple sociólogo, o historiador o filósofo."[8]

11. Considero a todos los que nos encontramos aquí, pues, obispos y teólogos, como hermanos y hermanas en el Señor. Somos uno en la fe y en el bautismo. Compartimos la llamada fundamental de todos los cristianos a la santidad de vida, que implica la progresiva conversión. Entiendo que la llamada a la santidad está intimamente ligada con lo que significa ser obispo y con lo que significa ser teólogo.

12. Por Providencia de Dios, nos hemos reunido en al Año Jubilar del 2000. Escribo estas palabras en Roma; la ventana frente a mí mira a la Basílica de San Pedro bañada por el sol. Hace poco tiempo el Santo Padre se dirigía a miles de peregrinos en la Plaza. En estos momentos veo a miles de peregrinos moviéndose lentamente hacia la Puerta Santa. Una y otra vez se nos ha recordado en este Año Jubilar que debemos abrir de par en par las puertas de nuestros corazones, a de la Iglesia, de nuestras diversas culturas y naciones a Cristo.

13. Aquí, en la Arquidiócesis de La Habana estamos en el umbral del Congreso Eucarístico. La existencia multisecular de la Iglesia nos ha revelado, con cada vez más claridad, que la Eucaristía es la fuente y cima de toda la vida de la Iglesia. En cada celebración eucarística, justo después que el sacerdote ha eucaristizado los elementos del pan y el vino, profesamos el Misterio de la Fe, *Mysterium fidei*.

14. Cada vez que hacemos esto, respondemos a la llamada a la santidad, aceptamos la llamada a la continua conversión, con todos los desafíos que implica esa conversión. Pues proclamar el Misterio de la Fe lleva consigo un impulso a una comunión más profunda con el Señor Resuscitado, en quien vivimos; es ser atraídos a una más profunda comunión con quienes comparten también Su vida y, por tanto son, con Él, su Cuerpo en el mundo.

15. Sabemos que la Eucaristía es un misterio de fe porque ha sido revelado sólo, a "los ojos de la fe," tal y como dijo Sto. Tomás de Aquino: el gusto, el tacto, la vista, el oído, ninguno de los sentidos es capaz de reconocer, bajo las apariencias de pan y de vino,[9] el Cuerpo, la Sangre, el Alma y la Divinidad de Cristo, real, verdadera y sustancialmente presente en este Santo Sacramento. Sólo el corazón que asiente al misterio como ha sido expresado, preservado y custodiado por la Iglesia, es capaz de abrirse a la realidad del Señor Eucarístico.

16. *Mysterium Fidei*. La misma exclamación puede ser aplicada al trabajo del teólogo en la Iglesia. Su vocación sigue siendo una vocación eclesial. Lo que hace diferentes las palabras del teólogo de las de otro estudioso

8. Ratzinger, "Church and the Theologian," *Origins* p. 765.
9. Himno *Adoro te devote*.

cualquiera, incluso de un estudioso de la religión, es que el teólogo depende de la Palabra revelada por Dios como ha sido proclamada en la Iglesia de Cristo, para desarrollar sus razonamientos. El entendimiento humano nunca es suficiente. El teólogo, como su nombre indica, habla acerca de Dios y de las cosas que conciernen a Dios, y habla de esas cosas según se nos han dado a conocer por medio de la Revelación divina. De otro modo, no sería un teólogo cristiano, no sería un teólogo que pudiera decir algo acerca de la Eucaristía, *Mysterium Fidei.*

17. Quisiera sugerir para vuestra subsecuente reflexión personal, un texto del Concilio Vaticano II que se ha convertido en el *leit motiv* del Magisterio posconciliar del Papa Juan Pablo II. Me refiero, por supuesto, al célebre texto de la "Constitución Pastoral sobre la Iglesia en el Mundo Actual," *Gaudium et spes* (n.22). Los párrafos se encuentran bajo el título *De Christo novo homine:* sobre *Cristo, Hombre Nuevo.* Aprendemos allí que es sólo en el misterio del Verbo Encarnado donde encontramos la luz que ilumina el misterio de lo que significa ser hombre. En el tiempo de que disponemos apenas puedo sugerir los temas para una más completa meditación sobre este texto en relación con la Eucaristía. Podríamos llamar a esa meditación: "Jesús, Pan de Vida, creador de un Mundo Nuevo." El Misterio de la Fe que anunciamos en cada celebración de la Eucaristía, es la presencia de Cristo Resuscitado, bajo las apariencias de pan y de vino. En la medida en que nos hacemos uno con Él, al recibirlo en la Eucaristía, nos volvemos más plenamente humanos. Nuestra comunión con Él implica una comunión en Él con quienes co-participan de esa comunión. El Espíritu de Dios crea una única comunión de fe, de amor y de esperanza entre los que proclaman el Misterio de la Fe.

18. Las ideologías humanas están condenadas a fracasar en sus intentos de construir algo nuevo, algo mejor para este mundo. Es sólo en Él, en el nuevo Adán, donde se encuentra el inicio de un nuevo cielo y una nueva tierra.

19. Escuchemos de nuevo esta parte central del texto conciliar: Él que es, 'imagen del Dios invisible' (Col. 1,15) es el hombre perfecto que ha restaurado la semejanza divina en el linaje de Adán, que había sido deformada desde el pecado original.[10] No sorprende que el Santo Padre vuelva una y otra vez a esta formulación fundamental del mensaje Cristiano. A este mundo deformado por la condición pecadora del hombre, deformado no por la acción de Dios, sino por nuestras propias acciones, viene por la generosa y paternal benevolencia de Dios, Uno como nosotros, excepto en el pecado, que restaura la criatura humana en algo que no es extraño a lo que significa ser humano, sino que es lo más connatural al ser del hombre, a lo que, desde el inicio fue querido para la criatura hecha a imagen divina, llamada a la vida de amistad e intimidad con Dios Padre, Hijo y Espíritu Santo.

10. Cfr. *Gaudium et spes*, n.22

20. Es sólo en esta comunión de bienaventuranza—que, aquí abajo, se vive en la Iglesia de la fe y los sacramentos, y la que, por toda la eternidad, será contemplada en una visión de la gloria que esperamos alcanzar—donde el hombre descubre la auténtica profundidad de su propia humanidad. Esto constituye, por supuesto, un gran misterio de la fe, un *Mysterium Fidei.*

21. *Guadium et spes* (n.22) continúa explicando que nuestra humanidad caída ha sido elevada por la Encarnación del Hijo de Dios. Desde el momento que el Verbo Eterno tomó carne en el seno de la Bienaventurada Virgen María, todo cambió en la historia de la humanidad. La Anunciación marca el inicio de ese "mundo nuevo" que nos sugiere nuestra meditación sobre la Eucaristía. Pero la Encarnación no es mágica, y el trabajo de la gracia divina a través de la larga historia—ya bimilenaria—del Evangelio Cristiano adopta un ritmo de continua transformación. He aquí una de las razones del sufrimiento en el mundo: para crear lo "nuevo," lo "viejo" debe ser derrotado.

22. *Gaudium et spes* (n.22) se refiere al sacrificio de Cristo en la Cruz: Sufriendo por nosotros Cristo no sólo nos ha ofrecido ejemplo para seguir sus huellas, sino que también nos ha abierto el camino en el cual la vida y la muerte han sido santificadas y dotadas de un nuevo significado.

23. Una de las antífonas que nos es más familiar es la oración compuesta para el Oficio del *Corpus Christi: O Sacrum convivium, in quo Christus sumitur, recolitur memoria passionis eius, mens impletur gratia, et futurae gloriae nobis pignus datur.* "¡Oh Sagrado banquete, en que Cristo es nuestra comida; se celebra el memorial de su pasión; el alma se llena de gracia, y se nos da la prenda de la gloria futura!" Se refiere, por supuesto, a la Eucaristía, Pan de Vida para establecer el mundo nuevo. La Eucaristía es un banquete sagrado, en el que el Pan de Vida y de los Ángeles se nos da como alimento a nosotros. Este alimento, más que nosotros consumirlo, nos consume en el fuego de la caridad y en el vínculo de la unidad.

24. La antífona *O Sacrum convivium* anuncia esta nueva humanidad; el alma humana, esto es, toda persona, todo hombre, la criatura humana, es colmada con la gracia divina, fuente de la nueva vida en nosotros y de nuestra unión de amistad con Dios. Sólo el misterio del Verbo Encarnado revela—en el sentido estricto de sus manifestaciones y efectos—el misterio del hombre. Si las estrategias humanas que excluyen la ayuda de la gracia en sus esfuerzos para perfeccionar la raza humana pudieran responder a las más profundas aspiraciones del corazón humano, seguramente hubieran tenido más éxito del que han tenido en el curso de los siglos. El ateísmo, en cualquiera de sus formas, es una ideología sin futuro.

25. Y finalmente, la Eucaristía, Pan de Nueva Vida, Fuente de todo lo que es Nuevo, apunta hacia el futuro, a una plenitud—donde toda lágrima será enjugada—que no está condicionada por los límites de la naturaleza caída y que se nos promete como un tiempo no de sufrimiento sino de

gloria: Allí esperamos disfrutar de la visión de Su gloria. Ya no un *Mysterium Fidei,* ni un asentimiento del corazón hacia lo que la mente puede apenas vislumbrar, sino ya entonces, una visión. El pensamiento de una prenda de la gloria futura, una visión de la futura gloria que la Eucaristía ofrece, nos transporta a otra isla que tiene un lugar importante en la difusión del Evangelio Cristiano, como esta isla de Cuba lo tiene en la evangelización de América. Me refiero a la isla de Patmos en el Mar Egeo, donde se nos dice que el evangelista S. Juan vivió en el exilio: "Vi un cielo nuevo y una tierra nueva, pues el primer cielo y la primera tierra desaparecieron, y el mar ya no existe. Vi también la ciudad santa, la nueva Jerusalén, que bajaba del cielo del lado de Dios, ataviada como una novia se engalana para su esposo. Y oí una fuerte voz procedente del trono que decía: He aquí la morada de Dios con los hombres: habitará con ellos y ellos serán su pueblo, y Dios, habitando realmente en medio de ellos, será su Dios. Y enjugará toda lágrima de sus ojos; y no habrá múerte, ni llanto, ni lamento, ni dolor, porque todo lo anterior ya pasó."[11]

26. Esta es la visión del mundo nuevo que la Eucaristía crea en nosotros y en el mundo de hoy. Dios sabía que una vez que la visión de la bienaventuranza fuera revelada al género humano en Cristo, querríamos tomar parte de esa bienaventuranza de una vez y no tener que esperar hasta después de la muerte. Es por eso que Cristo se nos da a Sí mismo en la Eucaristía, para que en este sacramento gustemos de la alegría del Pan de Vida, que ya, ahora, alegra a los bienaventurados en el cielo, mientras avanzamos en nuestro camino para unirnos a ellos.

27. Es tarea de los Pastores en la Iglesia traer a la memoria lo que la Iglesia cree, presentar los artículos de la fe. Nos dirigimos a los teólogos, cuyas reflexiones están apuntaladas por estos mismos artículos de fe, para que examinen las implicaciones de la fe Eucarística de la Iglesia en la vida de la comunidad cristiana y del mundo.

THE EYES OF FAITH: A THEOLOGICAL REFLECTION PRIOR TO THE EUCHARISTIC CONGRESS, HAVANA, CUBA, 1 DECEMBER 1998 (ENGLISH TRANSLATION)

1. How grateful I am to the good and generous God for allowing me to share with you this time of theological reflection in preparation for the Eucharistic Congress. How appropriate it is that the Eucharist is the unifying theme of our study as bishops and theologians. How much are we taught by recognizing our unity in and through the Eucharist. We are all one in our Lord: the Archbishop of Boston and the Archbishop of Havana;

11. *Apocalipsis* 21,1–4.

the church in the United States and the church in Cuba. St. Paul's words come to mind: "For as many of you as were baptized into Christ have put on Christ. There is neither Jew nor Greek, there is neither slave nor free, there is neither male nor female; for you are all one in Christ Jesus."[1] This unity in the faith, this communion we share through the Eucharist, is a miracle of grace that transcends the barriers of division created by man's sinful condition.

2. Some of you are theologians in the more precise meaning of the word. Others are priests particularly dedicated to the office of transmitting the faith as catechists and teachers. All of us gathered together here are committed to proclaiming the faith. The Catechism of the Catholic Church states: "Bishops, with priests as co-workers, have as their first task 'to preach the Gospel of God to all men,' in keeping with the Lord's command (cf. Mk. 16:15). They are 'heralds of faith, who draw new disciples to Christ; they are authentic teachers' of the apostolic faith 'endowed with the authority of Christ' (LG 25).[2]

3. It is useful for us to repeat this first task the bishops have: "to preach the Gospel of God to all men." Their message, then, does not come from themselves. It is not their own thoughts, their wisdom acquired through the combination of their intellect and their experience that they should give others. The Catechism clearly states that the bishops are:

- preachers of the faith;
- who draw new disciples to Christ;
- authentic teachers of the faith transmitted by the Apostles;
- endowed with the authority of Christ.

4. As a bishop I am very aware of the need for co-workers in fulfilling my responsibility of proclaiming the Gospel and preaching the faith. In the first place, my co-workers are the priests and deacons. In ever growing numbers, lay people, men and women, have also taken their place alongside the religious as co-workers. In the Archdiocese of Boston of the sixteen thousand catechists, the majority are lay persons.

5. However, today, I want to focus principally on the theologians and bishops. According to the *Instruction of the Ecclesial Vocation of the Theologian,* published by the Congregation of the Doctrine of the Faith on May 24, 1990, with the approval of Pope John Paul II, the theologian has the particular function of achieving an ever deeper understanding of the Word of God found in the inspired Scriptures and handed on by the living tradition of the church. He does this in communion with the Magisterium

1. Galatians 3:27–28.
2. Catechism of the Catholic Church, n. 888.

which has been charged with the responsibility of preserving the deposit of the faith.[3]

6. The same Instruction notes that by its nature, faith calls for reason because reason reveals to man the truth about his destiny and the way to reach it. . . . "Theology, which seeks the 'reasons of faith' and offers these reasons as a response to those seeking them, thus constitutes an integral part of obedience to the command of Christ, for men cannot become disciples if the truth found in the word of faith is not presented to them."[4]

7. In a clear affirmation that beautifully defines the relation between theology and the Magisterium, the Instruction declares: "The living Magisterium of the Church and theology, while having different gifts and functions, ultimately have the same goal: preserving the people of God in the truth which sets free and thereby making them 'a light to the nations.' This service to the ecclesial community brings the theologian and the Magisterium into a reciprocal relationship. The latter authentically teaches the doctrine of the Apostles. And, benefiting from the work of theologians, it refutes objections to and distortions of the faith and promotes, with the authority received from Jesus Christ, new and deeper comprehension, clarification, and application of revealed doctrine. Theology, for its part, gains, by way of reflection, an ever deeper understanding of the Word of God found in the Scripture and handed on faithfully by the Church's living tradition under the guidance of the Magisterium. Theology strives to clarify the teaching of Revelation with regard to reason and gives it finally an organic and systematic form."[5]

8. How tragic is the polarization that has characterized the relation between theologians and bishops in some places in recent times! For example, some have taken advantage of the *Ex Corde Ecclesiae* to place the bishop *outside* of the Catholic university. They regarded the *mandatum* as an unbecoming imposition on the theologian rather than a sign of ecclesial communion. In view of the tendencies of some organized expressions of the theological community, it is understandable that one can speak of what appears to be a methodology of dissent. Rather than with a resounding "credo," they begin with denial, doubt, or, at least, the suspension of the assent of faith.

9. We can compare the emptiness that characterizes some contemporary theologies with these words of Cardinal Ratzinger: "The church and her dogmas should be considered a thundering, powerful force in theology, not a chain. It is in fact this thundering force that can open theology up to its greatest horizons."[6]

3. Cf. *Instruction*, nos. 6 and 16.
4. *Instruction*, n.7.
5. *Instruction*, n.21, citing Paul VI, "Address to participants in the international congress on the theology of the Second Vatican Council," October 1, 1966.
6. Ratzinger, Card. Joseph, "The Church and the Theologian," *Origins*, May 8, 1986; Vol. 15, n.47, p. 768.

In that same conference which I recommend to you to study, Cardinal Ratzinger says: "faith is part of theology, and thinking is part of theology. It would fall apart without one or the other. This means that theology presupposes a fresh start for thinking which is not generated by our own reflections, but comes from its encounter with a word which always precedes us. We can call this fresh start 'conversion'."[7]

10. For St. Paul, as Cardinal Ratzinger explains, "the believing Christian is a person who has been converted to, taken over by, the Lord Jesus. This happens in and through the Church which is Christ's own body in the world.

Through her sacraments, especially in baptism and in the Eucharist, the Church makes it possible to root ourselves in Christ. . . . When we apply this to theology, one can immediately see that the theologian, who is presumably a believer, is such only in and through the church. If this is not true, if the theologian does not live and breathe Christ through the Church, his body, then I suggest that we are not dealing with a theologian at all, but a mere sociologist, or historian, or philosopher."[8]

11. I consider all who are here, then, bishops and theologians, as brothers and sisters in our Lord. We are one in faith and in baptism. We share the fundamental call of all Christians to holiness of life, which implies progressive conversion. I understand that the call to holiness is intimately linked with what it means to be a bishop and what it means to be a theologian.

12. By divine providence we are gathered together in the Jubilee Year 2000. I am writing these words in Rome. From my window I can see St. Peter's basilica bathed in sunlight. A short while ago, the Holy Father spoke to thousands of pilgrims in the square. Right now I see thousands of pilgrims slowly moving toward the Holy Door. Again and again we have been reminded in this Jubilee Year that we should open wide the doors of our hearts, the doors of the Church and of our different cultures and countries.

13. Here in the Archdiocese of Havana we are at the threshold of the Eucharistic Congress. The centuries-old existence of the Church has revealed to us, with ever greater clarity, that the Eucharist is the source and summit of the whole life of the Church. In each eucharistic celebration, just after the priest has consecrated the elements of bread and wine, we profess the mystery of faith, *Mysterium fidei.*

14. Every time that we do this, we respond to the call to holiness, we accept the call to a continual conversion, with all the challenges that this conversion implies. For to proclaim the mystery of faith bears with it an impulse to a deeper communion with the risen Lord in whom we live; it

7. Ratzinger, "Church and the Theologian," *Origins*. p. 766
8. Ratzinger, "Church and the Theologian," *Origins*. p. 765

means to be drawn to a deeper communion with those who also share his life and who thus are, with him, his body in the world.

15. We know that the Eucharist is a mystery of faith because it has been revealed only to "the eyes of faith" just as St. Thomas Aquinas said: none of the senses, whether taste, touch, or sight, is capable of recognizing under the appearances of bread and wine,[9] the body, the blood, the soul, and the divinity of Christ, really, truly, and substantially present in this holy sacrament. Only the heart that assents to the mystery as it has been expressed, preserved, and guarded by the church is capable of opening itself to the reality of our eucharistic Lord.

16. *Mysetrium Fidei.* The same acclamation can be applied to the theologians' work in the church. His vocation continues to be an ecclesial vocation. What makes the theologian's words different from that of any other scholar, even a scholar of religion, is that the theologian depends on the word revealed by God as proclaimed in Christ's church to develop his thoughts. Human understanding is never sufficient. The theologian, as his name indicates, speaks about God and about the things related to God, and he speaks of these things as they have been made known through divine revelation. Otherwise, he would not be a Christian theologian; he would not be a theologian who could say something about the Eucharist, *Mysterium Fidei.*

17. I would like to suggest for your personal reflection a text of the Second Vatican Council which has become the leitmotiv of the postconciliar Magisterium of Pope John Paul II. I am referring of course to the well-known text of the "Pastoral Constitution on the Church in the Modern World," *Gaudium et spes* (n. 22). The paragraphs are found under the heading *De Christo novo homine:* on *Christ, the new man.* There we learn that it is only in the mystery of the Incarnate Word that we find the light that enlightens the mystery of what it means to be man. In the time we have I can only suggest topics for a more complete meditation on this text in relation to the Eucharist. We could call this meditation, "Jesus, bread of life, creator of a new world." The mystery of faith which we proclaim in every celebration of the Eucharist is the presence of the risen Christ under the appearances of bread and wine. To the extent that we make ourselves one with him upon receiving the Eucharist, we become more fully human. Our communion with him implies a communion in him with those who also share in that communion. The Spirit of God creates a single communion of faith, love, and hope among those who proclaim the mystery of faith.

18. Human ideologies are condemned to fail in attempting to construct something new, something better for this world. It is only in Him, in the new Adam, that the beginning of a new heaven and a new earth is to be found.

9. Hymn *Adoro te devote.*

19. Let us listen once more to this central part of the Council's text: "He who is the 'image of the invisible God' (Col. 1:15), is himself the perfect man who has restored in the children of Adam that likeness to God which had been disfigured ever since the first sin."[10] It is not surprising that the Holy Father returns again and again to this fundamental formulation of the Christian message. To this world deformed by man's sinful condition, deformed not by God's doing but by our own deeds, there comes from the abundant and paternal divine benevolence One like us except in sin, who restores to the human creature something which is not foreign to what it means to be human, but which is most connatural to man's being, which, from the beginning, was willed for the creature made in the divine image, called to a life of intimate friendship with God Father, Son, and Holy Spirit.

20. Only in this communion of blessed happiness—which, here below, is lived in the Church through faith and the sacraments, and which, for all eternity, will be contemplated in the vision of glory that we hope to attain— does man discover the authentic depth of his own humanity. This constitutes, of course, a great mystery of faith, a *Mysterium Fidei.*

21. *Gaudium et spes* (n.22) goes on to explain that our fallen humanity has been raised by the Incarnation of the Son of God. From the moment when the eternal Word took on flesh in the womb of the blessed Virgin Mary, everything changes in the history of mankind. The Annunciation marked the beginning of that "new world" we considered in our meditation on the Eucharist. Yet the Incarnation is not magic. The work of divine grace throughout the long history of two thousand years of the Christian gospel takes on a rhythm of continuous transformation. Here is to be found one of the reasons for suffering in the world: in order for the "new" to be created, the "old" must be defeated.

22. *Gaudium et spes* (n.22) refers to Christ's sacrifice on the cross. By suffering for us, Christ has not only offered us an example to follow in his footsteps. He has also opened up for us the way in which life and death have been sanctified and received a new meaning.

23. One of the antiphons that is most familiar to us is the prayer composed for the Office of Corpus Christi: *O Sacrum convivium, in quo Christus sumitur, recolitur memoria passionis eius, mens impletur gratia, et futurae gloriae nobis pignus datur.* "O holy banquet, in which Christ is received, the memory of his passion is renewed, the soul is filled with grace, and there is given to us a pledge of future glory!" This refers to course to the Eucharist, the bread of life to establish the new world. The Eucharist is a holy banquet in which the bread of life and of the angels is given to us as our nourishment. This food, rather than being consumed by us, consumes us in the fire of charity and in the bond of unity.

24. The antiphon *O Sacrum convivium* announces this new humanity.

10. Cf. *Gaudium et spes*, n.22.

The human soul, that is, each person, every man, the human creature, is filled with divine grace, the source of new life in us and of our union of friendship with God. Only the mystery of the Incarnate Word reveals—in the strict sense of its manifestations and effects—the mystery of man. If human strategies that exclude the help of grace in their efforts to perfect the human race could meet the deepest aspirations of the human heart, then they would surely have been more successful than they have been throughout the centuries. Atheism, whatever form it takes, is an ideology that has no future.

25. Finally, the Eucharist, bread of new life, source of all that is new, looks to the future, to a fullness—where every tear will be wiped away—that is not conditioned by the limits of fallen nature and which is promised us as a time not of suffering but of glory. There we hope to enjoy the vision of his glory. No longer will it be a *Mysterium Fidei* nor a yearning of the heart towards that which the mind can hardly discern, but a vision. The thought of a pledge of future glory, a vision of the future glory that the Eucharist offers, transports us to another island that has an important place in the spread of the Christian Gospel, like this island of Cuba has for the evangelization of America. I refer to the island of Patmos in the Aegean Sea where we are told St. John the Evangelist lived in exile: "Then I saw a new heaven and a new earth; for the first heaven and the first earth had passed away, and the sea was no more. And I saw the holy city, the new Jerusalem, coming down out of heaven from God, prepared as a bride adorned for her husband; and I heard a great voice from the throne saying, 'Behold, the dwelling of God is with men. He will dwell with them, and they shall be his people, and God himself will be with them; he will wipe away every tear from their eyes, and death shall be no more, neither shall there be mourning nor crying nor pain any more, for the former things have passed away.'"[11]

26. This is the vision of the new world that the Eucharist creates in us and in today's world. God knew that once the vision of happiness had been revealed to mankind in Christ, we would want to share in that happiness once and for all and not have to wait until after death. This is why Christ gives himself to us in the Eucharist, so that in that sacrament we might taste the joy of the bread of life which already now makes the blessed in heaven rejoice while we advance along our way to being united to them.

27. It is the task of the pastors in the Church to recall what the Church believes, to present the articles of faith. We address the theologians whose reflections are shored up by those same articles of faith, so that they examine the implications of the eucharistic faith in the Church and in the life of the Christian community and the world.

11. Revelation 21: 1–4.

45

According to History and Law

A Statement about the Crisis in Kosovo

1 April 1999

At the end of his Mass last Sunday, Palm Sunday, Pope John Paul II spoke these words concerning the unfolding and widening tragedy of Kosovo: "There is always time for peace. It is never too late to meet again and negotiate."

The day before yesterday the Holy See addressed the nations of NATO and the Security Council of the United Nations concerning Kosovo.

The Cardinals of the United States, in solidarity with these efforts of the Holy See, have sent letters to President Clinton and President Milosevic. We have asked the Serbian leader for an immediate cessation of Serbian military and police operations against the population of Kosovo. We have also asked President Clinton for a cessation of NATO bombing.

A time of cease fire should be utilized by all parties, including other neighboring states and the United Nations, to seek a just peace which would guarantee the populations of Kosovo that degree of autonomy which respects their legitimate aspirations, according to history and law.

The rhetoric and actions of war will not bring all the parties to a negotiating table without further, incalculable loss. A NATO military victory would not ensure a just and stable peace in the region. Obviously, an immediate cessation of Serbian military and police action against the Kosovo population is essential.

This is Holy Week. Today is the first day of Passover. For Catholics and many other Christians next Sunday is Easter. For Orthodox Christians,

Easter falls on April 11. During these most holy days, I join my brother U.S. Cardinals in pleading for an end of armed conflict and an international effort to achieve a just and peaceful resolution to this crisis.

I am asking that during the Prayer of the Faithful at all Masses in the Archdiocese there be a special intention for a just and lasting peace in the Balkans.

46

+

At Our Best, We Affirm Self-Evident Truths

To the Missouri Catholic Conference at the State Capitol

Jefferson City, Missouri, 4 September 1999

It is a privilege for me to be here with you, and I congratulate you for your keen sense of civic responsibility which makes you a part of the annual Assembly of the Missouri Catholic Conference. Archbishop Rigali, I am most grateful to you, to Bishop Gaydos, to Bishop Leibrecht, to Bishop Boland, and to all the Bishops of Missouri for letting me come back.

I recall with fondness and gratitude my work with this conference from 1973 until 1984. Allow me to pay special tribute to Lou DeLeo. He has a keen lawyer's mind, an unshakable commitment to the social doctrine of the Catholic Church, and a quiet determination that make him an invaluable asset. The extent to which he has recently been the object of unjustified, seemingly hysterical criticism proves that he is doing his job well. Thank you, Lou.

This annual assembly, meeting in this place, is a distinctive gathering. It speaks of the strength of our democracy, and it gives flesh to the founding genius of this nation. It is an echo of "We the People" who spoke the principles by which this nation remains true to itself. These were not principles resting upon the authority of a majority vote; they were and are self-evident principles rooted in the human mind and heart by the Creator—God.

We are here as men and women of faith and as citizens of this state and nation to deliberate on matters of public policy. What a testament to the freedom of this nation is our gathering! There are places where such a gathering could not take place. Think, for example, of Vietnam, Cuba, or China. It would be unthinkable that in those nations such a group as this could be gathered in a facility of the government for the purpose that is ours.

Freedom cannot be taken for granted, however. Think again of the awful tyranny of the Soviet Union or the demonic totalitarianism of Nazi Germany. In these and in all totalitarian regimes the state, the government, is the all-embracing reality, and the individual human being is valueless. In such regimes, the rights to life, liberty, and the pursuit of happiness are considered subversive of the all important good and interests of the state.

The self-evident truths which are the substance of our nation have been and are a challenge to us as a people. We need only think of slavery, and the perduring racism which robs us of our birthright as a nation. The assaults on democracy are unending. There is a built-in altruism in our national aspirations which runs counter to the selfishness in us all. A democracy holds in balance the legitimate interests of the individual with the common good. At our best we balance rights and responsibilities, and thus protect the rights of even the weakest among us. At our worst, we degenerate into a tyranny of the majority, or we parody the rights and responsibilities of the individual with an unfettered individualism which rides roughshod over the rights of others.

At our best we affirm self-evident truths. At our worst we deny any truth as absolute and universally binding. At our best we affirm as a nation that our rights as individuals are endowed by God. At our worst we proclaim ourselves to be the only gods that are.

Is our gathering here for the purpose that unites us an anomaly? Do we, as men and women of faith, belong in this place to deliberate on matters of public policy? There are some in our society who would limit access to such a place and for such a purpose to those who have first checked their faith at the door. To those who question the propriety of what we are about, we emphatically state that we belong here, and we belong here as women and men of faith.

Not only is our faith not an impediment to our responsibilities as citizens, it is—rather—an asset. It is precisely *because* we are men and women of faith that we should be dedicated and involved citizens. The noble, national aspirations enshrined in our Declaration of Independence are aspirations totally congruent with our faith vision concerning the inviolable dignity of the human person.

At a time when there are disturbing signs that we are losing our mooring as a nation, at a time when self-evident truths are ignored if not denied, at a time when a rampant individualism is waxing, and a sense of responsibility for one another is waning, at a time such as our own, the citizen who is inspired by the social doctrine of the Church is needed more than ever before.

What a gift is ours in that body of social doctrine which the Church preserves and constantly develops. We must never be ashamed of the Church's social doctrine, we must never hide it under the bushel basket of political expediency. Ours it is to speak, and to *do,* the truth in season, and out of season, when convenient and inconvenient; ours it is to speak the truth, but to speak it always in love.

Let us never cease to affirm our rejection of violence, of *all* violence. In his great encyclical *Evangelium Vitae* (the Gospel of Life), the Holy Father, Pope John Paul II, speaks of the lights and shadows of this time. He says: "We are facing an enormous and dramatic clash between good and evil, death and life, the 'culture of death' and the 'culture of life.' We find ourselves not only 'faced with' but necessarily 'in the midst of' this conflict: we are all involved and we all share it, with the inescapable responsibility of choosing to be unconditionally pro-life."

This is who we must be in the public forum, in the marketplace of ideas, in wherever it is that our work and responsibilities place us: we must be unconditionally pro-life. That means that, unlike Cain who murdered his brother Abel, we understand that we are our brother's and sister's keeper. That means that we live as one human family with God as our common Father. That means that the people of Turkey and the Sudan and China are not strangers to our hearts. Our love for everyone, wherever they live, and especially the poor, the weak, the sick, the dying, and our younger sisters and brothers not yet born, must know no bounds. To be unconditionally pro-life means to champion the cause of the unborn and the dying, to make the support of the family of paramount importance, and to be unrelenting in our effective solidarity with the poor. This is who we should be as Catholic citizens, with apologies to no one.

How sad it is to see Catholics as voters or as elected officials mute the passionate defense of the inviolability of the human person with the weak and illogical explanation that they are personally opposed to abortion, but. But what? But their willingness to sanction the destruction of over a million human beings each year? But their inability even to muster the moral courage and backbone to ensure a law on partial birth abortion? We have been subjected to so much legal double talk and mental gymnastics in an effort to cloud the meaning of presidential and gubernatorial vetoes of bills which would prohibit partial birth abortions! The fact of the matter is that the proponents of abortion, the abortion industry, and those dependent upon it, are determined that no effective banning of partial birth abortion will be enacted. Why is this so? Because they fear that the truth about abortion will then become more widely known, and they fear that with this truth the people will see this barbarous practice for what it is, the wanton destruction of innocent human life. Make no mistake about it. The opponents of a ban on partial birth abortion are not concerned with the *language* of this or that bill, they are concerned with the *substance* of the bill. The only bill that will satisfy them is a bill which, in the end, maintains the status quo.

Scripture says "You shall know the truth and the truth shall make you free." We believe that. We believe that things should be called what they are, not coated with deceptive labels. Our nation was not founded on the principle of freedom of choice. Choice must be directed toward the good. No one has the choice to take the life of another human being. The right to life of the innocent trumps the choice of another to kill for whatever reason. This right to life is fundamental. When it is at risk, then all rights are at risk.

Today, in our nation, Catholics and many others with us affirm that the greatest assault on our nation, our democracy, is the assault on the right to life. The weakest in our midst, the child not yet born and the person who is dying, are the most vulnerable in our society. To an alarming degree we see the movement of the state to exercise arbitrary control over the right to life.

How blessed we are in the Church today to have the inspired leadership of Pope John Paul II. I have already referred to his encyclical, *Evangelium Vitae,* which I commend to you as an indispensable resource. In that document the Holy Father writes that, "The Church is becoming more aware of the grace and responsibility which come to her from her Lord of proclaiming, celebrating, and serving the Gospel of Life." Note what the Holy Father says. He speaks of the Church "becoming more aware of the grace and responsibility . . . of proclaiming, celebrating and serving the Gospel of life."

Clearly, the Social Doctrine of the Church is not a static body of truth. Perennial truths are applied to the new reality of succeeding ages and yield a rich resource of authoritative teaching for us. The Holy Father's contribution to this teaching is immense. Presently there is a work in progress, initiated and authorized by the Holy Father, to prepare a Catechism of the Social Doctrine of the Church which will parallel the *Catechism of the Catholic Church.* These two works will serve the Church well as we enter the new millennium.

You are well aware that there are efforts to minimize the Holy Father as a teacher of the faith. He is sometimes characterized as out of touch with the modern mind, as hopelessly imprisoned in a narrow cultural outlook. Nothing is further from the truth. The Holy Father, firmly rooted in his unshakable faith in Jesus Christ, who shows us the human face of God and the divine face of man, is a witness to hope as we move from this most violent of centuries to the new millennium.

George Weigel has recently completed a biography of Pope John Paul II which he aptly entitles: "A Witness to Hope." Let me read from this biography, which will be published later this year, a passage which relates to Karol Wojtyla's seminary days: "In the autumn of 1942, Karol Wojtyla walked to the seventeenth-century residence of the archbishops of Krakow at Franciszkanska 3, a few blocks from the Old Town market square, and asked to be received as a candidate for the priesthood. The rector of the seminary, Father Jan Piwowarczyk, accepted him, and Karol began to lead a new, double life.

"In the first days of the Occupation, the Gestapo had tried to control the seminary, intending to downgrade it to a kind of clerical trade school with no instruction by university-level professors. The seminary, with the agreement of Archbishop Sapieha, simply ignored these instructions. The Gestapo's next move was to ban the reception of new seminarians. The archbishop's response was to hire the young aspirants as "parish secretaries," place them in local parishes, and have them attend classes clandestinely at the Krakow seminary. Raids were frequent. On one occasion five students were arrested, immediately executed by firing squad or dispatched to Auschwitz.

> The archbishop then decided to take the seminary fully underground. Candidates would be accepted secretly. They would continue their work, telling no one of their new position. They would study in their free time, occasionally presenting themselves to professors for examination. And in due course, it was hoped, they would complete their studies and be ordained, having managed to avoid the Gestapo in the interim.
>
> Karol Wojtyla was among the first ten seminarians chosen for this extraordinary process of clandestine priestly formation. . . .
>
> While living his double life, Karol often went to the archbishop's residence to serve Archbishop Sapieha's morning Mass, a practice he continued after recovering from his accident. One morning in April 1944, his fellow server and another clandestine student for the priesthood, Jerzy Zachuta, didn't show up at Franciszkanska 3. After Mass, Karol went to Zachuta's home to see what had happened. In the middle of the previous night, the Gestapo had taken his classmate away. Immediately afterward, the name of Jerzy Zachuta appeared on a Gestapo poster listing Poles to be shot. One was taken, the other remained. In the designs of Providence, there are no mere coincidences.
>
> Four months later, on August 1, Poland's capital exploded in the Warsaw Uprising, the desperate attempt by the underground Polish Home Army to rid the nation's capital of the Germans and establish the legitimacy of an independent Polish government before the Soviet army arrived. After two months of indescribably fierce fighting, including pew-by-pew, hand-to-hand combat in St. John's Cathedral, the city fell while the Soviet army sat just across the Vistula, doing nothing; better for the Germans to exterminate the Home Army than to have to do it themselves. Warsaw was then leveled on Hitler's personal order. Nothing more than two feet high was to be left standing. (George Weigel, *Witness to Hope* [galley proof], pp. 53–55)

These words express the crucible of fire that tested the faith of this young Polish seminarian. When, as a Pope, he speaks of the inviolable dignity of the human person, of the precious gift of freedom, these are no throwaway lines cheaply bought. They are sentiments nourished in the darkest of days of Nazi and Soviet totalitarian rule. Pope John Paul II is himself a testament to hope: hope in God, and hope in man nourished by God's Holy Word.

Last November, at our annual meeting, the Bishops of the United States overwhelmingly approved a statement entitled, *Living the Gospel of Life: A Challenge to American Catholics*. Addressing our brothers and sisters in the Lord, we began in this way:

> At the conclusion of the 1998 Ad Limina visits of the bishops of the United States, our Holy Father Pope John Paul II spoke these words:
>
> "Today I believe the Lord is saying to us all: Do not hesitate, do not be afraid to engage the good fight of faith (cf. 1 Tim. 6:12). When we preach the liberating message of Jesus Christ we are offering the words of life to the world. Our prophetic witness is an urgent and essential service not just to the Catholic community but to the whole human family."
>
> In this statement we attempt to fulfill our roles as teachers and pastors in proclaiming the Gospel of Life. We are confident that the proclamation of the truth in love is an indispensable way for us to exercise our pastoral responsibility.

I commend this document to you. I urge you to study it prayerfully, and to share it with others. Catholic elected officials should be aware of and held accountable to this document. It does not represent *a* Catholic position; it articulates *the* Catholic position on matters related to the issue of the defense of life.

We, the bishops of the United States, state in this document that "the nobility of the American experiment flows from its founding principles, not from its commercial power."

We observe that "we are now witnessing the gradual restructuring of American culture according to ideals of utility, productivity, and cost-effectiveness. It is a culture where moral questions are submerged by a river of goods and services and where the misuse of marketing and public relations subverts public life.

"The losers in this ethical sea change," say the bishops, "will be those who are elderly, poor, disabled, and politically marginalized. None of these pass the utility test; and yet, they at least have a presence. They at least have the possibility of organizing to be heard. Those who are unborn, infirm, and terminally ill have no such advantage. They have no utility, and worse, they have no voice. As we tinker with the beginning, the end, and even the intimate cell structure of life, we tinker with our identity as a free nation dedicated to the dignity of the human person."

These are sobering words, but we need only recall the chilling push for euthanasia and physician assisted suicide, the relentless assault on the life of the unborn, even to the point of federal and state executive vetoes on a ban of partial birth abortions, the efforts to redefine marriage and the family, the organized and well funded efforts to maintain the monopoly of government schools to the exclusion of vouchers or tax credits for poor and working class parents. Add to this the so-called welfare reform legislation, signed by President Clinton, which has made of single mothers and their children an underclass ever poorer. As if this were not enough there is the growing gulf between informed Catholics and those who champion capital punishment.

Not infrequently, but always erroneously, the Church is accused of being narrowly focused on the child in the womb. By contrast, hear what we bishops said to our fellow American Catholics in our statement of last November.

> Respect for the dignity of the human person demands a commitment to human rights across a broad spectrum: Both as Americans and as followers of Christ, American Catholics must be committed to the defense of life in all its stages and in every condition. The culture of death extends beyond our shores: famine and starvation, denial of health care and development around the world, the deadly violence of armed conflict and the scandalous arms trade that spawns such conflict. Our nation is witness to domestic violence, the spread of drugs, sexual activity which poses a threat to lives and a reckless tampering with the world's ecological balance. Respect for human life calls us to defend life from these and other threats. It calls us as well to enhance the conditions for human living by helping to provide food, shelter and meaningful employment, beginning with those who are most in need. We live the Gospel of Life when we live in solidarity with the poor of the world, standing up for their lives and dignity. Yet abortion and euthanasia have become preeminent threats to human dignity because they directly attack life itself, the most fundamental human good and the condition for all others.

The fact of the matter is that no other institution in the United States, with the exception of the government with its vast resources, provides the array of social, educational, and health services that are provided by the Catholic Church. To accuse the Church of being singularly focused on the life of the unborn is a bold-faced lie born either out of ignorance or as a strategy to undermine the Church's credibility. The Catholic Church does not only talk the talk, the Catholic Church walks the walk.

My hope in addressing you is that these words might underscore the urgency of the task that is ours to proclaim the Gospel of Life. In a few moments you will be in workshops to define the task more specifically as you address public policy issues facing the state of Missouri.

As you begin your workshops, let me echo again the U.S. Bishops' statement of last November: "As Americans, as Catholics and as pastors of our people, we write therefore today to call our fellow citizens back to our country's founding principles, and most especially to renew our national respect for the rights of those who are unborn, weak, disabled, and terminally ill. Real freedom rests on the inviolability of every person as a child of God. The inherent value of human life, at every stage and in every circumstance, is not a sectarian issue any more than the Declaration of Independence is a sectarian creed."

At the end of this Assembly we will gather together again around the altar at St. Peter's Church for the celebration of the Eucharist. What a fitting conclusion to this day that will be. The Eucharist, source and summit of the church's life, strengthens our communion with the Lord and, in Him, with one another. In the Eucharist we glimpse—we experience the Heavenly Father's will for us to live as his children, as brothers and sisters in a communion of Divine Life and love. I look forward to joining you at God's Holy Altar.

47

Chilling Parallels with Nazi Germany

On Human Life and Biotechnology

7 April 2000

Ideas have consequences. A book soon to be published, entitled *Hitler, The War and the Pope,* records the sad history of Hitler and refutes clearly the scurrilous attacks that are made against Pope Pius XII. The author, Ronald J. Rychlak, recounts that a "euthanasia" program had long been part of the Nazi plan. He writes: "In 1929, at the Nazi convention in Nuremberg, Hitler had proposed the annual 'removal' of 700,000 to 800,000 of the 'weakest' Germans as a means of rapidly improving the overall health and capabilities of the German race. . . . This led to the creation of the 'Reich Commission for the Scientific Registration of Hereditary and Constitutional Severe Disorders,' and doctors soon began conducting the experiments which would lead to the gas chambers of World War II."

This evil idea of Hitler, with its diabolic consequences, unfolded with the official recognition of the 'right to die.'

> Then, in 1939, doctors began to give "mercy deaths" to the "incurably sick." Carbon-monoxide chambers were built to carry out the euthanasia. Next came deformed children, who were said to adversely affect the race and not to have very happy lives anyway. At first, these children were identified while still very young (not more than three years old), but the age gradually edged up to 17 and then to adulthood. Moreover, the standards were changed. Originally only the severely deformed were included in the program. Eventually, children with misshaped ears, bedwetters, and those who were found difficult to educate were marked for elimination.

> Between December 1939 and August 1941, about 5,000 children and 100,000 adults were killed by lethal injections or in gas chambers that were built to look like shower rooms. The victims were all deemed to have a "life unworthy of living" because they were handicapped, retarded, deformed or otherwise considered "undesirable."

I have quoted at length from this forthcoming book, to be published by Genesis Press, because it is so vitally important that we realize where erroneous ideas about the value of the human person can lead. There are chilling parallels between abortion and the push in this country today for euthanasia and physician-assisted suicide with what unfolded in Nazi Germany after 1929.

A story in the Tuesday, April 4, issue of the *Boston Herald* reports that "Britain may be poised to allow the cloning of human embryos for medical research, a step that could push the United States to approve public funding of such experiments."

The *Herald* article reports that "James Robi, a University of Massachusetts scientist who was involved in the cloning of transgenic cows, said public anxiety will decrease as soon as the practice is shown to benefit patients. 'Then people will become more accepting,' he said."

George Annas, professor of medical ethics at Boston University, is reported to have agreed with Robi's assessment. "They aren't going to make babies," the *Herald* quotes him as saying.

If not babies, then what? The *Herald* describes that "the idea is to clone human embryos and use them as a source for embryonic stem cells which scientists believe can be used to treat a number of medical ailments."

Certainly it is a noble and laudable purpose to seek a cure for diseases. The morality of donor transplants is clear; many people are alive today because of the donation of a kidney by a living person. The bad idea at work here, however, is the creation and destruction of a human being solely for the purpose of harvesting cells.

Just last Monday Pope John Paul II addressed 2,500 participants of an international congress on Gynecological and Obstetrical Medicine with the theme "Fetus as a Patient." The Holy Father said: "In recent decades, when the sense of the humanity of the fetus has been undermined or distorted by reductive understandings of the human person and by laws which introduce scientifically unfounded qualitative stages in the development of conceived life, the Church has repeatedly affirmed and defended the human dignity of the fetus. By this we mean that 'the human being is to be respected and treated as a person from the moment of conception; and therefore from that same moment his rights as a person must be respected.'"

The Holy Father affirmed, "whatever the mode of conception—once it happens—the child conceived must be absolutely respected."

Unfortunately, another idea about the respect due for a child in the early stages of development has been the justification for the laws sanctioning abortion in this country. Our national conscience has been conditioned to accept the notion of destroying the life of an unwanted child, unwanted because unplanned, or unwanted because he or she suffers an illness or disability. It is not too difficult to move from that to the development of human beings for the purpose of harvesting cells and then destroying the child at the beginning of his or her life. Where will this end?

48

The Simplicity of the Case Is Overwhelming

On What To Do with Elian Gonzalez

18 April 2000

A great deal has been made about the complexity of the case of Elian Gonzalez. Indeed, there is a convergence of many factors which have been woven together in the endless analyses and legal actions which his case has inspired.

For many, the case turns on a decision concerning the intrinsic superiority of a democratic system of government over a communist inspired dictatorship, or vice versa, depending on where you live and how you think. In either case, Elian becomes the latest in a series of incidents which will continue as long as the present relationship between the two nations is maintained.

Enough ink has been spilled on the complexity of the case. For me, it is rather the simplicity of the case which is so overwhelming. It is not necessary to wait for a state, or federal, or even a Supreme Court decision to inform us where a young boy who has lost his mother under the most tragic of circumstances should be placed. Absent clear evidence of the father's unsuitability as a parent, Elian belongs with his father. He needs the reassuring embrace of his father's love to help him begin to deal with the terrible loss he has sustained in his mother's death.

It is true that Disney World is much farther from Cuba than the map records. It is also true that chocolate milk is not readily available to little Cuban children. It might be argued that Disney World could be brought closer and chocolate milk could be made more readily available if the United States would lift the embargo.

Presuming that this will not happen immediately, it should be said that weighed in a balance, the natural bond between a father and son is of far greater value than a visit with Mickey or a glass of chocolate milk or even the superiority of a system of government.

Over the past ten years or more I have had occasion to visit Cuba many times. Those visits certainly do not make me an expert on that island nation. I am under no illusions about the regime's shortcomings.

At the same time, I have come to know families in Cuba. I have seen happy children in a loving relationship with their parents. As a matter of fact, a better future for Cuba, as for any nation, is rooted in the family.

Perhaps Elian will someday choose to come to this country. Perhaps his father will also make that choice. Perhaps Elian will stay in Cuba and help to build a better future for his country, and help to restore the relationship which should exist between neighboring states.

In the meantime, however, we should let the circus end, and allow the return of Elian to his father so that they might mourn together all that has been, and allow them the privacy and the time to get on with their lives.

49

✢

The Church Must Always Be Unambiguously Pro-Life

Funeral Homily for a Friend, John Cardinal O'Connor

New York, New York, 8 May 2000

Your Eminence, Cardinal Sodano, your presence as our Principal Celebrant is a deeply appreciated sign of our Holy Father's pastoral solicitude for this great Archdiocese of New York and a sign also of the Holy Father's and your own friendship and esteem for Cardinal O'Connor. Thank you for your presence. Cardinal O'Connor's family has asked me, Your Eminence, to acknowledge with their heartfelt gratitude the pastoral solicitude which Archbishop Gabriel Montalvo manifested towards Cardinal O'Connor particularly during his illness. The bishops of the United States join me in thanking this splendid representative of the Holy Father in this country.

My intent and your expectation is not that I deliver a eulogy. Cardinal O'Connor's often repeated request was that we gather at this time to pray for him. That we do, in the context of the Eucharistic sacrifice which is the source and summit of the Church's life, and was so clearly the source and summit of the life of the brother, the uncle, the friend, the priest, the bishop whom we bury this day.

We turn to the Scripture passages just read, and we look to the book of Cardinal O'Connor's life for consolation in our sadness and for inspiration in our lives.

Last Wednesday evening, when it became evident that death would come very soon, his family, his closest collaborators and friends began the

Preparing for the Annual March for Life with seminarians and Barbara Thorp, Director of the Archdiocesan Pro-Life Office.

Church's prayers for the dying. In the midst of those prayers, there was a moment of profound grief as each of us realized with a sudden clarity what was happening. Just as suddenly, we realized our tears were not for him, but for ourselves. Our hearts were consoled by "that mystery hidden from ages and generations past but now revealed to his holy ones," that mystery which Saint Paul explained to the Colossians as the "mystery of Christ in you, your hope of glory."

The inspired insight of the author of Wisdom spoke of "the hope full of immortality" in the souls of the just. He consoles us as we ponder his words in the light of their fulfillment in the Risen Christ:

"The souls of the just are in the hand of God . . . they are in peace." Jesus, who suffered, died, and rose from the dead, is our peace. Our hope, as was the hope of Cardinal O'Connor, is to drink of the fruit of the vine again in the reign of God.

The wondrous Passover meal which Jesus shared with the apostles the night before he died fulfills the deepest longings of every human heart for freedom. "This is my body," he said over the bread. And over the wine he said, "This is my blood, the blood of the covenant, to be poured out on behalf of many." He instructed us to do this in memory of him. And so we do, in this and in every Mass. The meal is forever linked to the sacrifice in which Christ offered himself for us, taking upon himself the burden of our sins and our death so that we might have forgiveness and everlasting life.

To have known John Cardinal O'Connor is to have known that what we do at this altar was at the heart of his life each day. Just a few weeks ago in a visit to his home we concelebrated Mass. It was so clearly for him the highlight of that day. The course of his illness had made it impossible for him to read. Already his ability to carry on a sustained conversation was impaired. With strength and conviction he was nonetheless able to recite from memory the Eucharistic Prayer. So much was the Mass a part of his life that when some things began to fade, the Eucharist did not.

He was a man of profound and uncomplicated faith in a good and gracious God who has revealed Himself in Christ Jesus. He believed in the Holy Catholic Church. He was unswerving in his loyalty to the Holy Father as the successor of Saint Peter. The words of Saint Paul found resonance in his life:

> I became a minister of this Church through the
> Commission God gave me to preach among you
> His word in all its fullness.

Certainly he did not shy away from the task of preaching. He made this pulpit unique in the history of the Catholic Church in the United States. God gifted him with a keen and subtle intellect, an uncommon rhetorical skill, a knack for the dramatic gesture, a sharp wit, and an outrageous sense of humor, all of which he used in the service of preaching.

No one proclaimed what Pope John Paul II has called the *Gospel of Life* with greater effectiveness than Cardinal O'Connor. It was in proclaiming that Gospel of Life that he became a national and international public figure. Inevitably there is an effort to categorize public figures as conservative or liberal. Cardinal O'Connor, like the Church herself, defies such categorization. He was eloquent and unremitting in his defense of the life of the unborn as well as his support of the value of human life to the moment of natural death. Perhaps his most lasting testament in support of life will be the work of the Sisters of Life, a religious community he founded and loved so dearly.

As he was dying last Wednesday, as a result of a disease with terrible consequences, he bore witness one last time to the moral evil of euthanasia and physician assisted suicide. He denounced capital punishment. He championed the rights of workers. He worked for a just peace in the Middle East and Northern Ireland. Were he in this pulpit today, he would applaud the hope for peace in the IRA's announcement on decommissioning. He preached by his example the necessity of seeing in every human being, particularly the poor, the sick, the forgotten, the image of a God to be loved and to be served. What a great legacy he has left us in his consistent reminder that the Church must always be unambiguously pro-life.

A former Navy chaplain, Bishop John McNamara, recalled for me his first meeting with Cardinal O'Connor. Let me quote from his reminiscence: "Father O'Connor, the division Chaplain of the Marines, came up from Vietnam to interview the new clergy. I remember his first words to me. 'I'm John O'Connor, what can I do for you?' I often thought of this meeting because those words, 'What can I do for you?' so characterize and personify the John O'Connor I have known for 35 years."

So many of us have heard him say, "What can I do for you?" There was no burden too heavy, no problem too complex for his genuine compassion and desire to help. To understand this in him is to understand that he was, to the core of his being, a priest. He ministered in the person of Christ. His life was configured to that of Christ as priest and as victim. Again, the words of Saint Paul to the Colossians found expression in the life of Cardinal O'Connor: "Even now," wrote Saint Paul, "I find my joy in the suffering I endure for you. In my own flesh I will fill up what is lacking in the sufferings of Christ for the sake of his body, the Church."

John O'Connor lived these words. He entered into the lives of countless thousands by identifying with their sufferings in union with Christ. It was thus that he viewed his final illness. He saw himself in solidarity with other cancer patients, and he offered up the sufferings of his illness with the sufferings of Christ. In all of this, he knew an incredible peace.

What a grace it was for his sister, Mary Ward, and other members of the Cardinal's family, for Monsignor Gregory Mustaciuolo, who could not have been a more loyal friend and attentive son in the Lord to the Cardinal, for Eileen White his Special Counsel, for his colleagues and friends to be gathered around his bedside when he breathed his last at 8:05 in the evening of last Wednesday, May 3, 2000. We prayed then, and we pray now:

> Saints of God, come to his aid!
> Come to meet him, angels of the Lord!
> Receive his soul and present him
> to God the Most High.

50

✢

Thousands Have Been Forced into Slavery

Statement on Conditions in the Sudan

14 November 2000

Sudan is the largest country, geographically, in Africa, followed by Algeria and the Democratic Republic of Congo. It is larger than the continental United States, east of the Mississippi. It is located in the Horn of Africa and is surrounded by a number of countries, including Ethiopia, Somalia, Kenya, Uganda, and the Democratic Republic of Congo.

There are approximately 28 million people living in the Sudan. It is, however, a very diverse country with more than 600 ethnic groups and more than 100 distinct languages. Muslims make up more than 40 percent of the population, living primarily in the north, but there are many Muslims living in the south. More than half of the population lives in the south. Christians make up more than a third of the population, with approximately 4.5 million Catholics living in the south and the north.

My brother bishops: The cry for peace in the Sudan rises up from the ashes of more than two million men, women, and children who have died in the seventeen-year civil war, which continues there unabated. The indiscriminate bombing of churches, schools, hospitals, markets—all civilian targets—continues unabated. Four million Sudanese refugees and internally displaced peoples have been forced to live in inhumane conditions both within and outside of Sudan.

The Church in Sudan, which numbers some 4.5 million members, experiences harassment of its apostolic workers, confiscation and destruction of its properties, and the forced conversion of its members. Catholics are among the thousands who have been forced into slavery. Religious liberty is persistently violated in the Sudan. Non-Muslims are considered second-class citizens by the ruling party and are treated accordingly. The brief statement before you calls upon the government in Khartoum to respect the rights and dignity of all Sudanese, Muslims, Christians, and practitioners of traditional African religions. It calls on the world not to stand by and simply watch the destruction of our Sudanese sisters and brothers.

The Church and the people of Sudan find themselves isolated, their cry muted by the indifference and inaction by the international community. Our message is one of solidarity. Our call to the international community and our government in particular is greater engagement in the search for a lasting peace. Following the thought of the Sudanese bishops, the statement calls for an immediate end to the bombing of civilian targets by the government in Khartoum. It urges all parties to commit themselves to the peace process and to the Declaration of Principles which provide the framework for resolving critical political, economic, social, and religious issues. It also calls upon all those involved in oil exploration and development in Sudan to use their influence to promote basic human rights and to urge equitable distribution of the benefits of the country's oil reserves for the good of all.

This situation in the Sudan is a complex one. There is a religious dimension as well as a cultural dimension. There are also political and economic factors in play. However complex may be the situation in Sudan, what is indisputable is the unconscionable disregard for human life and fundamental human rights, and the incredible crimes visited upon millions of our brothers and sisters for whom Sudan is home.

We join our voice to that of His Holiness Pope John Paul II, speaking in Rome at the canonization of the first Sudanese saint, Josephine Bakhita, when he said:

> In the name of suffering humanity, I appeal once more to those with responsibility: open your hearts to the cries of millions of innocent victims and embrace the path of negotiation. I plead with the international community: do not ignore this immense human tragedy.

Bishop Fiorenza, I place this statement before this body for consideration.

51

+

On the Lay Vocation

An Address to Catholic Lawyers

14 January 2001

A friend recently mentioned to me this exchange between an inquirer and Cardinal Newman. As repeated to me, the exchange went like this:

"What do you think of the laity, Your Eminence?"

The Venerable Servant of God is said to have replied: "Well, we'd look pretty silly without them, wouldn't we?"

Indeed, we would! If we add together all bishops, priests, permanent deacons, sisters, brothers, and major seminarians in the world, they come to 1,416,273. The worldwide total of laity in the world, on the other hand, is 1,016,840,727. As a matter of fact, the number of laity in the Archdiocese of Boston is greater by 880,000 than that worldwide number of bishops, priests, etc. We would look pretty silly, indeed, if our ranks were bereft of the laity.

When he began his ministry as Supreme Shepherd of the Church, John Paul II addressed us, each one of us, who with him and in Christ constitute the Church. Hear those stirring words again, so appropriate in this Jubilee gathering: "Do not be afraid! Open, indeed, open wide the doors to Christ! Open to his saving power the confines of states, political and economic systems, as well as the vast fields of culture, civilization, and development. Do not be afraid. Christ knows 'what is inside a person.' Only he knows! Today too often people do not know what they carry inside, in the deepest recesses of their soul, in their heart. Too often people are uncertain about a sense of life on earth. Invaded by doubts they are led into despair. Therefore–with humility and trust I beg and implore you–allow Christ to speak to the person in you. Only he has the words of life, yes, eternal life."

The Holy Father some years later wrote: "To all people of today I once again repeat the impassioned cry with which I began my pastoral ministry" (*Christifidelis Laici*, no. 34). To *all* people of today! Implicit in this Shepherd's charge are the insights of *Lumen Gentium:* "Protected by such great and wonderful means of salvation, all the faithful of every state and condition are called by the Lord, each in their own way, to that perfect holiness whereby the Father is perfect" (*Lumen Gentium*, no. 11). And again, "It is the special vocation of the laity to seek the kingdom of God by engaging in temporal affairs and ordering those in accordance with the will of God" (*Lumen Gentium*, no. 31).

It is the Magisterium of Pope John Paul II, rooted so firmly in the Second Vatican Council, which helps the Church make her way with courage and great hope through the doors of the new millennium. It is precisely the Council's focus on the laity, so powerfully reflected in the teaching and life of Pope John Paul II, which strengthens my hope for the future. In these two texts from *Lumen Gentium* are summarized the two poles of the vocation of the laity: the call to holiness, and the call to give witness to Christ specifically in the midst of the world, "by engaging in temporal affairs."

Boston was established as a see only in 1808. Catholics have grown from a very small minority to the majority of the population. What was one diocese in 1808 is now two archdioceses and nine dioceses. The Archdiocese of Boston today numbers 2.1 million faithful and 368 parishes.

As this particular Church moves into the third millennium, the lay faithful constitute a source of great hope. On December 8 I appointed my third chancellor in sixteen years: each of them has been a layman. Our next chancellor, typical of the others, is sixty years of age. He studied at the University of Notre Dame and Harvard Business School. He has been very successful in business, having begun and sold several businesses. He and his wife are deeply committed Catholics who have continued their education in the faith and who are committed to spiritual growth.

Many archdiocesan offices are headed by laywomen and men, including Family Life, Pro-life, Young Adults, and Catholic Charities. The competence brought by laypersons to various boards is indispensable. The Archdiocesan Pastoral Council and Finance Council are of great help to me in my administration, and are paralleled by Pastoral and Finance Councils in each parish.

The Pastoral Plan of the Archdiocese is rooted in our Eighth Synod in which laity had a key role. Our Catholic schools are staffed primarily by laywomen and men. The parish catechetical programs for those not in Catholic schools are carried out principally by lay volunteers numbering 16,000 Catechists.

One development of recent years which should directly impact the profile of the laity in the third millennium is the emergence of young lay theologians. Many of these young theologians represent a departure from what might be termed the theological establishment controlled by their older peers. These new theologians are rooted in the Church's teaching and represent something of a recovery of theology.

Laity play a much more significant role in the Archdiocese of Boston's internal life today than they did twenty years ago. This phenomenon is replicated in other parts of the United States, and will accelerate in the future.

As important and as positive as this development is, however, there is a danger that lay involvement in the mission of the Church be reduced to her internal life. If all the laity thus involved in the Archdiocese and in the parishes were to be numbered, they would constitute but a fraction of the laity of Boston. Moving into a time of greater lay participation in the internal life of the Church, it is of paramount importance that we not "clericalize" the laity.

A failure to appreciate the specific vocation of the laity to bring the light of Christ into the temporal order can lead to a misplaced emphasis on lay service *within* the life of the Church as a validation of active lay involvement. Such a line of thinking can place totally out of context the importance of roles such as extraordinary minister of the Eucharist and lector. Important as these are, they certainly do not define the active layperson.

A further misunderstanding of roles is fueled by the contemporary obsession with power. Unfortunately, holy orders are not infrequently characterized as the source of power in the Church. In this construct, the exclusion of women from holy orders is perceived as a discriminatory exclusion of women from access to power. This subversion of the meaning of holy orders is more facilely accomplished to the extent that the universal call to holiness is obscured.

The Holy Father has written of the laity: "Their responsibility, in particular, is to testify how the Christian faith constitutes the only fully valid response—consciously perceived and stated by all in varying degrees—to the problems and hopes that life poses to every person and society. This will be possible if the lay faithful will know how to overcome in themselves the separation of the Gospel from life, to again take up in their daily activities in family, work, and society, an integrated approach to life that is fully brought about by the inspiration and strength of the Gospel" (*C.L.* no. 34).

Early in the document he underscores two temptations which the lay faithful have not always been able to avoid on the post-conciliar path: "The temptation of being so strongly interested in Church services and tasks that some fail to be actively engaged in their responsibilities in the professional, cultural, and political world; and the temptation of legitimizing the unwarranted separation of faith from life, that is, a separation of the Gospel's acceptance from the actual living of the Gospel in various situations in the world" (*C.L.* no. 2). I have already dealt with the first temptation.

It is the second, the separation of faith and life, which represents the greater threat. Even as I write these words, my mind is flooded with examples of lay faithful who are just that—full of faith and aware of the necessity of an integration of faith and life. These include young legislators in a very hostile political environment, a Harvard professor of law, a Nobel laureate in medicine, the Chief Executive officer of a Catholic Health Care System, several business entrepreneurs, several financial analysts. There are many other examples of persons whose work would not impact the culture as strongly as these.

Those whom I have listed in my memory, however, stand as exceptions to the rule. These few have committed themselves to the hard task of integrating the faith with their professional life. In a culture increasingly more hostile to the faith, a culture characterized by skepticism concerning truth, and by moral relativism, a culture which can rightly be termed a culture of death, it is both difficult and demanding of great courage to allow the truths of faith to permeate the whole of life. The consequence of this failure is all too painfully evident in those politicians who explain their support of legalized abortion by saying that they are personally opposed but that they cannot impose their personal views on others.

If the numbers of those lay persons in positions of critical influence in the dominant culture of this country is to increase, then, it seems to me, Catholic universities must be more effective in challenging students to engage the culture from the perspective of faith. All too often graduates from Catholic universities seem indistinguishable from their peers from secular universities in the pursuit of their professional goals. The vocation of the layperson with a mission to the temporal order appears not to be understood or accepted. To be a Catholic for many young laypersons is reduced to religious practice and a few narrowly circumscribed personal, moral choices.

For some, participation in movements or other association of the faithful may help to heighten a fuller appreciation of the lay vocation. The larger Catholic universities, however, have not been successful in instilling an appreciation of the lay vocation. My presumption is that this temptation to separate faith from life is present in other nations and cultures as well.

To speak of the third millennium one must consider the phenomenon of globalization. Because of it, it is possible to speak of a world-culture even as we acknowledge the particularities of individual sub-cultures.

As we deal with this growing challenge, these words from the Second Vatican Council provide inspiration and direction: "Among the signs of our times, one particularly worthy of note is the increasing, unavoidable sense of solidarity between all peoples. It is the task of the apostolate of the laity to cherish this and to convert it into a true and genuine desire for fellowship" (*De Apostolate laicorum*, no. 14).

And again: "This duty of the Church (i.e., to declare with greater clarity to the faithful and the entire human race the nature of the Church and its universal mission) is made more urgent by the particular circumstances of our day so that all people, more closely bound together as they are by social, technological, and cultural bonds, may also attain full unity in Christ" (*L.G.*, no. 1).

In a very realistic way, the Council accepted globalization as a fact, and urged the Church to utilize this phenomenon as a means for evangelization of culture. It was a similar thought which undergirded the suggestion of the Extraordinary Synod of 1985 to the Holy Father that there be prepared a compendium of the truths of faith, or a Catechism; the result of this suggestion is *The Catechism of the Catholic Church* promulgated by the Holy Father on October 11, 1992.

Is it too much to hope that the Church might more effectively utilize the methodologies of globalization to establish worldwide networks of faithful, grouped around specific professional areas of interest, who could mutually reinforce one another in overcoming the separation of faith and professional life? There is a new world of instant communication which could be put at the service of a Catholic laity awakening to the challenge of evangelization of the dominant culture.

Encouraged as I am by the exemplary lay faithful attempting to do in their lives what is the life goal of each of you, I believe there must be a new intensity of effort to inspire millions of others around the globe who are indispensable to the mission which is ours as the Church.

Among the challenges of the third millennium is the evangelization of feminism. Not to mention this would be to fail in acknowledging what is at once a challenge and an opportunity for the Church. The Holy Father has been a leader in the articulation of a Christian feminism. It is, however, the special task of the lay faithful, and specifically Catholic laywomen, to give credible expression to this new feminism. The U.N. World Conference on Women at Beijing illustrates both the dauntless challenge of a secular feminism and the way to effectively meet that challenge. The head of the Holy See's delegation was our own Mary Ann Glendon, a distinguished professor at Harvard Law School. She and her colleagues were able to mount an effective effort in support of the integral advancement of women. This type of leadership will, hopefully, be more the rule as the Church continues to develop and champion Christian feminism.

I have been most heartened by what has been done by a group of women in Boston, and what now has become a national and even an international effort, through an organization called *Women Affirming Life.* Focusing on the abortion question, a pivotal question in secular feminism, these women give witness to a contemporary feminism which embraces motherhood as a constitutive element of what it means to be a woman.

The culture of death can only be overcome if we unambiguously affirm the inviolability of every human life. We will be successful in this to the extent that Catholic women, under the banner of an authentic, Christian feminism, have an evident, leadership role in the Church's efforts to engage the culture. Here again, we need to develop a global network with a global strategy.

Such a global strategy for evangelization of the dominant culture, and the myriad of subcultures, might be expressed, albeit all too glibly, in these terms: Pro-life, Pro-family, Pro-poor. There is where the Church must be, and there is where the laity can be most effective: in proclaiming the inviolability of every human life, in championing the rights of the family as the basic unit of every society, and in standing in the solidarity of justice and love with the poor and whomever else is weak and marginalized. It has been said that the Social Doctrine of the Church is our best-kept secret.

The Church is sometimes vilified for an alleged exclusive concern for life in the womb. Nothing could be farther from the truth. While we need make no apology, quite the contrary, for our insistent defense of life from the first moment of conception, the fact is that there is no other non-governmental institution in the United States which provides more service to the poor and destitute than the Catholic Church. Our focus is simple. We *are* pro-life. We are pro-family. We are pro-poor. Each one implies the others.

As future ages look back on our own, the Church will be praised for having been often a lone voice in defense of the fundamental right to life. The same will be said of our advocacy on behalf of development and peace. The Holy Father ceaselessly attempts to focus world attention on the forgotten continent of Africa, for example. His has been a persistent voice in support of relief from the debt that is burdening third world nations. The faithful laity of the third millennium will, hopefully, find new and effective ways of translating the Church's social teaching into the cultures of politics, business and academe.

The way of the family is the way of the Church, as the Holy Father has reminded us. It is the way of humankind. It is in and through the family that the lay faithful make their greatest contribution to the Church and to society. Please God, the third millennium will see an ever stronger focus on marriage and the family in the life of the Church. Here is where the world so desperately needs the light of the gospel and the Church's teaching.

When *Lumen Gentium* was promulgated, I can still recall the enthusiasm generated by the document's emphasis on the universal call to holiness. Certainly this was not a new teaching. For too many, however, it had become obscured by an exaggerated emphasis on what distinguished different states in the Church. Our fundamental unity in the order of grace is through baptism. We are one in Christ. We can say with St. Paul, each one of us, "I live now, not I, but Christ lives in me." Our communion with

Christ through baptism, and our communion with one another in consequence of our communion with Him, is the truth that can set us free from the divisions, the polarities which are so destructive of human society. Called to live in Christ through baptism, we are therefore called to be holy. In that fundamental unity of grace and vocation we can meet one another with gratitude and respect as lay faithful, religious, deacon, priest, or bishop, as man or woman, as young or old, as strong or weak, as rich or poor, as professional or worker.

It is a paradox but nonetheless true that we are able to witness more effectively within the world to the extent that we realize we are not of the world. As we look to the laity in this new millennium, the Church bids us reflect on the Kingdom beyond all millennia. As we seek to respond to the challenges and opportunities of history, the Church stretches our thoughts to a day beyond time.

This passage from a treatise on John by Saint Augustine serves as a challenging conclusion to these remarks:

"I implore you to love with me and, by believing, to run with me; let us long for our heavenly country, let us sigh for our heavenly home, let us truly feel that here we are strangers. . . . I am about to lay aside this book, and you are soon going away, each to his own business. It has been good to be glad together. When we part from one another, let us not depart from him."

52

+

Intermediate Agencies Can Never Replace the Government

On a Visit to the White House

9 February 2001

Last week, President Bush invited a number of clergy to the White House to discuss his proposal that domestic programs to aid the needy be entrusted to faith-based agencies. At the present time the proposal of the President has not yet been fully developed, and many details remain to be completed. The wide discussion it has provoked will continue as new details become known and as the original idea comes to be fleshed out with specifics.

My own thoughts on this idea are based upon the principles of Catholic social teaching. That teaching places the human person at the center of its reflection and measures proposals and policies from the perspective of whether or not the human person, with all the dignity and rights that adhere to the person, is protected, advanced, and promoted.

From that perspective, there is every reason to be positive about the general approach the President has outlined. This is so, first of all, because the proposal responds to Church teaching on subsidiarity. This principle teaches us that the government should not arrogate to itself actions and activities that can be better carried on by other organizations that are closer to the needs of people and better able to respond to those needs. Subsidiarity recognizes that individuals and groups who are close to the social issue know it better and are better able to respond flexibly to what that issue demands. Education is a good example of this. Traditionally our federal government has left it to local communities to set the standards and administer the education of young people. That American tradition reflects very much what the Church teaches about subsidiarity, provided that the primary right and obligation of parents in the education of their children be both recognized and supported.

Second, I believe this proposal recognizes the value of intermediate institutions in our society. The tendency to have government take over all aspects of social life offends not only against subsidiarity. It reduces, and even possibly can eliminate, the existence of voluntary organizations that make any society healthier and richer. In the last several decades, intermediate organizations and free associations of citizens have become fewer and fewer. This reduces the number of ways citizens can participate in improving the lot of the community and achieving goals that serve everyone. At the same time, an all-powerful government can tend to take over more and more, leaving a society in which the only real institution with any effectiveness is the government. This is not healthy.

The involvement of citizens in a wide variety of faith-based and non-faith-based voluntary agencies that help those in need is a benefit to society as a whole. This is certainly to be encouraged across our society. Faith-based and secular organizations involve more people, extend the sharing of responsibility, and use the resources made available by the government in ways that often correspond better to the real needs of people. It should be noted, however, that practices that are essential to the identity and activities of faith-based agencies must be respected by the government.

For their part, however, intermediate agencies can never replace the government or assume the responsibility the government has for the common good of all. In Catholic social teaching, the government is a positive force that guarantees the common good and ensures the conditions for the flourishing of every citizen. The government must see to it that freedom is guaranteed, that rights are respected, and that the basic needs of all, especially the poor, are provided. Thus there will always remain both the government's own unique responsibility for the common good and its particular responsibilities for specific social needs and goals.

Pope John Paul II has recently written "Now is the time for a new 'creativity' in charity, not only by ensuring that help is effective but also by 'getting close' to those who suffer so that the hand that helps is seen not as a humiliating handout but as a sharing between brothers and sisters." (NMI, 50) From this perspective, President Bush has made a promising start with this new and creative initiative.

III

A PASTOR SPEAKING TO THE FAITHFUL

53

✣

Church Suffers from Faith Illiteracy

On Faith as a Kind of Knowing

28 August 1992

Pilate looked at Jesus and asked, "What is truth?" (Jn 18:38). It was the right question, but somehow it does not seem genuine on his lips. It seems more like a statement questioning the reality of a binding truth. In a way, Pilate's question is echoed many times over in our age.

Our knowledge of God, even without the further illumination of faith, is able to affirm that God is truth. To know God, therefore, is to know truth. Scripture says that, "You shall know the truth and the truth shall make you free" (Jn 8:32). It is our faith conviction that our freedom as human persons is linked to our acceptance of the truth. The truth is what Jesus reveals to us in Himself. He says: "I am the way, the truth, and the life" (Jn 14:6).

Catholic faith affirms that the Church has been commissioned by Christ to teach the truths of salvation until the end of time. Church teaching, therefore, is not an option for a life of faith. Furthermore, that thirst for freedom which is in every human heart can only be satisfied through a life lived in conformity with the truth, the truth revealed by God and taught by the Church.

Some currents of contemporary fashion, throwbacks to errors of earlier ages, attempt to contrast freedom and truth. The message of some contemporary movements would demand a choice: either freedom or truth. Indeed, some would deny the possibility of attaining the truth about God or about morality.

A Catholic view, by contrast, would maintain that freedom is realized in proportion to one's personal knowledge of the truth, which is to say, one's holiness of life. The "knowledge of the truth" which leads to freedom is not simply an intellectual exercise. To "know the truth" is to live the truth. Jesus said, "Not everyone who says, 'Lord, Lord,' shall enter the kingdom of heaven, but he who does the will of my Father shall enter the kingdom of heaven."

There is another false contrast that is often current in today's thinking. It is the false contrast of truth and love. It leads to a caricature of a person of faith as a zealot who stands in self-righteous condemnation of all those who do not agree with him or her. This is not the attitude of a person of authentic faith towards one whose life contradicts the truths of faith. The measure of a Christian's love must always be the cross of Jesus. Love, as St. Paul writes, never fails. Indeed, our effort must always be to speak the truth in love.

We live in an age in which truth is denied and faith is ridiculed. This has its adverse effect even on those of us striving to walk by faith. For this reason, I so look forward to the publication of the *Catechism for the Catholic Church.* In many ways the Church today suffers from faith illiteracy. It manifests itself even among those who write about and teach the faith. We are in need of a profound renewal in catechesis, in the teaching of the faith. I hope and pray that here in the Archdiocese of Boston this Catechism will be seen as an instrument to further that renewal.

May we hear more clearly the words of Jesus to Thomas, "Do not be faithless, but believing" (Jn 20:27).

54

+

The Constant Need for Evangelization

Words Addressed to the Holy Father at the Promulgation of the *Catechism of the Catholic Church*

Vatican City State, 8 December 1992

Santissimo Padre,

Con indicibili sentimenti di umiltà, nel nome di miei con-fratelli del Collegio Episcopale, voglio esprimere la nostra profonda gratitudine a Sua Santità per la promulgazione di questo nuovo Catechismo della Chiesa Cattolica.

It is even years ago to the day, Most Holy Father, that you addressed the last working session of the Extraordinary Synod of 1985 and indicated that you accepted the recommendation of the Synod concerning a catechism. On that occasion you said: "The desire expressed to prepare a compendia or catechism of all Catholic doctrine to serve as a point of reference for catechisms or compendia on this theme in all the particular churches . . . responds to a real need both of the universal Church and of the particular churches."

Today, in accepting that Catechism on behalf of my brother bishops around the world, I am aware that it will be up to us and our helpers to translate its proclamation of the faith of the Church into the many cultural languages of the human communities from which we come and into which we have been sent as evangelizers and catechists. I am referring, of course,

Presentation of the New Cathechism—Cardinals Law and Ratzinger with Pope John Paul II.

to what has been called inculturation. In so doing we must remember that inculturation is much more than an adaptation of vocabulary, terminology, and methodology. However necessary this aspect of inculturation is, it is not its heart. Furthermore, in our own day of rapid transportation and instant communication, cultural boundaries often blur into a universal culture as is evident among youth and in the fields of business and science. In a sense, the Gospel gives rise to its own language, to its own culture, as faith finds expression in hope and love.

Our most important task is to ensure that the Gospel is proclaimed in its entirety; evangelization will occur through the power of the Gospel itself. Pope Paul VI reminded us in *Evangelii Nuntiandi*: "The Church is an evangelizer, but she begins by being evangelized herself. She is the community of believers, the community of hope lived and communicated, the community of brotherly love; and she needs to listen unceasingly to what she must believe, to her reasons for hoping, to the new commandment of love. In brief, this means that she has a constant need of being evangelized." In carrying out the mission of proclamation, this new Catechism of the Catholic Church will be an invaluable and rich resource, as well as a clear norm, as we strive to transmit the Gospel to all the nations and as we are constantly evangelized ourselves.

Es profundamente significativo que este nuevo Catecismo de la Iglesia Católica sea promulgado en el Quinto Centenario de la proclamación del evangelio en las tierras del Continente Americano. Como tan acertadamente aclaró el Santo Padre durante su reciente visita a Santo Domingo, y como lo han repetido los obispos de la América Latina, esta ocasión marca un nuevo comienzo, un nuevo amanecer, una nueva evangelización. Apunta así, de esta manera, hacia el futuro, sin negar las ambigüedades en la historia de la obra evangelizadora, contradicciones que se originan en el pecado del hombre cuyos trágicos frutos vemos claramente tanto en el presente como en el pasado, por ejemplo, en el sufrimiento desgarrador de las poblaciones de Somalia, el Sudan, y Bosnia-Herzegovina. Este nuevo catecismo, este nuevo compendio de la fe de la Iglesia promulgado hoy en la alborada del tercer milenio será un instrumento indispensable para la proclamación de la esperanza que esta en nosotros (cf. 1 Pedro 3:15), según respondemos a los oportunidades y desafíos de esta época dramática que estamos viviendo. Como tal, este nuevo Catecismo representa un inestimable don de nuestro Santo Padre quien, fiel a la misión encomendada al Apóstol San Pedro, confirma así a sus hermanos en la fe.

Santissimo Padre, nel nome di tutti i miei con-fratelli, i Vescovi in piena communione con il sucessore di San Pietro, ringrazio Vostra Santità con profondo amore ed intensa devozione. Grazie, Santissimo Padre!

55

A Woman of Quiet Strength and Deep Faith

Funeral Homily for Rose Fitzgerald Kennedy in the Church where She Had Been Baptized

24 January 1995

To you, Senator Kennedy, and to your sisters, Mrs. Eunice Shriver, Mrs. Patricia Lawford, Ambassador Jean Smith, Rosemary, and to all in your family, I wish to express the heartfelt, prayerful sympathy of the Church of Boston. Bishop Sean O'Malley of Fall River joins me in this expression, as do my brother priests who are concelebrating with us.

Yesterday I received a telegram from the Vatican which it is my privilege now to read:

> The Holy Father was saddened to learn of the death of Mrs. Rose Fitzgerald Kennedy and he asks you kindly to convey his heartfelt condolences to the Kennedy family and to all gathered for the Mass of Christian burial. Commending her soul to the loving mercy of God our Father, he prays that the Risen Christ, judge of the living and the dead, will grant her eternal rest and the fulfillment of her deep faith and patient trust in his promises. Upon all who mourn her in the hope of the resurrection, His Holiness cordially imparts his Apostolic blessing as a pledge of consolation and strength in the Lord.
> (Signed) Cardinal Angelo Sodano, Secretary of State

It is so appropriate, Ted, that you and your family have chosen St. Stephen's as the place for your mother's Mass of Christian Burial. By her own words, she has said that faith was her greatest gift. Here her life of faith began in baptism. She spoke of that gift as her legacy to you. She told an interviewer: "I have asked them to hold on to it and to foster it." You have honored that gift in the loving way in which you have helped to plan this liturgy.

It was quite a different gathering, and quite a different world when Rose Fitzgerald Kennedy was brought to this church for baptism over a century ago. The changes from then to now challenge our ability to imagine: from social relationships to communication to medicine to political systems and nation states to travel to the moon and beyond.

We can reasonably conjecture that it was a very small congregation that came here on July 23, 1890, for her baptism. The faith of her parents gave them a vision of life which saw it as God's gift—a gift destined to last forever in that newness of life won for us through the saving death of Jesus on the cross. Baptism, then, was a new beginning for Rose Fitzgerald—it was a moment of grace in which the Church claimed for her the responsibility and the rewarding fulfillment of discipleship. Jesus' words in today's Gospel so beautifully summarize that responsibility and that reward:

> As the Father has loved me,
> so I have loved you.
> Live on in my love . . .
> All this I tell you,
> that my joy may be yours
> and your joy may be complete.

The words of Jesus and the faith of the Church give us a living link to her baptism 104 years ago. The Paschal Candle which stands at the foot of her coffin as a symbol of the Risen Lord's triumph over death, reminds us that she is destined to live forever in Him. Our consolation is not only nor principally in her life on earth these past 104 years, but rather our consolation and hope is in the promise of fulness of joy in God's eternal love.

On the occasion of her baptism, which in those days were not large affairs, we know the principals were here: Rose herself, the celebrant of baptism, Father John E. Hickey, and her godparents, Edward Fitzgerald and Emily Hannon. Today, by contrast, millions are gathered with us in ways that would have been unimaginable then. Indeed, "her works praise her at the city gates."

A nation pays honor to a woman of quiet strength and deep faith who is unequaled in the way her life was at the service of the commonweal. In a message to the Kennedy family, President Clinton has written: "Rose Kennedy was the heart and soul of a family of leaders. Guided by an abiding faith that withstood overwhelming tragedy, she taught by example the importance of compassion and service, and Americans everywhere are grateful for her enduring contributions to our world."

Every life is a mixture of joys and sorrows. In that, her life was ordinary.

Few lives, however, have been so intertwined with the joys and sorrows of the nation's life as was hers. Her joys have been moments of triumph for millions. Her personal losses and sorrows have been epic tragedies which have moved the world.

In good times and in bad, she has been "clothed in strength and dignity," and because her life was rooted in faith she was able "to laugh at the days to come." There is, indeed, cause for rejoicing here, as Peter reminds us in the second reading. She has suffered the distress of many trials, but through these, the genuineness of her faith has been made manifest as a gift "more precious than the passing splendor of fire-tried gold."

One hundred and four years ago in this sacred space the Church welcomed Rose Fitzgerald as its newest member. Today, the Church is gathered here once again, this time to pray for Rose Fitzgerald Kennedy, that she may forever rejoice with inexpressible joy touched with glory because she believed, because she hoped, because she loved.

56

+

The Legacy of History Not Overcome

Homily on St. Patrick's Day

Armagh, Ireland, 17 March 1995

Coming as I do from a land where a century is the measure of almost half our history as a nation, it is an awesome thing to contemplate a span of time which links more than fifteen hundred years. These years, this history which we mark, is the measure of lives lived, of triumphs and tragedies, of saints and scholars and sinners. It is the measure of violence and of peace, of despair and of hope.

History as the world knows it is made up of what we see in the record of past ages and what we experience in our own lives. Paul gives us a different perspective than that of the world. He writes: "We do not fix our gaze on what is seen but on what is unseen. What is seen is transitory; what is unseen lasts forever" (2 Cor. 4:18).

Patrick, like Paul and Barnabas before him, took heart from these words of Scripture: "I have made you a light to the nations, so that my salvation may reach the ends of the earth." Brought to these hills first as a captive of an evil wordly power, Patrick returned in the freedom of the sons and daughters of God. What he "saw" in his day was an island divided against itself into more than a hundred kingdoms, kingdoms which did not live in peace with one another. As he strove to bring the reconciling love of Christ to the land he freely chose as his own, he experienced resistance not only from unbelievers but also from within the household of the faith itself.

Yet, Patrick saw beyond whatever adversity the moment brought to the enduring presence of Christ the Lord, and he confidently prayed: "Thy kingdom come." Like the Prophet Jeremiah, he came to God in prayer overwhelmed by his own inadequacies for the task before him. God spoke to Jeremiah: "Do not say, 'I am a child.' Go now to those to whom I send you and say whatever I command you. Do not be afraid of them, for I am with you to protect you—it is the Lord who speaks."

God spoke to Patrick as well. He tells us himself in his *Confession*: "God showed me how to have faith in Him forever, as one who is never to be doubted. He answered my prayer in such a way that in the last days, ignorant though I am, I might be bold enough to take up so holy and so wonderful a task."

That Patrick did, making this place holy by his apostolic ministry. Pope John Paul II, in his words at Kilineer near Drogheda on September 29, 1979, gave eloquent testimony to the reason why we hold Armagh in special honor. The Holy Father said:

> Hence I desired to make my first Irish journey a journey towards the 'beginning,' the place of the primacy. The Church is built in her entirety on the foundation of the apostles and prophets, Christ Jesus Himself being the chief cornerstone (cf. Eph. 2:20). But in each land and nation the Church had her own particular foundation stone. So it is towards this foundation, here in the Primatial See of Armagh that I first direct my pilgrim steps. The See of Armagh is the Primatial See because it is the See of Patrick. The Archbishop of Armagh is Primate of all Ireland today because he is the Comharba Padraig, the successor St. Patrick, the first bishop of Armagh.

St. Patrick came to Armagh with the words of Jesus in his heart: "Whatever house you go into, let your first words be, 'Peace to this house.'" He came to Armagh to preach the truth that "the Kingdom of God is very near." In the face of a hundred different Irish kingdoms Patrick gave witness to the one enduring Kingdom—God's Kingdom. That Kingdom, to which Patrick committed his life, is a Kingdom of Truth, of Justice, of Peace, of Reconciling Love.

We pray every day, we pray in this Mass—*Thy Kingdom come.* We know too well the shortcomings of the kingdoms of this world. One of my treasures is a gift which Cardinal Tomas O'Fiaich gave me shortly before his death, a copy of his book on his prececessor Oliver Plunkett. In that book, the Cardinal quotes a report on the Archbishop's execution, probably by an English Jesuit, sent to Rome. The report states:

> All write with one accord that this innocent victim has done and yet performs great good in England, not only by the edification which he gives to the Catholics, but moreover by the change of ideas and sentiments which he occasioned in many Protestants, who now commence to regard all these conspiracies as malicious fictions; and these are great grounds for believing that the fruit which England will derive from his blood will not end here.

Cardinal O'Fiaich added: "The prophesy was quickly shown to be true. The first of July was the day when the people of England finally turned against the Popish Plot and its makers. . . . Oliver Plunkett was the last man to be martyred for the Catholic faith in England."

Yet we know how heavy have been the hearts of Patrick's successors as violence and injustice have so long marked the lives of the faithful, and made their bishops martyrs of another kind. The violence of recent years suffered by Catholics and Protestants alike, has been a grim reminder that violence begets violence. The systemic injustices against the spiritual heirs of St. Patrick have borne their rotten fruit.

How poignant it is to recall the words of St. Patrick's present successor, Cardinal Daly, spoken on the occasion of the funeral Mass of Cardinal O'Fiaich:

> Cardinal O'Fiaich was totally opposed to all use of violence purporting to advance nationalist aims. In Germany in 1987 he had said: "God has placed our two communities, Protestant and Catholic, Unionist and Nationalist, side by side on the island of Ireland. His intention was certainly not that we should be warring communities, but, in the words of St. Paul, "That out of the two he might make a new creation." The validity of both identities in Ireland and the right of both to continue must be accepted as the basis for future peace.

The then Bishop Daly added:

> May those committed to violence listen at last in death to this plea from the heart of that great Irishman who was Cardinal Tomas O'Fiaich.

I was in this Cathedral when those stirring words of Bishop Daly were spoken over the coffin of Cardinal O'Fiaich. I was here not long after for the installation of Bishop Daly as successor of Father Tom and of Oliver Plunkett and of St. Patrick.

For 1,550 years, Patrick has proclaimed from Armagh the Kingdom of God. The present primate did so again in this Cathedral on Sunday, February 19 of this year on the occasion of the episcopal ordination of Archbishop Sean Brady as his Coadjutor. The Cardinal spoke of his belief that the Irish Catholic Church was "emerging from its winter time" with signs of new life ranging from the renewal of lay spirituality to a greater commitment to ecumenism and reconciliation. He said: "There is no terminal illness in the Church in Ireland; there are no preparations for the Church's burial."

Indeed, the history of these past 1,550 years attests to the truth of Jesus' promise to be with His Church until the end of time. Again and again the Paschal rhythm of death and resurrection has been manifest in the Church of Armagh, the Church in Ireland, and the churches around the world who are the grateful heirs of the prophecy of Patrick fulfilled. He wrote in his *Confession*: "He gave me the great grace that through me many peoples should be reborn in God . . . one people gathered by the Lord from the ends of the world."

The ends of the world converge on Armagh this Jubilee Year with grateful hearts for the gift of faith received through Patrick and his successors. As Patrick first preached in this place, Armagh echoes again the words of Jesus: "The kingdom of God is very near." Ireland is not a hundred separate kingdoms now, but rather an island divided more by mutual distrust and war than by lines on a map, an Ireland weary of war and violence, determined to walk the way of truth, of justice, of reconciliation and peace. *The New Framework* says that "the most urgent and important issue facing the people of Ireland, North and South, and the British and Irish governments together, is to remove the causes of conflict, to overcome the legacy of history and to heal the divisions which have resulted."

Surely this is true when we speak of that history which records the perversity, violence, and sin of which the human heart is capable. There is another legacy of history, however, and it is that which we celebrate today. It is the legacy of Patrick's gift of faith to this Island that belongs in a unique way to the whole world. This legacy of history is not to be overcome; it remains to be fulfilled.

A better future must be rooted in that legacy of faith, that legacy of history expressed for 1,550 years through Patrick and his successors at Armagh. This legacy affirms the dignity of the human person, the sanctity of the family, and the implications of human solidarity. To hear Patrick is to know that we are to live in unity and peace. He says, quite simply, "This is our faith: believers are to come from the whole world."

What we *see* in our world today is different from what Patrick saw 1,550 years ago. Now, like then, there are lights and shadows. Like Patrick, however, we do not fix our gaze on what is seen, which is transitory, but on what is unseen and lasts forever: God's Kingdom, which is an eternal and everlasting kingdom: a kingdom of truth and life, a kingdom of holiness and grace, a kingdom of justice, love, and peace. We pray now and always: "Thy Kingdom come."

57

✣

You Are Ordained for Sacrifice

At the Ordination of Three Dominican Priests

Washington, D.C., 26 May 1995

The rite of ordination instructs me at this point to address the families and friends of the ordinandi. That first word is one of gratitude to the parents of these three deacons. It was through you that the gift of life came to be in them, and it was through you that the gift of faith was mediated to them. On behalf of the Church I thank you and rejoice with you.

It is good to remember gratefully all those whose lives have been a grace for these ordinandi. We think in particular of all those who have been their teachers.

Father Voll, this day has special meaning for you, for Father Folsey and for all your confreres in the Order of Preachers. These three brothers of yours have found strength and inspiration in religious community as Dominicans. They seek ordination as priests conscious that this new ministry will draw strength from that community of brothers which claims St. Dominic as father. As the burden of Moses was lightened by the ministry of the seventy elders, so will the burden of their ministry be lightened by that fraternal spirit which they cherish as Dominicans.

The responsery to the second reading from the Office of St. Philip Neri, whose feast day that is, speaks beautifully to your common life as Dominicans:

> Rejoice, brothers. Strive for perfection; encourage one another. Live in harmony and peace and the God of peace and love will be with you.

It is important that we be clear about the ordained priesthood. Jesus Christ is Priest. In his sacrificial death upon the cross, he showed Himself to be at once both priest and victim. Jesus has defined Priesthood in Himself so that, as Cardinal Suhard observed, the priesthood is not something, it is someone—Christ. Because we share, through baptism, in His life—we share in His Priesthood. This truth concerning the priesthood of all believers must in no way obscure the fact that the ordained priesthood is distinct from the priesthood of all believers. Catholic faith speaks of an ontological difference between the ordained priesthood and the priesthood of all believers. It is through the ministry of the ordained priest that the Lord Jesus wills to make present in the Church his priestly ministry. The ordained priest acts in *persona Christi*—in the person of Christ.

Far from being a ministry of worldly status and power, the ordained priesthood makes incarnate in a wondrous way the priestly service of Jesus Christ—pre-eminently in His sacrificial death under the appearance of bread and wine. It is above all in the Lord's sacrifice that the ordained priesthood finds its identity. Pray for your brothers—commend them now to the Lord, and "to that gracious word of his which can enlarge (them) and give (them) a share among all who are consecrated to him.

Now—my brothers—the Church bids me to speak to you. The hour has arrived for you. What was that hour for the first priests of the Church? It was an hour which linked together and forever the Passover meal, Christ's death upon the cross, and the unique service of the ordained priest. The burden of your shepherd service is to make present in the bread, the wine, and in your pastoral love of the new and everlasting covenant signed in his blood.

You are to preach Christ crucified to a world in desperate need to hear of God's endearing love revealed in Him. In a world adrift in moral relativism you are to be shepherds preaching a higher and enduring vision about God, about God revealed in Christ Jesus, about the Church, about the human person, and about the implications of human solidarity.

You will be good shepherds, you will be worthy priests to the extent that you are configured to Christ, and to Him crucified. In our world, *benefactor* has a nice ring. You, however, are to be more than benefactors—those who are honored for doing good to others out of their abundance.

You are ordained for sacrifice—which means, literally, to make holy. Priesthood is encountered in Christ Jesus—and in Him as Victim on the cross. You are called to make holy by being configured to Christ as

Victim. Your life as priest will be more effective to the extent that your lives reflect the sacrificial love of Jesus Christ. The good shepherd lays down his life for the sheep. *This* is priestly service.

May Mary, Mother of God and Mother of the Church, intercede for you now and throughout your lives that you may be priests after the heart of her Divine Son.

58

✢

The True Witness of a Political Figure

The Catholic Vision of John F. Collins, Former Mayor of Boston

1 December 1995

Yesterday Mayor John Collins was buried. The Mass of Christian Burial at the Cathedral of the Holy Cross was beautiful in its prayerful simplicity. He expressed his wishes to his wife within the year of his death, suggesting that talks and speeches belonged elsewhere, not at Mass.

This tells us a lot about Mayor John Collins. He understood and loved the Mass; he was a man of vibrant faith; he understood that what was ultimately important was a life lived in accord with God's will, a life lived in accord with the teaching of the Church.

He loved the Church, and he was distressed to see her message distorted, her role ridiculed, and her place in the public square questioned.

There was a consistency about Mayor Collins. These days following his death he has been remembered as the person responsible for a new Boston, and we are invited to look at the skyline as proof of that. He has been credited for the change of image of Boston, so that it became more attractive to outside investment, thus permitting economic revitalization. These are fair characterizations, understanding always that what one person accomplishes depends upon what others have done before.

Mayor Collins' concern, however, was not with skylines and image. He was concerned about the quality of life that makes possible a habitable city. He was concerned about how we view one another.

If someone had asked him if he were satisfied now with Boston, and its fine new skyline and its financially active business center, I think the answer would obviously be no, he was not satisfied.

There is so much more building to be done in the city of Boston and in all the cities of this commonwealth and nation. How important it is that we attend to that more fundamental fabric of human relationships.

The media are filled with discussions about the Bosnian peace plan and the appropriateness of the deployment of U.S. troops there. Part of the discussion hinges on whether or not it is in the national interest that U.S. troops be deployed. Surely there are real and serious questions which must be answered before such deployment. What is disconcerting, however, is how narrowly national interest appears to be defined by some.

Certainly it is in our nation's interest that peace be secured in the place of barbarous hostilities anywhere in the globe. Whether that national interest demands U.S. troops or not is a fair question. It cannot be said, however, that humanitarian intervention on behalf of peace, even if it means the deployment of troops, is only in the national interest if some material benefit or some imminent danger to us as a nation be involved. The containment of armed struggle must be in the interest of every nation, or else the world must adjust to being an armed jungle.

We need not only to discuss the peace of Sarajevo, we also need to discuss the peace in Boston and in the other cities of this nation. How great the distance is from some suburban communities and the streets of cities where youngsters are gunned down or left stabbed and bleeding within minutes of their homes.

Last week, Barrington Nevins became another in an all-too-long succession of victims. A gifted student with a great future, his mistake was apparently wearing the wrong jacket. It is almost impossible to comprehend an environment in which a teenager is at risk in his own neighborhood simply by virtue of what he wears, or simply by virtue of being there.

The work of building this city remains an unfinished task. "This city" is the Boston that Mayor Collins served so well, and it is Lawrence and Brockton and Lowell and Lynn and every other city in this Commonwealth and nation. It is so important that we realize, each one of us, that it is very much in our personal interest to be involved in changing the quality of life of "this city."

In his later life, Mayor Collins focused a great deal on such issues as the dignity of every human being from the first moment of conception to the last moment of natural death. He focused on the importance of the family, he focused on the need to make room in the public debate for the voice of moral teaching, and to include in that, very specifically, the voice of the Catholic Church.

Were these later interests of the Mayor a break from his earlier commitment to the rebuilding of Boston? I think not. Rather, I believe that in his later life he entered into the far more important phase of city building.

There are encouraging signs in every city, which too often fail to make the news. In Boston and in other cities of this Archdiocese, the Catholic Church provides educational opportunities, social services, and medical facilities which enhance the quality of life. Perhaps the most important contribution of the Church is encountered in the life of our parishes. The fact that men and women gather Sunday after Sunday to celebrate the mystery of God's love in the Eucharist, and to be nourished by His Word is the yeast, is the salt of God's kingdom in our midst, it is the building of the city of God in our midst.

The Ten-Point Coalition involving the pastors of many black Protestant churches as well as the pastors of inner city parishes in Boston, St. Mary's Women and Infants Center in Dorchester, and Laboure Center in South Boston are just some of the ways in which men and women of good will are seeking to build the city of God in our midst.

Earlier this week I visited Walpole Prison. I went into several of the maximum security units. They each have three levels with rows of single cells. What is our future? Are we going to build more prisons, or are we going to build up the quality of life within our cities?

In our choice is the latter, then we must attend to the moral fabric of our communities. We must hold everyone to greater accountability for their actions. We must ask some very serious questions about the messages that are given to our young. We must proclaim consistently a vision of human worth, of human dignity, of the value of every human being, of the sanctity of the family, of the implications of human solidarity.

Please God, there will be willing hands and hearts to continue the work of rebuilding Boston and all the cities of the Commonwealth and the nation. Let us build here the city of God.

59

✣

What a Wondrous Thing Is the Human Body

Reflections from a Hospital Bed

16 February 1996

These past few days have given me a new experience of God's presence. I have been blessed with good health and abundant energy all my life, and I recognize these as God's gifts. What appears to have been a virus, however, has left me sick and drained enough to land me in St. Elizabeth's Medical Center. All indications are that this afternoon I will return home, well on the way to full recovery.

What a wondrous thing is the human body! What an incredibly complex organism. The science of medical diagnosis reveals an amazing system or complex of systems which function in harmony when we are healthy, and which reveal illness when that normal harmony, that normal balance is affected.

I am not a stranger to hospitals because, like all priests, I see visiting the sick as part of my pastoral responsibility. St. Elizabeth's Medical Center is particularly well known to me because of the exquisite care it provided my mother. To be actually in a hospital bed, however, is a new experience. It has been an experience of God's love in the care provided me by doctors, priest-chaplain, nurses, medical technicians, dieticians, the patient hospitality associates, volunteers, and all with whom I have come in contact.

It has been a reassuring sign of God's love to see the young men and women interns giving themselves to such a noble profession. It is reassuring about the future to hear the enthusiasm of a young Haitian man who serves as a nurse's assistant, aspiring to become an R.N., and hoping later to become an M.D. It is good to hear a young resident speak of his desire to practice medicine in the inner city, with the desire to do so from a clearly religious perspective. It is good to hear wonderfully dedicated young nurses who balanced their lives with an evident love for their families and their patients. It is good to hear a nurse say, "I do this because I just like helping sick people."

The hospital is very much in touch with reality. It is one of those places where the truth about us is revealed. The x-rays, the sonogram, the blood and other lab analysis, the weighing of intake and output tells us things about ourselves that we have never known and perhaps things that we would rather not know.

Because the hospital is so rooted in the real, God is present here in a way that is more easily perceived than is usually the case in the world of business, government, or entertainment. I heard someone say recently that religion is the meaning we give to human existence. I do not think that is correct. We do not "give" meaning to human existence. That meaning has already been given by God. The hospital setting, in being open to the awe and wonder of the human organism, invites an openness to the awe and wonder of God's presence which is one of the gifts of the Holy Spirit.

It was words from the Book of Proverbs in today's Office of Readings which have triggered these reflections. In Proverbs we are reminded that, "The beginning of wisdom is the fear of the Lord, and knowledge of the Holy One is understanding." In moving from the very real subject that is a human being, the practice of medicine reinforces true wisdom and understanding. This is so because we can only appreciate the full wonder of the human being in God as He is manifest in Christ Jesus.

Next Wednesday, Ash Wednesday, the Church begins forty days of preparation for the great Paschal Mystery of Christ's Saving Death and Resurrection. As we seek to be more conscious of God's love for us revealed in the Paschal Mystery, the Church focuses our attention on ourselves. We are asked to remember who we are. The ashes are a reminder of our mortality. We are dust. But look what God has done with this dust! And look what God will do if we but die to sin and rise to newness of life in Christ Jesus.

Repent and believe the Good News. May we do this. May we live these days of Lent in prayer, in penance, and in good works so that we might come to a deeper knowledge and experience of the Paschal Mystery.

60

✢

The Church Already Has "Common Ground"

On the Catholic Common Ground Project

12 August 1996

Cardinal Bernardin of Chicago has announced today a project which he has agreed to lead that is called "The Catholic Common Ground Project." He is joined in this effort by a group of Catholics including bishops, priests, religious, lay women and men. The several signatories from within the Archdiocese of Boston are persons for whom I have great esteem.

In connection with the announcement of this "Project," a statement has been released which was prepared by the National Pastoral Life Center. This statement entitled "Called to be Catholic," is proposed as "a good framework for fostering careful reflection on issues of concern."

It is, I think, unfortunate that the Cardinal's initiative has tied itself to this statement. The statement is not very helpful. Throughout there are gratuitous assumptions, and at significant points it breathes an ideological bias which it elsewhere decries in others. The fundamental flaw in this document is its appeal for "dialogue" as a path to "common ground."

The Church already has "common ground." It is found in Sacred Scripture and Tradition, and it is mediated to us through the authoritative and binding teaching of the Magisterium. The disconnect that is so often found today between that Catholic common ground and the faith and practice of some Catholics is alarming.

Dialogue as applied to this pastoral crisis must be clearly understood, however. Dissent from revealed truth or the authoritative teaching of the

Church cannot be "dialogued" away. Truth and dissent from truth are not equal partners in ecclesial dialogue. Dialogue as a pastoral effort to assist in a fuller appropriation of the truth is laudable. Dialogue as a way to mediate between the truth and dissent is mutual deception.

The statement raises the issue of the faithful's "reception" of a truth or in the incorporation of a decision or practice into the Church's life. Surely this is an issue worthy of on-going theological consideration. Reception by the faithful cannot be measured by polls which are subject to all the pressures of contemporary culture, however, any more than the schism of all the bishops save one in Henry VIII's England can be ascribed to an exercise of collegiality.

Recent Pastoral Statements of the bishops of the United States on peace and on the U.S. economy were not universally well received by the faithful. If polls are to be believed, the position of the bishops of Massachusetts in opposition to capital punishment does not enjoy overwhelming support from the faithful. The Church must teach "in season and out of season, when convenient and inconvenient." Careful discernment must be used in assessing what is called "reception."

The statement proposes as the sixth of seven "working principles" for dialogue the following: "We should not rush to interpret disagreements as conflicts of starkly opposing principles rather than as differences in degree or in prudential pastoral judgments about the relevant facts." Fair enough, as long as it is admitted that "conflicts of starkly opposing principles" *can* occur. When such conflict involves dissent from authoritative Church teaching, that conflict cannot be dialogued away. Dissent either yields to assent, or the conflict remains irresolvable.

In paragraph eighteen of twenty-seven, the statement introduces the thought that "Jesus Christ, present in Scripture and sacrament is central to all we do; he must always be the measure and not what is measured." I would have preferred to have the statement begin at that point. The crisis the Church is facing can only be adequately addressed by a clarion call to conversion. Jesus' question to Peter must be responded to by each of us: "Who do you say that I am?" Only with this beginning will institutional renewal and reform be authentic.

61

✣

The Pain of Separation Is Particularly Acute at the Altar of God

In Rome with Orthodox and Catholic Pilgrims

25 October 1996

I write this column in Rome. It is Wednesday, and by the miracle of fax *The Pilot* deadline will be met.

It is only our second day of pilgrimage in Europe and already the grace of this trip is evident. We are about 120 pilgrims, Orthodox and Catholic. Bishop Methodios and I are privileged to lead the group. The *fact* that we are together in pilgrimage is its own story. From here we go to Istanbul to visit the Ecumenical Patriarch and then to Athens.

For more than a thousand years, the Churches of East and West were one at the table of the Lord. For almost a thousand years we have suffered the effects of schism. Our separation has been reinforced by cultural differences, political considerations, and bitter memories.

As we prepare for the next millennium, it is imperative that Catholic and Orthodox Christians do all in their power to reverse the course of schism and re-establish that communion that was ours from the beginning.

That is the intention in the hearts of those of us traveling together. When we arrived yesterday, we made our way to the Basilica of St. Paul—Outside the Walls. There, at the site of St. Paul's martyrdom and burial we prayed together for unity and for the spread of the Gospel. Later, we joined in prayer again as Mass was celebrated at a church near our hotel. The pain of separation is particularly acute at the altar of God. Our present inability to express our communion of faith in one Eucharist is a compelling motive for working in the cause of unity.

This morning we got an early start in order to be in time for a 7:30 a.m. Mass at St. Peter's Basilica. I never cease to be awed by the quiet beauty and splendor of St. Peter's in the early morning hours. It is a time reserved for prayer—the tourists come later. This morning's Mass was celebrated in the crypt at an altar facing the small casket holding the remains discovered in St. Peter's grave.

It is always a moving experience to celebrate Mass at St. Peter's, and especially is this so when Mass is celebrated at such a special spot. Today, however, our pilgrimage Mass was particularly moving. To be at the spot of Peter's burial, and to be joined as Catholics and Orthodox in prayer for the unity of the Church which Peter served even to the shedding of his blood, gives an added urgency to our prayer.

Following the Mass, Bishop Methodios led us in prayer, and then we knelt in quiet before the remains of St. Peter.

Later this morning, the Holy Father appeared at his window overlooking St. Peter's Square. There were thousands of persons gathered to receive his blessing. The Holy Father, before granting his blessing, greeted several of the groups gathered in the square. He acknowledged the presence of our pilgrimage, he thanked us for our initiative and begged God's blessing upon our efforts.

Needless to say, it was a special moment for us. After the Holy Father departed from the window and the crowds began to disperse, it was picture-taking time. Not only were there the Orthodox-Catholic pilgrims with cameras in hand, but others, seeing them, also wanted pictures. Within a short while Bishop Methodios and I were photographed with Polish students, a Mexican couple, a group from Scotland, several persons from Ethiopia and Germany, a family from Holland, an Australian and a Japanese person. It seemed as though all roads do lead to Rome, and we began to wonder if we would get out of the Square before dark.

The only thing missing so far is time to sleep!

62

Sacrifice Is Alien to Rampant Consumerism

To an International Eucharistic Conference in Europe

Poland, 26 May 1997

What a singular grace it is to be here at this Eucharistic Congress. We are poised on the eve of the new millennium. We are focused in this year of millennial preparation on the truth that Jesus Christ is Lord, the same yesterday, today, and forever. We look forward with a hope borne of faith in Him to the year 2000. We are one in prayer with Mary, the Mother of God and the Mother of the Church, imploring the outpouring of the Holy Spirit upon the whole Church that we might be a light unto the nations as we leave this most violent of centuries.

We gather in Poland. Here the tragedy of two world wars was experienced in all its violence. Here the memory of Nazi and Communist oppression is still fresh in its horror. Here the slavery that comes with systems devoid of God has given Poland its martyrs. Here the indomitable power of God's Spirit moving in the minds and hearts of Poland's sons and daughters has brought the hope of a new spring of freedom.

We come, from all over the world, to give thanks to God for the freedom that is ours in Christ Jesus. The words of Isaiah were fulfilled in Jesus: "The Spirit of the Lord God is upon me, because the Lord has anointed me . . . to proclaim liberty to the captives, and release to the prisoners." He it is who has freed us from sin and from death by his sacrifice on the cross. He bore our iniquities; he bore our death. He put death itself to death on the cross.

A Visit to Poland.

Whenever we gather to celebrate the Eucharist, we show forth the death of the Lord until he comes again, as St. Paul reminds us. In the Eucharist there is made present on our altars, under the appearance of bread and wine, the all-sufficient sacrifice by which Jesus Christ, both priest and victim, redeemed the world. Paul also teaches us the consoling truth that Christ unites our offering to his. Paul says: "we make up the sufferings that are wanting in Christ." Jesus' sacrifice is the total gift of Himself out of love for us. Greater love than this no one has. It is to this sacrificial love that we are called. Listen again to Jesus' words in today's Gospel: "If a man wishes to come after me, he must deny his very self, take up his cross and begin to follow in my footsteps."

To understand the truth of Eucharist as sacrifice it is not enough to *say*, "I believe in the Mystery of Faith." It is necessary to enter into the Sacrifice of Christ by offering our lives in faithful discipleship. It is in knowing the truth, who is God, who is revealed to us in Christ Jesus, who is present in Eucharist, that we become free. Jesus Christ reveals to us what it means to be fully human, what it means to be fully free. Only in leaving all to follow Him can we know freedom in the fullest sense.

How much to the point for us are the words of Jesus to his first disciples and to all those of any age who would be his disciples: "What profit would a man show if he were to gain the whole world and ruin himself in the process? What can a man offer in exchange for his very self?" These words cut to the heart of contemporary culture which is driven by an insatiable thirst for monetary profit. This profit in turn is fueled by a rampant consumerism that appeals to every conceivable human instinct and desire.

Contemporary culture misunderstands freedom as an ability to choose, regardless of the object. By contrast, true freedom, as Jesus reveals to us in his redemptive death, is the freedom to love even to the point of laying down our lives for another. What a grotesque caricature of freedom is the hollow claim of choice: the bell of choice tolls for the lives of millions of unborn babies and threatens the lives of the terminally ill, elderly and disabled. A disordered consumerism logically reinforces a culture of death because it focuses on individual gratification, on individual convenience. The notion of sacrifice is alien to a rampant consumerism.

Sin is disruptive of communion with God and communion with one another. Adam and Eve hid from God in the shame and fear that their sin brought them. Cain's murder of his brother Abel is a chilling foreshadowing of all the violence that has set brother against brother, sister against sister throughout human history. We hold in mind our brothers and sisters in Africa, in the Middle East, in Northern Ireland, and wherever it is that sin works its way through wars and other manifestations of violence. We remember those who suffer violence in the sanctuary of their marriages and families. We remember especially women and children whose equality and dignity are so often abused in our world. We call to mind the way in which ethnic, racial and religious differences are used as excuses for the most violent forms of discrimination. We remember all this as the sin from which the Lord Jesus has delivered us.

The Eucharist as communion teaches us that if we are one with our Eucharistic Lord, then we are one with one another. Again St. Paul is our guide as he teaches that "the body is one and has many members, but all the members, many though they are, are one body; and so it is with Christ." We receive the Body of Christ, the Risen Lord, each one of us, in the Holy Communion of this Mass. As each of us is brought into a deeper communion with the Lord Jesus, so are we brought into a deeper communion with one another. We discover one another in Him in a new way. No longer are we blinded by our differences, but we are drawn by the Lord who is present in each of us.

Just as faith in the Lord brings us as individuals out of ourselves and into relationships of sacrificial love with others, so too does the Spirit empower the church to go into the whole world to make disciples of all peoples, of all nations. It is the task of the Church to evangelize the cultures of the world. It is the task of the Church, which is to say it is our task, to proclaim liberty to those who are captives of sin, to proclaim release to the prisoners of all forms of oppression and violence. It is for us "to announce a year of favor from the Lord, and a day of vindication by our God."

As we move towards that year of favor 2000, we proclaim Jesus Christ as Lord yesterday, today, and forever. We acknowledge the presence of the Risen Lord in the Eucharist. We proclaim that the Eucharist makes present His redemptive sacrifice, the new and everlasting covenant under the appearance of bread and wine. We acknowledge our communion with Him and, in Him, with one another in Eucharist. In Eucharist we experience the freedom which He alone can give, for in Him we know the full splendor of the truth.

63

+

The Church Creates Her Own Culture

Intervention at the Vatican Synod for America

Vatican City State, 16 November 1997

Most Holy Father, my brother bishops, brothers and sisters all in Christ, this intervention is a reflection on paragraph 35 of the *Instrumentum Laboris*.

St. Paul gives us great courage in declaring: "When I am weak, then I am strong." In the face of the phenomenon of globalization, in the face of the hegemony of the United States which has led to what some have called "the Americanization" of popular culture, a culture too often one of death, the Church frequently finds herself marginalized. We can and we must stand with and for the poor, the most vulnerable, in our world. The concerns expressed in this aula on the external debt of nations, for example, or on the hardships of economic embargoes, are certainly appropriate. Often the most we can do, however, is to lift our voice in advocacy for a more just social and economic order. In all candor we must acknowledge our weakness.

We do not have in hand the economic and political forces which move the world. While we are in the world, we are not of it. Paradoxically, however, therein lies our strength. Like Peter, we have neither the silver nor gold of this world's power. What we have is the freedom that flows from revealed Truth. What we have is the transcendent power of God's love revealed in His Incarnate Son. What we have is faith in Jesus Christ as Lord and Savior, the same yesterday, today, and forever.

The work of proclaiming the Lordship of Jesus understandably involves the evangelization of culture. Can we not say, however, that the Church, in a very real sense, creates her own culture? Is it not possible to catch a glimpse of this Catholic culture in the theme of this Special Assembly: *Encounter With The Living Jesus Christ, The Way To Conversion, Communion, and Solidarity?*

We must always be ready to give an account of the hope that is within us. With great confidence not in ourselves, but in the Holy Spirit's abiding presence in the Church, we must be more clearly who we are as the One, Holy, Catholic and Apostolic Church. We are a light, through our ecclesial communion, unto the nations.

To this end, I would suggest that this Special Assembly underscore:

1. The universal call to holiness.
2. The bond of unity with the ministry of Peter in our midst, recognizing the Petrine office as a constitutive element of the Church, as an element of the *esse,* not simply the *bene esse* of the Church and of each local Church.
3. The role of bishops as confident teachers of the faith in the face of a widespread faith illiteracy. We have in the *Catechism of the Catholic Church* a great help in this.
4. The vocation of theologian in its relation to the authoritative teaching of the Church.
5. *Communio* expressed in an unambiguous Catholic identity as a service to the cause of ecumenism.
6. A commitment to sanctify and strengthen marriage and the family.
7. A commitment to follow the lead of our Holy Father in championing the role of women in Church and society.

May the intercession of Our Lady of Guadalupe grant us the grace of a deeper communion as the Church in America so that we may more clearly appear as the icon of the living Jesus, so that the words of St. Augustine might be verified in our life together as the Church in this hemisphere: "The Church is Christ, extended in time and space."

64

✛

Priesthood Is Not Something but a Someone

Ordination of a Priest under the Exceptional Terms of the "Pastoral Provision"

30 May 1998

The Church places on the ordaining bishop two tasks at this point in the liturgy. First, to address those who are assembled concerning the meaning of priestly ordination, and, second, to address the candidate himself.

You who know Richard Bradford longest and best, his wife, his children, the congregation he has shepherded, have walked the path to this day through your love, your encouraging support, and your prayers. Mrs. Bradford, would you and your children please stand so that we might all express our gratitude to you for your part in bringing us to this moment of grace.

All of us, by virtue of baptism, share in the life of Christ, who is the eternal high priest. "One does not take this honor on his own initiative, but only when called by God as Aaron was. Even Christ did not glorify himself with the office of high priest; he received it from the One who said to him:

> You are my son;
> today I have begotten you;
> just as he says in another place—
> "You are a priest forever, according to the
> order of Melchizidek."

These words in the Letter to the Hebrews have moved the hearts of the faithful throughout the centuries as the meaning of priesthood has been contemplated. Cardinal Suhard, Archbishop of Paris, during World War II, wrote that "the priesthood is not something, it is someone, Christ." Christ, who is Priest, altar, and Lamb of Sacrifice, has given new meaning to Priesthood—forever Priesthood can be properly understood only in terms of all that Jesus Christ is.

Since, by baptism, we have died to sin and risen to newness of life in Him, we live now, not we, but Christ lives in us. We share, then, in the priesthood of Christ, we are a priestly people, because Jesus Christ *is* the Eternal High Priest.

From among our number, however, God calls men to minister in the name, in the very person of Christ—in *persona Christi;* as ordained priests. The distinction between the priesthood of all believers and the ordained priestly ministry is not simply a difference of degree. The outpouring of the Holy Spirit and the laying on of hands transfigures the one ordained in such a way that for all eternity he will bear the mark of priestly character.

Pray for Richard—that the presence of Jesus Christ, the eternal high priest, might be ever more evident as the ministers in the person of Jesus Christ. Pray that he might never forget that Jesus came, not to be serviced but to serve.

Richard—I commend to you Paul's words to the elders of the Church at Ephesus: "Keep watch over yourselves, and over the whole flock the Holy Spirit has given you to guard. Shepherd the Church of God, which he has acquired at the price of his own blood."

"Keep watch over yourselves." How absolutely fundamental it is that you watch over yourself by nourishing a life of prayer. Called though you are to serve the Church as a priest, your prior and enduring call is to holiness of life. Before all else—you must ever strive to be a holy man. This fresh anointing of the Holy Spirit will bring also the gift of deeper prayer. Be open and eager for this gift.

While the efficacy of your priestly ministry will not depend on your holiness, since you minister in the person of Jesus Christ, the eternal High Priest, the Church nonetheless teaches us that priestly ministry is rendered more effective as the priest is more holy. Strive, then, for holiness of life.

For you Richard, the call to holiness embraces the sacrament of marriage and the blessing of fatherhood. The Church looks to her priests as ministers of love and peace because Jesus Christ, the eternal high priest, *is* love incarnate, *is* our peace. That love and that peace is to characterize your ministry in the Church—and should be reflected in your relationship to your wife and children. The notion of the family as the domestic church should have special meaning for you.

Our Lord's dialogue with Peter is so consoling to us. Peter had thrice denied the Lord as we do whenever we sin. Again and again the movement of the Holy Spirit in our minds and hearts enables us to proclaim that Jesus Christ is Lord and to profess our love of Him. The priestly ministry of Jesus is one of forgiveness and reconciliation. Be always ready to receive that gift yourself even as you minister Divine Mercy to others in the person of Christ.

Hear well Christ's mandate to Peter. Feed my sheep. It is the flock of Christ whom we are privileged to serve as priests. The food we bring is the bread of life and the chalice of everlasting life. The Church which we shepherd as priests has been acquired at the price of Christ's own blood. Our priestly identity is never more evident than when we stand at the altar of God, take the bread and chalice of wine into our hands, and say—or better—Jesus Christ, the Eternal High Priest says in us—This is my Body, this is my Blood.

Pope John Paul II, the successor of Peter, is in our midst in a special way. He has fed you, Richard, and the community you have served by making it possible for this ordination to occur. He has fed the Church in deepening our understanding of ministerial priesthood by his focus on the truth that the priest ministers in *persona Christi*, in the person of Christ. He feeds us by the outstanding witness of his zeal, his love for the flock of Christ. Be always close to the Holy Father in your priestly ministry. Remember always that he is the pastor, the shepherd of the universal Church.

To love with a priestly heart, Richard, is to love as did Christ. Greater love than this no man has, than a man lay down his life for a friend. Jesus did this for us. Peter gave witness to his love by a martyr's death. You, by this ordination, lay down your life for the flock.

On this eve of Pentecost we are gathered in prayer—not alone, but with us are Mary—Mother of the Eternal High Priest and Mother of the Church, St. Peter and all the Apostles, St. Athanasius and all the Saints. With great confidence we pray—Come, Holy Spirit.

NOTE

The Pastoral Provision, established by the Holy See in 1980 and for which Cardinal Law serves as the Ecclesiastical Delegate of the Congregation for the Doctrine of the Faith, allows for the ordination, on a case by case basis, of former Episcopal clergymen who are married.

65

Belief in Christ Releases from All Fear

Words of Encouragement at a Home for the Elderly

14 March 1999

Jesus, after his encounter with the woman who had been caught in adultery, said to the Scribes and the Pharisees who thought she should be stoned:

> I am the light of the world.
> No follower of mine shall ever walk in darkness;
> no, he shall possess the light of life.

These words are recorded in the eighth chapter of St. John's Gospel, and help us to understand the meaning of today's Gospel reading from the ninth chapter of John.

This episode in the life of Jesus is, at one level, self-evident. There is a spectacular miraculous cure which the enemies of Jesus refuse to acknowledge, in spite of clear and compelling evidence.

It is not so much the physical fact that the one born blind was able to see which claims our greatest attention. It is, rather, what Jesus says to the man after he had been expelled. Jesus sought him out and asked him: "Do you believe in the Son of Man?" When the man asked Jesus in return, "Who is he, sir, that I may believe in him?" Jesus answered, "You have seen him, and the one speaking with you is he." The man born blind responds: "I do believe, Lord," and he worshiped him.

This Gospel is about the gift of faith which enables us to see Jesus as He

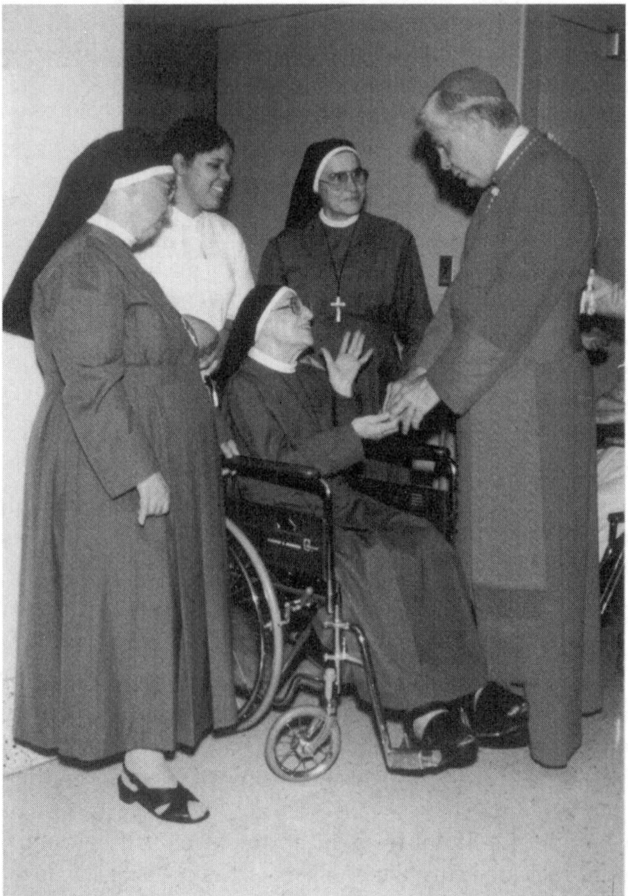

is—the Eternal Son of God, the Messiah, Our Lord and Savior. We hear this Gospel in the context of our Lenten journey to Easter. We accompany with our prayers all those catechumens who will be baptized at Easter. The new life that will be theirs through their rebirth in the waters of baptism will enable them to live in Christ who is the light of the world.

Paul reminded the Christians at Ephesus how transforming is the sacrament of baptism when he wrote: "You were once darkness, but now you are light in the Lord. Live as children of light, for light produces every kind of goodness and righteousness and truth." In another place Paul writes: "We walk by faith."

Faith is the greatest gift we can have. Recall Jesus' words, "Not everyone who says 'Lord, Lord,' shall enter the kingdom of heaven, but he who does the will of my heavenly Father." Faith is not simply a matter of professing the creed in words, it is rather a matter of living that creed in all that we do.

Again, Paul helps our understanding when he says: "Try to learn what is pleasing to the Lord."

The gift of faith is the way God grants us the ability to see Jesus as he is. The words of the Lord which came to Samuel when he met Jesse's youngest son, David, are read today in the Mass because those words are fulfilled in Jesus, the Christ, the anointed one. The Lord said to Samuel: "There—anoint him, for this is the one."

Jesus is the one, and there is no other, by whom salvation comes. If we walk in the light of his teaching, a teaching which comes to us through the Church, then we will never walk in darkness. The darkness cannot overcome the light that is Christ. Even should we walk through the shadow of death, the light of Christ will illumine our way.

To believe in Christ is to be released from all fear—it is to experience the deepest meaning of freedom. Scripture says: "you shall know the truth, and the truth shall make you free."

We are surrounded by points of view that are blind to the truths of faith. Our sight, our insight can at times appear overwhelmed by the darkness all around us. Today's readings encourage us to accept wholeheartedly the gift of faith which enables us to see that Jesus is the one, and enables us to walk in His light.

Each day the Church concludes her morning prayer with these beautiful words from Zechariah's Canticle:

> In the tender compassion of our God the dawn from on high shall break upon us, to shine on those who dwell in darkness and the shadows of death, and to guide our feet into the way of peace.

May the light of dawn, who is Jesus Christ, shine on us.

66

+

We Must Help Others Hear the Call

Vocation Awareness in a Period of Crisis

VOCATION AWARENESS WEEK, 14 JANUARY 2001

This is Vocation Awareness Week. Our focus in prayer is especially on vocations to religious life and to priesthood.

I wonder, however, if we do not do better by beginning our reflection on vocations with the fundamental call to holiness which is implicit in baptism. The vocation common to all in the Church is the vocation to holiness.

This week, then, is an invitation to each of us to consider God's call to holiness of life. Through baptism, we die to sin and death and rise to newness of life in Christ Jesus. The weeks of the Christmas season which concluded last Sunday have brought to mind in the beauty of the liturgy the saving truth of the Incarnation. This little baby, born of Mary, is the Eternal Son of God made flesh.

When the voice of God the Father proclaimed that Jesus was His beloved Son at the river Jordan, those words had reference also to every person rising from the waters of baptism. Through the new birth of baptism we are able to say "Abba, Father" to God because we live now in Christ.

It is precisely because of baptism and the new life it brings that we are called to be saints, that we are called to holiness.

Many of the more popular saints who are woven into the church's piety were religious or priests. Most of the saints in heaven, however, are undoubtedly laymen and women. They are wives and husbands, mothers and fathers. Again and again I find examples of great holiness among the lay faithful.

Without naming names, but with specific persons in mind, I think of someone suffering in patience and prayer the terrible effects of a debilitating illness. I think of someone whose life has been dedicated to the care of elderly parents so that other siblings might have their own families. I think of persons richly blessed materially who give most generously of their resources to help others. I think of someone who has overcome the assaults of racial discrimination in a life of service to the sick regardless of race. I think of a young woman with Down's Syndrome who is a source of blessing for all who know her.

The lives of each of these persons is rooted in faith and prayer. Faith for them is not just a gloss, it is the very basis of their existence. Prayer is to their spiritual lives what oxygen is to maintain our human existence. These friends understand that their vocation is holiness, they understand that God calls them to be saints.

In this week dedicated to vocation awareness, then, it is good for each of us to remember that we are called to be saints. Sanctity is not something bestowed upon us after we have died. There are no saints in heaven who were not first saints on earth. The call to holiness is about our lives here and now.

The Holy Father has prepared a message for the 37th World Day of Prayer for Vocations which is celebrated May 14, 2000, on the Fourth Sunday of Easter. The theme for that observance is: The Eucharist, source of all vocations and ministries in the Church." In that message Pope John Paul II writes: "It is in the Eucharistic Presence that Jesus reaches us, places us within the dynamism of ecclesial communion and makes us prophetic signs for the world."

I read those words in preparation for last Sunday's Mass at the Cathedral marking the Sesquicentennial of the foundation of the Sisters of Charity of Halifax. Those words immediately brought to mind Saint Elizabeth Ann Seton, the foundress of the Sisters of Charity in this part of the world. While not yet a Catholic, she was drawn to Jesus through the Eucharist as she prayed before the tabernacle. It was the Eucharistic presence of the Lord which drew her into the dynamism of ecclesial communion as a Catholic. It was her deep Eucharistic piety which made her such a powerful prophetic sign of God's love in the world. She responded in prayer to the call of Jesus which came to her through the Eucharist.

May the focus of our prayer these days be on the young women whom God may be calling to become saints as religious. May the example of Saint Elizabeth Ann Seton encourage them to say "yes" to God's gracious call.

May the focus of our prayer be also on those young men whom God may be calling to priesthood or religious life. I will meet with some of these young men this weekend, and will give a discernment retreat for another group in February.

In a world of much noise and many options, it is sometimes difficult to be still enough to hear God's voice. We join our prayer to that of the Holy Father:

> Holy Mary, Mother of all who are called,
> make all believers have the strength
> to answer the divine call with generous courage,
> and let them be joyful witnesses of love toward God
> and toward their neighbor.
> Young daughter of Sion, Star of the morning,
> who guides the steps of humanity
> through the Great Jubilee toward the future,
> direct the young people of the new millennium
> toward Him Who is "the true light which enlightens all men." (Jn 1,9)
>
> Amen.

WE MUST HELP OTHERS HEAR THE CALL, 16 JANUARY 2000

Today's readings remind us how necessary it is for us to be helped to hear the voice of God, to know his will for us.

Samuel thought that it was Eli who was calling to him, awakening him out of his sleep. After the third time that Samuel came to Eli, thinking it was he who had called him, Scripture tells us: "Then Eli understood that the Lord was calling the youth. So he said to Samuel, 'Go to sleep, and if you are called, reply, Speak Lord, for your servant is listening.' When Samuel went to sleep in his place, the Lord came and revealed his presence, calling out as before, 'Samuel, Samuel!' Samuel answered, 'Speak, for your servant is listening.'"

What a tremendous grace it is to listen to the voice of the Lord, yet so often it is so difficult for us to hear God. There are so many other voices, contrary voices, and so many conflicting emotions which make it difficult for us to hear God.

John the Baptist, like Eli, was one of those blessed figures who help us to know and to hear the Lord. "Behold the Lamb of God." With those words he directed his own disciples to Jesus. Andrew, one of those disciples of John the Baptist who followed Jesus, immediately went to his brother Simon to tell him that Jesus was the Messiah.

Paul, in his first letter to the Corinthians which was our second reading, was helping his brothers and sisters at Corinth and helping us to hear the word of the Lord. Listen again to his words: "The body is not for immorality, but for the Lord. . . . Avoid immorality. . . . Do you not know that your body is a temple of the Holy Spirit within you?"

These direct words of Saint Paul invite us to respond to Jesus' call to each of us when he says, "Be holy." God calls us to holiness of life. God calls us to live conscious of the fact that we are temples of the Holy Spirit. God calls us to a vision of human dignity which recognizes that all of life is to be lived in accord with God's will. Religion is not to be an occasional attitude, one mood among others in our mood swings. True religion calls for an integral life where every word and thought and action is formed in accord with God's will, a will revealed in Christ Jesus and his Church.

Holiness, the vocation of each one of us, is not a part-time career.

Last Sunday we were reminded of the special call which God gives to some as religious as we marked the sesquicentennial of the Sisters of Charity of Halifax. Just as God called Samuel, and as Jesus called the disciples of John the Baptist, Simon, and the other Apostles, so God, in the silent prayer of the heart, calls some to be religious, deacons, and priests today.

We must help others hear the call. We must be like Eli, John the Baptist, and Andrew for them. It is not easy in our world today to hear the call to priesthood and religious life. Through our prayers, through our positive attitude about priesthood and religious life, and through our encouragement of our brothers and sisters we can help them hear God's voice in their hearts, help them hear God's call.

Yesterday I met with a group of twelve young men, mostly high school seniors with a few juniors, who were at Saint John's Seminary for a twenty-four-hour visit. They are disposing themselves, like Samuel, to hear the Lord's call to them. Will they all be called to be priests? Probably not. But as they listen more attentively to God in their hearts, they will surely hear the Lord calling them to holiness of life.

Last evening I heard the good news that a young couple I know have become engaged to be married. This young man and woman have helped one another to hear God calling them into the sacramental bond of marriage.

Eli, John the Baptist, Andrew, and Saint Paul remind us that we have an obligation in love to help our brothers and sisters hear the call of God in their hearts, the call to holiness and to whatever special way we are to live out that holiness.

God calls to us constantly, not just in those extraordinary moments of great decision. God calls to us in all the circumstances of our lives, even the most ordinary.

Hear God now as He speaks to us through the words of the Psalmist: "Be still, and know that I am God."

67

✣

Boston Is Proud of the First African-American Bishop in the United States

A Salute in an Ecclesial Context to Black History Month

13 February 2000

Leprosy was a disease which conjured up fear not only in the ancient world, but well into our own time. Some of you will remember the poignant news accounts some years ago about a segregated community of persons with leprosy in Carville, Louisiana. This place was entrusted to the Daughters of Charity of Saint Vincent de Paul who made of it a place of loving care. Because of medical advancements, segregation became no longer necessary, and the facility was to be closed. Some of the persons who had only known that place in Carville, Louisiana, as their home were reluctant to leave, and feared entering into the wider world beyond the gates.

In Jesus' time, absolute segregation of those with leprosy was considered the only way to insure against the spread of the dreaded disease. So it was that the leper would make his presence known so others could avoid him. Perhaps the great pain of the disease was the separation from others, the isolation it demanded.

A leper was not allowed in the temple or synagogues. A leper was considered ritually unclean. Someone who touched a leper was also considered unclean.

Against this background, listen again to the beginning of today's Gospel.

> A leper came to Jesus
> and kneeling down begged Him and said,
> "If you wish, you can make me clean."
> Moved with pity, He stretched out His hand,
> touched him,
> and said to him,
> "I do will it. Be made clean."

Notice that the leper came to Jesus. His faith in Jesus allowed him to recognize that Jesus turns away no one. Whatever the illness, the fear, the anxiety, the sin, we are free to come to Jesus. The leper sought healing from Jesus, believing in Jesus' power to grant it.

Jesus was moved with pity. While Jesus' miracles of healing were signs of His Messianic power, the "healing" He had come to bring was far more profound. He had come to save us from sin and death. Jesus saw the leper before Him, and He was moved with pity.

Jesus stretched out His hand, and He touched him. He touched the leper. What a powerful expression of Divine Love. Jesus overcame the separation, the isolation that had gripped the leper's life, and He made Himself one with him. Healing flowed from this Divine encounter as Jesus said to him: "I do will it. Be made clean."

Thank God for the medical advances which have developed effective treatment for leprosy. For us, however, these advances have not affected the meaning of today's Gospel account.

The Gospel speaks to us, not of a physical illness, but of the far more serious affliction of sin. In its most radical form, sin is the choice we make to separate ourselves from God with the consequence that we also separate ourselves from one another. The original sin of Adam and Eve, and the fratricide committed by Cain when he killed his brother Abel teach us that sin results in isolation from God and, ultimately, from our brothers and sisters.

Yesterday at a Mass at Immaculate Conception parish in Everett, I called the children into the sanctuary and engaged them in discussion about Jesus. One young boy explained that we are all God's children, and so we are brothers and sisters and should live as family. How beautifully he expressed the truth that Jesus proclaimed in His saving death upon the cross.

Yet, not everyone, not all Catholics, perhaps none of us all of the time lives the truth of our unity with God and with one another in Christ Jesus.

Our isolation is not because of leprosy, but it is often caused by the sin of prejudice. It is appropriate to consider that as we mark Black History Month. Prejudice means making a judgment about a person without knowing him or her as an individual, but seeing the individual in terms of a negative stereotype, usually of race, or nation, or tribe. It is not wrong to make judgments; as a matter of fact we must make judgments all the time in attempting to live virtuous lives. If we are to avoid evil we must judge what is evil in the light of God's revelation and the Church's teaching. Certain acts are evil, and to make such a judgment is not an act of prejudice.

Prejudice, on the other hand, is a denial of our human solidarity as children of God. Its evil consequences are evident in the troubles in Northern Ireland, the tensions of the Middle East, the tribal conflicts in Africa, the ongoing nightmare of Kosovo, and so many other places plagued by division and violence.

As we mark Black History Month here in the Cathedral of the Holy Cross, as we give thanks to God for the ways in which we are learning, black Catholics, white Catholics, and all Catholics to live as family, we remember in a special way Bishop James Augustine Healy, the first African-American Bishop in the United States. Before he became the Bishop of Portland, Maine, he was the first Chancellor of the then Diocese of Boston. This Archdiocese is rightly proud of him and his role—not just in black history, but in the history of the Church in this country.

U.S. Black History must be seen in the context of a prevalent racism which has marked our nation's life, and which is not yet removed from our midst. In spite of the clear teaching of Scripture about the dignity of every human person made in the image and likeness of God, a teaching clearly proclaimed by the Second Vatican Council, the Catechism of the Catholic Church, and the eloquent teaching of Pope John Paul II, Catholics have all too often succumbed to the dominant culture. The racial prejudice in the lives of Catholics is too often indistinguishable from the racism in the dominant white culture. To our shame, we made our peace with slavery, with racial segregation, with racism.

As the white Archbishop of Boston, I give thanks to God for the long history of black Catholics in this country who did not give up the faith in the face of racism because they knew who they were; they knew they were the Church because Jesus had touched them and made them whole. They were able to see beyond the sins of prejudice and its demeaning structures to the mystery of the Church which is Christ-with-us.

Today may we approach Jesus in this Eucharist, each of us personally, and ask the Lord to heal us of whatever sinful prejudice may be in our hearts. We all need to do this, for prejudice can inflict blacks as well as whites as well as every human being. We ask Jesus, through the mystery of the cross made present in this Mass, to touch us, to make us whole, to let us live as the children of God we are, as brothers and sisters in Christ, as family.

68

✢

Sin Impeded the Spirit's Working in the Hearts of Many

Reconciliation during the Great Jubilee of the Year 2000

11 March 2000

"Now is the acceptable time! Now is the day of salvation!" Our *now* is the eve of the first Sunday of Lent. Lent is for the Church a spiritual pilgrimage to Easter. We prepare to enter into the Paschal Mystery of Christ's death and resurrection through these forty days of prayer, penance, and almsgiving. Our *now* in these forty days of Lent is understood in terms of that earlier "now" of those forty years which marked the exodus of God's chosen people from the land of bondage into the promised land, from slavery into freedom. Our *now* takes us from sin and death to forgiveness and eternal life.

In my pastoral letter of Ash Wednesday addressed to the faithful of the Archdiocese, I have stressed the importance of the sacrament of penance in our Lenten pilgrimage to Easter. Each of us must confess to God in that profoundly personal encounter with Christ through the sacrament of penance. No one else can say for us, "I confess." With all my heart I urge my brothers and sisters in the Archdiocese to approach the throne of Divine Mercy during this most acceptable time of our Lenten pilgrimage.

Tonight we situate the "now" of our Lenten pilgrimage in that other "now" of the Great Jubilee 2000. Our Holy Father, in anticipation of this Jubilee year, wrote: "Hence it is appropriate that as the second millennium of Christianity draws to a close the Church should become ever more fully conscious of the sinfulness of her children, recalling all those times in history when they departed from the spirit of Christ and his Gospel, and, instead of offering to the world the witness of a life inspired by the values of her faith, indulged in ways of thinking and acting which were truly forms of counter-witness and scandal. Although she is holy because of her incorporation into Christ, the Church does not tire of doing penance. Before God and man, she always acknowledges as her own her sinful sons and daughters."

These are courageous words from the heart of a man who loves the Church, and is not afraid to embrace that freedom which the truth about the past affords. In every age the Church has shone forth splendidly in her holiness through the witness of the saints. At the same time, sharing the "now" of these past two thousand years, generation after generation of Catholics have acknowledged before God their sinfulness. The Church is at once holy and ever in need of repentance until our "now" becomes one with the eternal "now" of God.

In our celebration of the Great Jubilee, the Holy Father has called us to a purification of memory. While we glory in our unity with the saints of old, it is also necessary to recognize that we are in the same communion of faith with those who have not reflected the life and teaching of Christ. As the Holy Father has written:

> Because of the bond which unites us to one another in the Mystical Body, all of us, though not personally responsible and without encroaching on the judgment of God Who alone knows every heart, bear the burden of the errors and faults of those who have gone before us. Yet we too, sons and daughters of the Church, have sinned and have hindered the Bride of Christ from shining forth in all her beauty. Our sin has impeded the Spirit's working in the hearts of many people. Our meager faith has meant that many have lapsed into apathy and been driven away from a true encounter with Christ.
>
> As the Successor of Peter, I ask that in this year of mercy the Church, strong in holiness which she receives from her Lord, should kneel before God and implore forgiveness for the past and present sins of her sons and daughters.

Tomorrow at Saint Peter's the Holy Father will kneel before God as the Universal Pastor of the Catholic Church and acknowledge those faults which weigh with sorrow on our memory as we contemplate our history.

Tonight, in this Cathedral, I seek with you God's forgiveness for the faults of Catholics throughout the history of this Archdiocese. I give thanks to God for the marvelous growth and countless witnesses to holiness which is our history since 1808. We ourselves have suffered, as a community of faith, the effects of discrimination and prejudice. All the greater should be our sorrow, therefore, for our own acts of discrimination and prejudice.

Within our life as Church, the mutual respect, love, and unity which should characterize our interpersonal relations have not always been evident. Intolerable situations have caused great pain and have sometimes resulted in alienation from the Church. There are the obvious cases of sexual abuse which have so seared us all, and the less celebrated cases of harsh words, as well as rough and unjust treatment which have affected clergy, religious, and laity.

As Catholics, we have too often been exclusive in our love and concern, defining ourselves erroneously by race or language or land of origin. To be the Church is to be Catholic, which means universal. To be less than that is to give an unclear witness of who we are as Church. The prejudices of others have too easily invaded our lives.

The Church should be a sign of unity, of hope, of justice, and of love in the world. To the extent that we have not been that, we acknowledge our faults and ask God's pardon.

Our prayer this night celebrates the Infinite Mercy of God which is made manifest in the suffering, death, and resurrection of Jesus Christ. We turn to God in total confidence that He will grant us the grace to turn from sin and to live more fully the life of the Risen Lord.

I am filled with profound gratitude by the presence of our beloved brothers and sisters in Christ with whom we are not yet in full communion, of our revered Jewish brothers and sisters with whom we share the memory of discrimination and persecution culminating in the Shoah, of our Islamic friends with whom we share the memory of the Crusades and their aftermath, and of brothers and sisters from many racial, ethnic, and national backgrounds. Please, in your goodness, pray for the Archdiocese of Boston as it exists today in me and in your Catholic neighbors. Pray that we might live out the spirit of this night. Pray that we might be more effective in building in our midst God's Kingdom of unity, of justice and of peace.

Now is the acceptable time. Now is the day of salvation. What a grace it is to be here, now, in this place.

69

✢

I Hope To March with Thousands of Young People

On the Jubilee Youth Rally at Fenway Park

24 March 2000

In the document inviting the Church to enter into preparation for the New Millennium which Pope John Paul II issued several years ago he wrote: "The future of the world and the Church belongs to the younger generation, to those who, born in this century, will reach maturity in the next, the first century of the new millennium." Inspired by this thought of the Holy Father, this Archdiocese embarked on a very ambitious program called Pilgrimage 2000. This is a remarkable spiritual renewal effort for all Catholic teenagers, college-age students, and young adults (those in their 20's and 30's). As you know, we began this effort in the Archdiocese of Boston last September 25, 1999, at Foxboro Stadium where 22,000 young people gathered with me.

Since then, tens of thousands of young persons in this Archdiocese, the other dioceses of Massachusetts, young Catholics in New Hampshire through the efforts of Bishop McCormack and his collaborators in the Diocese of Manchester, and members of the Ukrainian Catholic Church and Melkite Catholic Church have been engaged in a period of preparation which has involved small groups gathering regularly for contemplation, prayer, questions and answers, study, and discussion in an ongoing journey focused on a deeper understanding of what it means to live a new life in Christ.

On Saturday, April 29, 2000, there will be a culminating celebration of

Pilgrimage 2000. The event will begin with the morning gathering of participants in a welcome area on the Boston Common. This area will include musical and other performances; games; displays for various Catholic organizations; areas for Eucharistic adoration, confession, and vocation information; food; and other activities. After mid-day, there will be a great march by all the participants from the Boston Common to Fenway Park. I hope to march with the thousands of young people who will have gathered on the Common. At Fenway Park, the afternoon program will include inspirational speakers, musical performances, witness talks by young people, and a great deal of interaction with all the participants. The celebration will climax with a twilight Mass concelebrated by the Bishops of Massachusetts and New Hampshire, at which a representative group of teenagers, college students, and young adults will be baptized, confirmed, and will receive their First Holy Communion.

While this is a culminating event of Pilgrimage 2000, it is not the end of this effort. It is my hope and prayer that the thousands of young people who will be gathered with me at Fenway Park on April 29 will commit themselves to a life of ongoing formation and education. It is essential for all of us to recognize more clearly our responsibility to grow in our knowledge of the faith and to deepen our participation in the life of grace.

I have written to the pastors of this Archdiocese, to Catholic high school principals, and to those who are involved in college campus ministry to ask their help in ensuring the success of the culminating event of Pilgrimage 2000 on April 29. At this time, I appeal to everyone within the Archdiocese to assist in the success of Pilgrimage 2000 by doing three things.

First, I ask your help in ensuring that all teenagers, all college students, and all young adults in their 20's and 30's realize that they are personally invited to the culminating event. There are local leaders in every parish working to ensure that this invitation is understood. I have asked the pastors to help me in getting the word out. I now ask you to do that. I ask you to help me reach out to all baptized Catholics between grade 9 and the age of 40, and to urge them to register through their parishes for the Fenway event.

Second, I ask you to consider the possibility of assisting as a volunteer during this culminating event. In all, 1,200 volunteers are needed for April 29. To date, hundreds of volunteers are still needed. By volunteering, you will be able to participate personally in the culminating event, and will be able to offer direct service to the younger members of our Church. If you feel that you might be able to assist as a volunteer, I would ask you to let your pastor know of your willingness to offer your time and talent for the Pilgrimage 2000 Culminating Event. If there is any question about our need for volunteers, I would ask you to call Sister Marion Batho, C.S.J., at (617) 746-5637.

Third, and most importantly, I would ask you to join me in a crusade of prayer for the success of Pilgrimage 2000's Culminating Event. As I write these words, Pope John Paul II has arrived in the Holy Land. What a gift his pastoral leadership has been to the Church. What an inspired initiative it was for him to call the Church to celebrate this Jubilee Year as a year of spiritual renewal. Already in this Archdiocese I have seen extraordinary signs of that renewal. Pray that this culminating event of Pilgrimage 2000 will be a life-changing event for the thousands of young people who participate in it.

To summarize my requests:

1. Please help to register young people for the Fenway event;
2. Please consider serving as a volunteer for that event;
3. Please pray that the Culminating Event of Pilgrimage 2000 at Fenway Park will be a life-changing event for the young people of the Archdiocese.

70

✢

It Simply Is Not an Option That One No Longer Be a Priest

Words of Encouragement to the Priests of Boston

29 March 2000

Yesterday I celebrated the funeral Mass of Father John Maguire. He was ordained sixty years ago with the class of 1940. Father was older than his classmates by about ten years. He died at the age of 97. His younger classmate, Father Joseph Collins, only 86 years of age, was the homilist. As I prepared to incense the coffin during the Final Commendation, I thought of our meeting today. This faithful priest, who "retired" seven years before I was appointed Archbishop of Boston, has something to say to both you and me.

By comparison, we are both more active than John Maguire has been in his later years at Regina Cleri. You and I both struggle to maintain a balance in our schedules that allows sufficient time for prayer, for study, for relaxation. We live priesthood through a backbreaking succession of pastoral commitments.

The John Maguires in our midst help me to understand that priesthood is not about doing; it is, rather, a way of being. John Maguire was able to do very little by way of pastoral activity during his last years. He was nonetheless a priest, however. Talk of an onotological change implicit in priestly ordination can appear overly theoretical. Yet, as I reflect on the reality of this great grace that is ours in priesthood, as I enter more deeply into the mystery of it all through the awesome experience of ordinations each year, including your own, I am brought more and more to focus on the truth of that ontological change.

The fundamental call we have received with all the baptized is to holiness of life. To be a priest, however, is to strive for holiness in a unique way. The last question in the ordination rite before the promise of obedience is this:

"Are you resolved to consecrate your life to God for the salvation of His people, and to unite yourself more closely every day to Christ the High Priest, Who offered Himself for us to the Father as a perfect sacrifice?"

The candidate responds: "I am, with the help of God."

How blessed we are to have John Paul II as our Pope. He images for us what it means to *be* a priest. It is so evident that his life is consecrated to God. To have the privilege of concelebrating Mass with him in his chapel is to be invited into a far deeper communion with Christ the High Priest. To be with him in prayer is to be on retreat.

Are *you* resolved to consecrate your life to God for the salvation of His people? Am *I* resolved so to consecrate my life? That question, at ordination, is to be answered each day, and each moment of each day. It is not a matter of consecrating priestly actions or certain times in our lives. It is a matter of consecrating to God the whole of our lives. Priesthood cannot be put on and taken off. To live with integrity as a priest is to *be* a priest. Priesthood, as Cardinal Suhard wrote, is not *something*, it is someone, *Christ*.

Our Holy Father insists again and again on the notion that the priest ministers *in persona Christi*, in the person of Christ. We do this by virtue of our ordination, thank God, and not by virtue of our holiness of life. In the celebration of Mass, the Lord is made present under the appearance of bread and wine through the words of consecration by the ordained priest *ex opere operato*, or—more precisely, *ex opere operantis Christi:* The priest who is less than holy is able thus to serve the Church.

Yet, as the Second Vatican Council's Decree on the Ministry and Life of Priests reminds us, the efficacy of our priestly ministry *is* related to our holiness of life, to the degree that we have united ourselves more closely every day to Christ the High Priest.

It is at the altar of God that we experience most deeply and intimately what it means to *be* a priest. Here we stand before God's people to minister to them in the person of Christ, Christ the priest and Christ the victim of sacrifice. Here Christ asks us to lay down our lives for His flock. Here God invites us to enter into His sacrificial death through the many deaths which Christian living and priestly service demand of us.

Mother Teresa once asked me to always pray for her as I poured a drop of water into the chalice of wine at the preparation of the gifts. Recall the words: "By the mystery of this water and wine, may we come to share in the divinity of Christ Who humbled Himself to share in our humanity."

She helped me to appreciate that momentary ritual in terms of Paul's teaching that we make up the sufferings that are wanting in Christ.

With all the baptized we can say "I live now, not I, but Christ lives in me." To say that as priest, however, is to realize that Christ shares with us his priestly existence in such a way that we can make His priestly action present in the world. Without us, that presence would not be. Christ uses bread and wine and *us* to become present in Eucharist.

Small wonder then that the Church asks of us in the ordination ritual a resolution to consecrate our lives to God for the salvation of His people, and to unite ourselves more closely every day to Christ the High Priest, Who offered Himself to the Father as a perfect sacrifice.

I have been at the sickbed and the deathbed of many priests. It is humbling to see in their weakness the strength that is too often obscured or forgotten in my own life. We can so easily be overtaken by the many works, *good* works of our lives. There is the possibility of deception here, the possibility of placing ourselves, our talents, our programs at the center of the Church's mission. We know, however, in the clarity of faith, that Christ and He alone is the Center, the Alpha and the Omega, the Beginning and the End. The priest, struggling for the next breath, is breathing in union with Christ, the Eternal High Priest. He is joining the sacrifice of his illness, his dying, his fear to the sacrifice of Christ on the cross.

We call it "retiring," but there is no way by which the priest and priesthood can be separated. The ways in which priesthood is lived may vary, and some of those ways are conditioned by sickness or the frailty of years. But priests we remain for all eternity. We will take our place one day, please God, in the heavenly liturgy, and we shall be there as the priests we are.

The fact of an ontological change in ordination implies the perduring nature of priesthood. My sense is that this permanency of priesthood is a particularly difficult concept in our culture. *Change* is the dominant modality of our culture. Constancy in an individual or in relationships is viewed more as an aberration. The constancy of truth and moral good are widely denied in an age of relativism.

It simply is not an option that I no longer be a priest. Ordination is the opening of a door into a new life in union with Christ the High Priest, but it is also the shutting of a door. There is no turning back. Far from constraining us, this allows us the freedom to be a priest without playing forever the role of Hamlet, without wasting time in imagining how it might have been. For us, our fulfillment is in being more perfectly configured to Christ the Priest.

To be united more closely every day to Christ the High Priest implies the obvious. We are speaking about a dynamic, not a static relationship. We are in the realm here of "the already but not yet." Already we are one with Christ the High Priest by virtue of ordination, but we have not yet come to that fullness of unity in heaven where He will be all in all. The invitation to greater holiness of life always beckons us; the invitation to a more intimate communion with Him always lies ahead. To appreciate this truth, to live in this truth is to be saved from cynicism. If our focus is on Christ, there is no room for cynicism.

In our lives as priests, there is scarcely anything else more destructive than clerical cynicism. Such cynicism usually feeds on the imperfections and shortcomings of others. These imperfections and shortcomings abound. If we don't recognize that, all we need do is take a good look at ourselves in a mirror. If the Lord is our focus, then we can see our own shortcomings and those of others in the light of His redeeming, reconciling love.

What a gift is ours in the Sacrament of Penance. How helpful is this sacramental encounter with the Lord to redirect our focus. What a privilege is ours to be the minister of this Sacrament. In my own life, I have found weekly reception of the Sacrament to be a great grace. It is clearly an opportunity to refocus on the Lord. For me, this sacramental encounter with the Lord is also the occasion for spiritual direction. The more faithful and regular we are as priests in the reception of this Sacrament, the better we will be able to help others rediscover its power to bring pardon and peace.

We prepare for the Sacrament each day, particularly with the Examination of Conscience during Night Prayer. Let me suggest a practice which has been helpful to me. Begin the Night's Examination with a prayer of thanks for the blessings of the day. I find this prayer, which came to me on retreat last July, helpful:

> O God, I think you for this day—
> for the gift to call you Father.
> for the grace to approach You as Divine Mercy.
> I thank You for the knowledge that there is sin and guilt,
> because I know You as Creator, Lawgiver, Judge and Redeemer.
> Help me now to recall the grace of new life in You,
> the grace of ordination,
> and the special graces of this day.
> Help me to acknowledge my response and failure to respond to these graces.
> Reveal to me my sins and shortcomings.
> Guide me to see a recurrent weakness, sin or vice.
> Help me with a firm and focused purpose of amendment.

When I returned from retreat last July, I mentioned in a homily at the house that during retreat the thought had come to me that "Guilt is a gift." Later at breakfast, Paul McInerny and Mike MacEwen took off on that as only good friends might do. Yet it is true. Our ability to confess our sins, our ability to own our guilt is itself a great gift.

Guilt presupposes a belief in God. Faith is the primordial gift in the life of grace. How important it is for us as priests to be men of faith. Several weeks ago, the Holy Father made his annual Lenten retreat. The preacher this year was Archbishop Francis Xavier Van Thuan. The theme he used for his conferences was the virtue of Hope. This modern confessor of the faith spent almost twenty years in prison in Vietnam, a number of those years in solitary confinement. Cardinal Baum, who made that retreat with the Holy Father, told me that in his twenty years at the Vatican never had he been so moved by a Lenten preacher. Archbishop Thuan's presentation was simple and personal. He is a man of profound faith. What a difference that makes, as it did with Mother Teresa, as it does with the Holy Father.

"To Believe" is the first grace. To believe in God. Here the Catechism begins. Here our life of faith begins to believe in God. That is not so easy today. So much is literally at our fingertips, a click of a mouse away. A simpler world could more easily invite faith in God. We can be so easily but superficially surfeited with fact that God appears superfluous. The drama of life, however, its beginning and end, its deepest joys and sorrows cry out for meaning that only God can give. We must be profoundly men of faith.

Without apology, without temporizing, we must reflect the Splendor of the Truth as it is proclaimed by the Church. We must never be embarrassed by the teaching of the Church. If we are, we must make it our business to be better informed, and we must pray for an ability to witness to the faith without fear. We are to speak the truth in season and out of season, when convenient and inconvenient, as Paul instructs us.

To be men of faith implies being men of the Church. As priests, we *are* men of the Church. The Holy Father's invitation to us to reflect on the collective failures of Catholics in our past has caused us to reflect more deeply on the mystery of the Church. We proclaim her to be holy, and so she is, throughout the ages, because Christ is her Head, and His is the holiness of God. She is also holy in countless of her members. At the same time, we confess ourselves to be sinners whenever we gather as Church for the celebration of the Eucharist.

To be men of the Church is to embrace with gratitude and love the mystery of the Church. Here God dwells with us, here the Lord ministers to His people, here revealed truth is authoritatively proclaimed. To be men of the Church is to acknowledge with love and respect the ministry of Peter in our midst and the bishops in communion with him.

To be men of the Church is to burn with zeal for sharing the faith with others. To be men of the Church means to recognize our solidarity with every human being, particularly the most vulnerable, the unborn, the poor, the disabled, the elderly and sick, the imprisoned. The Church creates her own culture. What a treasure is ours in the social doctrine of the Church!

Pope John Paul II has challenged the Church in our day to create a culture of life, a civilization of love. In *The Gospel of Life,* he summarizes the many contemporary assaults against the dignity of the human person which challenge us in our efforts to follow the social doctrines of the Church.

Father John Maguire understood this as a curate, as then they were called, at St. Theresa's in West Roxbury when he addressed forthrightly the evils of racism. Father Joseph Collins, who spoke so beautifully at his classmate's Mass of Christian Burial, was a powerful preacher when I first heard him in 1949. At St. Paul's in Cambridge, where he was then a curate, he introduced us to a keener appreciation of the Church's liturgical life.

To be men of the Church, firmly rooted in the Church, demands that we develop an ecumenical spirit, a passion for interreligious activity, and a desire to engage in dialogue those who profess no faith.

The extraordinary pilgrimage of Pope John Paul II to the Holy Land expresses magnificently what it means to be men of the Church. He brought the Church, all billion of us, to the Western Wall of the Temple. Facing clearly the sins and failings of our past, it was by the power of Christ, the All-Holy-One, that he was also able to incarnate the reconciling love of God. In the midst of so many divisions dividing the human family, the Pope reflected the Light of the World which the Church is called to be.

So often in the Church we can be our own worst enemy. One of the signs of the times which impresses me is the number of clergy from other communities of faith who have become Catholics because of the mystery of the Church. The very things which sometimes cause anxiety in some Catholics are the marks of the Church which attract others to her. This is particularly true of the authoritative teaching office of Pope and bishops. There is an interesting body of literature detailing the journeys of faith of those who have found in the Catholic Church the fullness of what Christ intends for the Church. Such books, I have found, help to strengthen my own faith.

These reflections on priesthood are personal and summary. Any reflection of this type is of necessity autobiographical. That is always a risk, because any one of us is at once a priest and still becoming a priest. It isn't finished yet in my life or yours. Each day I stand in awe of this call and its sublime beauty, and I must deal with the banal in my failure to respond as I should.

For me as for you, however, prayer must be the oxygen of our priestly lives. We are, as priests, called to be men of prayer. The Eucharist is the source and summit of the Church's life, and is the source and summit of the life of a priest. As you have heard me say before, the daily celebration of the Eucharist is central to my life. Here we are united most intimately to Christ the High Priest, who offered himself for us to the Father as a perfect sacrifice.

The rhythm of prayer provided by the Liturgy of the Hours provides a structure for our priestly day. A strong devotion to Mary, expressed through the Rosary, is an integral part of priestly prayer. Quiet time spent with the Lord before the Tabernacle should be a part of our prayer life.

Preaching is also prayer. We come to it through prayer. We prepare for it through *Lectio Divina,* the meditative reading of the Sacred Texts as well as the Fathers and other Church writings. Preaching is the fruit of prayer and is profoundly personal. Our own life's experience is necessarily a part of our reflection on God's Word.

I have anticipated this opportunity to be with you today. We are co-workers in the Vineyard. You will labor here much longer than I. Perhaps my longer time in the Vineyard provides some insights which you might find helpful.

I give thanks to God for you. My desire is to serve faithfully as your father in the Lord and your brother in the priesthood.

These words from Paul's Second Letter to Timothy express what I have attempted to do in this presentation:

> For this reason, I remind you to stir into flame the gift of God bestowed when my hands were laid on you. The Spirit God has given us is no cowardly spirit, but rather one that makes us strong, loving and wise. Therefore, never be ashamed of your testimony to our Lord, nor of me, a prisoner for his sake; but with the strength which comes from God bear your share of the hardship which the Gospel entails.
>
> God has saved us and has called us to a holy life, not because of any merit of ours but according to his own design, the grace held out to us in Christ Jesus before the world began but now made manifest through the appearance of Our Savior. He has robbed death of its power and has brought life and immortality into clear light through the gospel. In the service of this gospel I have been appointed preacher and apostle and teacher, and for its sake I undergo present hardships. But I am not ashamed, for I know him in whom I have believed, and I am confident that he is able to guard what has been entrusted to me until that day. Take as a model of sound teaching what you have heard me say, in faith and love in Christ Jesus. Guard the rich deposit of faith with the help of the Holy Spirit who dwells within us.

71

✢

To Be a Priest Is To Minister in the Person of Christ

At the Cathedral of the Holy Cross on Holy Thursday

20 April 2000

Three realities converge in the solemn celebration of this night: Passover, Eucharist, and the ordained Priesthood.

Our Jewish brothers and sisters share with us the special character of this night as they mark the second day of Passover. This night reminds us of the spiritual heritage which is ours through the Jewish people. Jesus was very much an observant Jew as he gathered in the Upper Room with the twelve to do what Jews had done for centuries. The Passover meal, as we heard in our first reading from Exodus, was a ritual inspired by God through Moses and Aaron. It would stand as a yearly reminder of all that God had done in bringing the Jews from the slavery of Egypt into the Promised Land. This night was the beginning of that journey of forty years, a journey through which God led His chosen people.

"It is the Passover of the Lord," God revealed. "This day shall be a memorial feast for you, which all your generations shall celebrate with pilgrimages to the Lord, as a perpetual institution."

So it is, then, that Jesus went up to Jerusalem in pilgrimage with the twelve, for the memorial feast of Passover.

Paul, a faithful Jew brought by grace to faith in Jesus as Messiah, as Lord and Savior, writes to the Corinthians that he had received from the Lord, as Moses and Aaron had received from the Lord the Passover injunction, that which he had handed on to them in the Eucharist. Paul's words are direct and simple: "The Lord Jesus, on the night he was handed over, took bread, and, after he had given thanks, broke it and said: 'This is my body that is for you. Do this in remembrance of me.' In the same way also the cup, after supper, saying, 'This cup is the new covenant in my blood. Do this, as often as you drink it, in remembrance of me.'"

Jesus observes the ritual of the Passover meal, but he also fulfills its meaning. The second century Bishop Melito of Sardis wrote in a moving Easter homily:

> There was much proclaimed by the prophets about the mystery of the Passover: The mystery is Christ. . . . He was led forth like a lamb; he was slaughtered like a sheep. He ransomed us from our servitude to the world, as he had ransomed Israel from the land of Egypt. . . .
>
> He is the One who brought us out of slavery into freedom, out of darkness into light, out of tyranny into an eternal kingdom; who made us a new priesthood, a people chosen to be his own forever. He is the Passover that is our salvation.

Saul of Tarsus, filled with zeal for the faith of his fathers Abraham, Isaac and Jacob, thought he was honoring God and loving his neighbor when he sought out those Jews who had come to faith in Jesus, in order to turn them from what he considered the error of their belief. At that moment, Saul was moved by God's grace to realize that these early Christians shared in the life of the Risen Lord. God revealed to Saul that out of these Christians he had made a new priesthood, a people chosen to be his forever. Saul's conversion to Jesus was signaled by a new name, Paul, as he entered into a new life in the Risen Lord.

Paul came to believe that in His suffering and death upon the cross, Jesus saved us from sin and from death. He came to believe that in a new and definitive way God had made a covenant with his people—an everlasting covenant in the blood of Christ. Paul understood that Jesus is our Passover.

So it is that Paul teaches the Corinthians and reminds us: "as often as you eat this bread and drink the cup, you proclaim the death of the Lord until he comes."

We encounter the Risen Lord as our Passover in the Eucharist. As it was on the evening before He died when Jesus gathered in the Upper Room with the Apostles, the Eucharist is a meal. We eat, we drink, we are nourished by the Lord Himself.

The Eucharist is also Sacrifice.

Through the signs of bread and wine we enter into the Sacrifice which Jesus made on the Cross. It is the Lord Himself, Body, Blood, Soul, and Divinity, present on our altar this night under the appearance of bread and wine. It is the Risen Lord we receive in Holy Communion. He is our Passover from sin to grace, from death to life.

We become one in Him—one Holy People—the Church.

These two realities, Passover and Eucharist, demand a third: Priesthood.

The perennial faith of the Church is proclaimed by Bishop Melito of Sardis when he says that Christ has made us, the Church, a new priesthood. We are reminded of this whenever baptism is conferred: the newly baptized is anointed with chrism as a sign that he or she now shares in the life of Jesus, the Eternal High Priest. In a beautiful letter to the priests of the world for this Holy Thursday, a letter which he signed on March 23 of this year in the Upper Room of the first Mass in Jerusalem, the Holy Father recalls the Church's belief that the entire people of God participate in the priesthood of Christ by baptism. He then goes on to say that "The Vatican Council reminds us that, in addition to the participation proper to all the baptized, there exists another specific, ministerial participation which, although intimately linked to the first, nonetheless differs from it in essence."

This night, as we recall the Institution of the Eucharist, the Church also recalls the Institution of that ministerial priesthood through which the Eucharist is made present on our altars today, has been in the past, and will be until the end of time.

The priest is to lead God's Holy People as they gather about the altar to do that which Jesus commanded that we do in remembrance of Him. The priest is to minister in the very person of Christ the Priest, who is at once Christ the Victim. When Jesus went from Apostle to Apostle to wash their feet, he showed them what it means to serve. His loving service was to know no bounds, as he would prove on the Cross the next day. It is this willingness to lay down his life in loving service of us all that constitutes Jesus as our Passover. To be a priest is to minister in the person of Christ, our Passover.

This night we thank God for our Passover, Jesus Christ. We thank the Lord for the gift of His presence under the appearance of bread and wine in the Eucharist, and we thank God for the ministerial priesthood which makes possible the Eucharist in our midst.

72

+

For Me, To Live Is Christ

Easter Greetings to the Archdiocese

21 April 2000

Dearly Beloved in Christ,

> The Opening Prayer for the Easter Vigil Mass begins with the affirmation, "Lord God, you have brightened this night with the radiance of the risen Christ."

The sharp contrast between darkness and light expressed in the procession of the Paschal Candle into our darkened churches at the beginning of the Easter Vigil portrays in a dramatic way the truth that is, indeed, the radiance of the risen Christ who brightens this night.

It is not only the night that gives way to Easter morning which is illumined by the radiance of the risen Christ, however. It is every night, every darkness that is brightened by the radiance of the Risen Lord.

This night. What is this night for you or for me? The prevalence of the darkness and gloom of suffering, of sadness, of injustice, of violence, of sin, and of death all around us can make talk of the radiance of the Risen Lord seem a fantasy. A day does not pass but I receive a prayer request for a person in the most trying of circumstances. Beyond these individual cases of need, all of us are overwhelmed by the dramatic suffering caused by the lack of basic necessities of life by so many poor persons throughout the world. This is precisely the "night" of which our payers speaks.

It is that night of suffering and all suffering which Jesus took upon Himself. He, the Eternal Son of God, became flesh in the womb of the Blessed Virgin Mary precisely so that He might save us from sin and death. As our

Holy Father reminded us when he visited Bethlehem last March, the cross cast its shadow on the crib of the Infant Jesus.

Easter does not invite us to a momentary escape from the real world of our many relationships and responsibilities. The enemies of Christianity have characterized it as the opium of the people. Nothing could be farther from the truth. Jesus Christ is the supreme realist, and Christian discipleship demands that we face squarely and honestly all that our lives entail, the good and the bad, the happy and the sad, the successes and the failures, and to see all in the perspective of the saving death and resurrection of Jesus Christ.

Easter is the proclamation that the Risen Lord brightens every night of our lives, however deep the darkness may be. He even brightens the night of sin with the light of His pardon and peace, and brightens the night of death with the radiance of everlasting life.

He brightens the night of despair with the light of an unfading hope in His love. He brightens the night of loneliness and fear with the light of His enduring presence. He brightens the night of pain with the light of His suffering with us and for us.

Easter is the work of Divine Love, the revelation of Divine Love. The Risen Lord manifests to us even now something of the glory, the radiance, that He has won for all those who love and serve God.

During this celebration of Easter, we need to hear once again the Jubilee invitation: "Open wide the doors to Christ." We are invited to open wide the doors of our hearts, our lives to the radiance of the Risen Lord.

With all my heart I pray that the radiance of the Risen Lord might brighten whatever is of night in your lives. May the Easter gift of the Lord's peace be with you now and forever.

Devotedly yours in Christ,
Bernard Cardinal Law

73

+

Religious Reflect the Universal Call to Holiness

Instruction to a New Religious Community, the Brotherhood of Hope

1 July 2000

Brother Kenneth, God has brought you by an unlikely route to this moment of grace. We give thanks to God with you and with the Brotherhood of Hope for your religious vocation. Today the Church recalls the mystery of the Immaculate Heart of Mary, that crucible of love for God, which fashioned her perfect oblation, her Fiat. She is with us through her powerful intercession as Mother of the Church and Mother of Divine Hope.

In a few moments I will address you in these words:

"Dear Brother, in baptism you have already died to sin and been consecrated to God's service. Are you now resolved to unite yourself more closely to God by the bond of perpetual profession?"

Of course, you will answer "I am," or we will all be mightily surprised. The question the Church puts to you, however, is so instructive concerning the meaning of your perpetual profession. With all the baptized you share the fundamental vocation of Church which is to holiness of life, to sanctity. There is a radical equality in the Church through baptism. We have all been incorporated into Christ, we have all been called to live His life of sacrificial love, we have all been called to put God above everyone and everything else. Indeed, as Jesus tells us, "What profit would a man show if he were to gain the whole world and ruin himself in the process? What can a man offer in exchange for his very self?"

In marriage and in the blessed role of father you have attempted to live by this word of the Lord. Sanctity is the vocation of married couples, the simple lay state, priests and deacons, consecrated virgins and consecrated persons, religious women and men, bishops and the Pope. In this vocation, implicit in our incorporation into the Body of Christ through baptism, we discover the radical equality in the Church.

Religious stand within the Church as incarnations of that vocation through the vows of poverty, chastity, and obedience. The fiat of many, indeed the submission to the Father's will by Jesus are echoed in the three vows which will constitute your perpetual religious vocation.

As you so well know, and as the whole Church should always recall, these vows are radical ways of living out the double commandment of love: love of God and love of neighbor.

Today, your heart is overwhelmed by that vision which grasped the consciousness of John. With him you see "new heavens and a new earth." You see the Church as "a New Jerusalem, the holy city, coming down out of heaven from God, beautiful as a bride prepared to meet her husband." With John you hear a voice from the heavenly throne cry out: "This is God's dwelling among men. He shall dwell with them and they shall be his people, and he shall be their God who is always with them."

The Brotherhood of Hope, where all things are held in common, this Brotherhood of Hope which devotes itself to the apostles' teaching and the communal life, to the breaking of bread and the prayers, which is responsive to the needs of others, this Brotherhood embodies for you that vision of a new Jerusalem, this Brotherhood is to reflect within the church all that we are called to be as a holy people.

Through this perpetual religious profession, your fundamental vocation to holiness takes on a new dimension. More than anything else, the religious through the vows—are to reflect in the beauty of their lives the universal call to holiness.

There will, undoubtedly, be moments of desolation of your life. The greatest of saints have found themselves in the desert. Our Lord Himself knew the Agony of the Garden. Remember God's word through John: "To anyone who thirsts I will give drink without cost from the spring of life giving water."

In difficult moments, recall the words of that great religious and mystic, St. Teresa of Avila: Solo Dios basta (Only God is enough) God alone satisfies. St. Augustine put it this way: "Our hearts were made for Thee, O Lord, and they will not rest until they rest in Thee."

What you are about to do, Brother Kenneth, is to respond wholeheartedly to Jesus who said to his disciples: "If a man wishes to come after me, he must deny his very self, take up his cross, and begin to follow in my footsteps." You do that now through the vows of poverty, chastity, and obedience.

74

+

Every Sin Is Profoundly Personal

National Address on Reconciliation

Los Angeles, California, 7 July 2000

Sunday after Sunday we profess our faith in the one, holy, catholic, and apostolic Church. We affirm the Catholic Church to be holy. That holiness is reflected most perfectly in the Incarnate Son of God whose body the Church is. Saint Augustine, who had such a firm grasp on his own sinfulness, was able nonetheless to say that the Church is Christ, extended in time and space.

The Church's holiness is reflected through Mary whose very being proclaims the greatness of the Lord. From the beginning of our history, a history rooted in the pierced side of Christ and the Pentecostal overshadowing of the Holy Spirit, there have been saintly men and women who have shown the world the face of the Holy Catholic Church.

Saint Paul reminded the Galatians, and he reminds us, that in the Church "all are one in Christ." There is a radical equality among the disciples of Christ which is the consequence of our baptism. We have, through the waters of baptism, died to sin and death itself, and have risen to newness of life in Him. Because Christ is the Incarnate Son of the All-Holy God, the fundamental vocation of all the baptized is to holiness of life, to sanctity. Whatever else God may call us to, our radical call is to be holy.

Sin obscures the holiness of the Church. We are the Church, we who gather in this space, we who gather Sunday after Sunday and proclaim ourselves to be sinners. We are the Church, but the Church is always more than us, more than all billion of us scattered throughout the world. The Church is more than our brokenness, our prejudice, our violence, our sins.

We are the branches, but Christ is the vine. We are the members, but Christ is the body's Head.

Jesus prayed for the Apostles and for us in these moving words recorded by John the Evangelist: "I pray also for those who will believe in me through their word, that all may be one as you, Father, are in me, and I in you; I pray that they may be one in us, that the world may believe that you sent me."

Every sin is profoundly personal. Sin is a deliberate act of the human will by which a person turns away from God by a failure to love Him, another person, or oneself, or a failure to reverence God in the beauty of nature. We do not confess the sins of another, therefore, we confess our own sins. Yet, since we are bound together through grace as the Body of Christ, there is a sense in which no sin is only personal. When I sin, when you sin, when we are caught up in a systematic evil which we make our own, then we obscure the holiness of the Church. When we sin, we are not living that oneness of love which is the life of the Trinity. We make it difficult for others to come to know Jesus as the Son of God, as our Lord and Savior. We bear the burden of one another's sins, therefore.

Our Holy Father, in anticipation of this year of the Great Jubilee 2000, has written:

> Because of the bond which unites us to one another in the Mystical Body, all of us, though not personally responsible and without encroaching on the judgment of God Who alone knows every heart, bear the burden of the errors and faults of those who have gone before us. Yet we too, sons and daughters of the Church, have sinned and have hindered the Bride of Christ from shining forth in all her beauty. Our sin has impeded the Spirit's working in the hearts of many people. Our meager faith has meant that many have lapsed into apathy and been driven away from a true encounter with Christ.
>
> As the successor of Peter, I ask that in this year of mercy the Church, strong in holiness which she receives from her Lord, should kneel before God and implore forgiveness for the past and present sins of her sons and daughters.

That is what we do here today. We turn to God and acknowledge our sins, the sins which obscure the holiness of the Church today and the sins which have obscured that holiness in years past.

Within our life as Church, the mutual respect, love, and unity which should characterize our interpersonal relations have not always been evident. Intolerable situations have caused great pain and have sometimes resulted in alienation from the Church. There are the obvious cases of sexual abuse which have so seared us all, and the less celebrated cases of harsh words, as well as rough and unjust treatment which have affected clergy, religious, and laity. Within the memory and lived experience of so many of us gathered here, there is the pain and scandal of injustice and alienation.

As Catholics, we have too often been exclusive in our love and concern, defining ourselves erroneously by race or language or land of origin. To be the Church is to be Catholic, which means universal. To be less than that is to give an unclear witness of who we are as Church. The prejudices of others have too easily invaded our lives.

The Church should be a sign of unity, of hope, of justice, and of love in the world. To the extent that we have not been and are not that, we acknowledge our faults and ask God's pardon.

Our prayer today celebrates the Infinite Mercy of God which is made manifest in the suffering, death, and resurrection of Jesus Christ. We approach God in total confidence that He will grant us the grace to turn from sin and to live more fully the life of the Risen Lord.

We ask the grace to see ourselves in the light of our vocation to be holy men and women. We pray for the Church, the one Catholic and Apostolic Church, and we ask that her holiness might be reflected in our lives of love, love for God, for one another, and for every human being from the first moment of conception to the last moment of natural death. No human being, however young or old, strong or weak, poor or rich, of whatever race, language or ethnic background can be outside the circle of our love.

75

✢

If You Root Your Marriage in God's Love, Love Will Never Fail in Your Wedded Life

Words to a Young Couple on Their Wedding Day

15 July 2000

SAL DIDOMENICO AND TRICIA TANKEVICH
INCARNATION CHURCH, MELROSE

The three readings have love as their common theme.

When Trish and Sal chose the first reading from the Song of Songs, they saw their love for one another reflected in that beautiful poetry.

It is good that they see their love reflected in those words. Hear again the inspired author:

> Set me as a seal on your heart
> as a seal on your arm;
> For stern as death is love,
> relentless as the nether world is devotion;
> its flames are a blazing fire.
> Deep waters cannot quench love,
> nor floods sweep it away.

These are not words which can be lightly claimed as your own. The love for one another which you vow today, Sal and Trish, you want to be that kind of love. You want a love which will bind you together until death. Through whatever your life together might entail, your love for one another will remain.

It takes nothing away from your personal reading of the Song of Songs to remind you that the inspired author did not have you specifically in mind. Nor was he recalling the story of two young lovers of long ago. He was thinking rather of God's love for His Holy People and for each one of us.

To understand this is very important, for your love for one another can only be the kind of love we read of in the Song of Songs if first you love God, and allow God to love you.

It is no accident that you have chosen a church for your wedding, and the celebration of the Eucharist as the sacred context for your exchange of vows. God, who is love, is very much a part of what you are about to do. He created you, He redeemed you, He called you to be holy, and today he calls you to set one another as a seal on your hearts. At a time when marriage is so little understood and when enduring commitments seem out of reach for so many, God calls you to pledge your undying love for one another.

We who are here as ministers of the Church, as your families and friends to witness what you do, are grateful to you both for daring to risk real love.

Listen again to Jesus as he tells you:

> As the Father has loved me, so I have loved you;
> Live on in my love.

Saint Paul gives you both very good advice about the love you are to have for one another:

> Love is patient
> Love is kind
> Love is not jealous
> It does not put on airs; it is not snobbish;
> Love is never rude
> It is not self-seeking
> It is not prone to anger
> Neither does it brood over injuries.
> There is no limit to love's forbearance,
>   to its trust,
>   its hope,
>   its power to endure.
> Love never fails.

And love will never fail in your wedded life if you root your marriage in God's love, a love revealed in Christ's saving death upon the cross. It is that mystery of Divine Love which we celebrate in this and every Eucharist. As the Lord binds you together today in this Eucharist, so may the Mass always be at the center of your married life until finally you are gathered to the Heavenly Liturgy with all the angels and saints.

76

+

It's a Beautiful Document, Dominus Jesus

Clearing Up Certain Ambiguities in Press Accounts

17 September 2000

I would propose three points for our consideration in this homily. The first is Peter's confession of faith. The second is the centrality of the passion in our profession of faith concerning Jesus, and the third is a living faith. And to the first point, Peter's confession of faith, the setting is beautifully human, isn't it? Jesus is gathered with his apostles, and he inquires of them "What is the reaction to my teaching? Who do the people think that I am?" And the apostles respond. Then Jesus changes the question and he says, "But you, who do you say that I am?" And it is Peter who responds for the Twelve and he says quite simply, "You are the Christ." And then Our Lord as recorded by Saint Matthew in the 16th Chapter which is parallel to this Gospel from Mark says to Peter, "Blessed are you, Simon Bar Jonah, for flesh and blood has not revealed this to you, but my Father who is in heaven." This profession of faith that Peter made concerning Jesus is a profession that can only be made by the grace of God which we call the gift of faith and it is to that which Isaiah points when he says, "the Lord God opened my ears that I may hear and I have not rebelled and have not turned back."

"The Lord opened by ears that I might hear." And so it is with each one of us. Our ability to profess our faith in Jesus as Lord and Savior demands that gift of grace which we call the gift of faith, enabling us to go beyond the limits that human reason imposes upon our ability to understand, allows us to go beyond that to enter into the mystery of God in all its fullness, the gift of faith. And it's so interesting that it was Peter who responded, and in the parallel passage in the 16th chapter of Matthew, the 19th verse, the Lord goes on to say to Peter, "Thou art Peter, and on this rock I shall build my Church," and so it has been in every age since that Peter and his successors have led the Church in our profession of faith as to who Jesus is. And so it is also in our own time. On August 6 of this year the Holy Father through a document prepared by the Congregation of the Doctrine of the Faith responded to that question for our time, "Who do you say that I am?" a question put to the Church, indeed to all believers "Who do we say that Jesus is?" I have in my hand that document. This document of some thirty-six pages. I hold it before you because this is what the Church teaches, not what you might read in some op-ed page of a newspaper. There's been a lot of misinformation published this past week about this document. What this document is is an authoritative statement of what we believe as a Church concerning Jesus. It's a beautiful document, and its very name echoes the response of Peter to that question two thousand years ago when he said, "You are the Christ," and the document begins, "The Lord Jesus."

Now, in today's *Globe,* there is a very interesting and very good letter to the editor. I wish it had been printed as an op-ed piece, but it wasn't. But it is a letter to the editor on the last page of the Focus section, and in that letter the author criticizes last weeks' article—which was an op-ed piece—about this document. It said some terrible things about it—all wrong. This letter is interesting because it is written by a Protestant who is the President of Eastern Nazarene College in Quincy, Dr. Kent Hill, and it's a letter that he wrote spontaneously. He wasn't asked to write it. Let me just quote a little from that letter. He begins by saying "as a Protestant committed to genuine ecumenism and as a participant for eight years in the Evangelical and Catholics Together dialogue, I was disappointed to read in the *Sunday Globe* last Sunday Paul Wilkes' strong assertions that Pope John Paul II had somehow allegedly abandoned his earlier ecumenism and is moving the Catholic Church back towards "pre-Vatican triumphalism." That was Wilkes' term. So the charge was that in issuing this proclamation of what we believe about Jesus, the Church has taken a step backwards in terms of our commitment to ecumenical dialogue and interreligious cooperation, and this man is saying that's a lot of nonsense, as indeed it is. He says, "all of these criticisms surprised me because it did not sound at all like the spirit or the ideas of the Christian leader that so many of us, Catholic and Protestant alike, have come to respect and admire for decades. I wondered if perhaps John Paul II had suddenly changed his deepest convictions and so I downloaded from the Vatican the infamous thirty-six-page document and read it through line by line. I could barely recognize in its pages the caricature to which *Globe* readers had been subjected. Even the eleven paragraphs from *Dominus Iesus* cited in the *Globe* do not support the unfair and careless analysis of the reviewer. For example, Wilkes charges that the Vatican document bars Protestants "from the gates of heaven, despite their most sincere intentions and good lives." So clearly a lie as to what we do believe as Catholics. In fact the quotations given actually contend that even we Protestants who "have not preserved the valid episcopate" but have been baptized are "incorporated in Christ and thus are in a certain communion, albeit imperfect, with the Church. The position, this author says, is completely faithful with the ecumenism of Vatican II and is seen as a gesture of good will by most Protestants who appreciate the affirmation that the grace of God extends the membership of the Catholic Church. He says that this document affirms that which Vatican II repeatedly affirmed, namely that Jesus Christ is uniquely God Incarnate and the universal Savior of all humanity. We believe that. And when you enter into ecumenical or interreligious dialogue, one of the first rules is that you enter in by speaking the truth about your own belief. And the reason why this document was issued was because some within our Church, including some theologians, have been a little bit ambiguous about what we believe, and that doesn't serve the cause of ecumenism or interreligious dialogue, nor does it serve the cause of the Church herself.

Which brings me to the second point which is the centrality of the passion in our proclamation of faith about Jesus. The centrality of the passion. It is by virtue of his death that Jesus has saved us and has saved all humanity. Every human being who has ever lived, who lives, or who will ever live is saved by the Blood of the Lamb, Jesus, our Lord. As Scripture says, there is one name by which all salvation comes, and we believe that. So that after Peter professed his faith in Jesus as the Christ, we read that the Lord Jesus began to teach them then that the Son of Man must suffer greatly and be rejected by the elders, the Chief Priests, and the scribes, and be killed and rise after three days. And Matthew 16:21 has practically the same words, "from that time Jesus began to show his disciples that he must go up to Jerusalem and suffer many things from the elders and Chief Priests and scribes and be killed and on the third day be raised again." It is our faith that his death is the death of the one unique savior of all mankind, that there is no other name by whom salvation comes, and that our own life must be focused on the mystery of the cross and of the resurrection because the two go together. It is in his resurrection that we see the consequence of his saving death, not only in him but in our own lives.

Which brings me to the third point, ours is to be a living faith—a living faith in Jesus as Lord and as Savior. What does that men? Well, James tells us that faith without works is dead. In other words, if our faith is to be a living faith, then all that our life is, all of our works, our desires, our dreams—everything about us must reflect that faith. And how does it do that? When we are baptized we believe that we die. Baptism is a death, it is a death to sin and it is a death to death itself so that we might rise to newness of life so that we might share in the life of Christ. So much is that so that the Catechism of the Catholic Church, when it speaks about our human death at the end of the course of our days on this earth, says that that moment of human death simply completes what was begun in baptism, and so everything in between is in a sense an invitation to die to sin and to the claims of death upon us so that we may live, even now, this new life of Christ. It is what the Lord means when he says to us in today's Gospel, "Whoever wishes to come after me must deny himself, take up his cross and follow me. For whoever wishes to save his life will lose it. Whoever loses his life for my sake and that of the Gospel will save it." To lose our life for the sake of the Gospel means to die to sin, to selfishness, to a too-narrow vision of my brothers and sisters. To die to that and to live in the message of the Gospel, which is the message of universal love of every man, woman, and child on the face of the earth, from the first moment of conception to the last moment of natural death and every moment in between. That's what it means to have a living faith, to let our proclamation of Jesus as Lord and Savior find expression, not simply in the words we say but in the lives we lead.

And so the Church puts before us today Peter's profession of faith, the centrality of the passion in our belief concerning Jesus, and the necessity for us to have a living faith.

77

+

How Well I Remember the Day of His Death

On Blessed Pope John XXIII

13 October 2000

Today is Wednesday, October 11. It is the day chosen by Pope John Paul II as the Church's memorial of Blessed John XXIII. How well I remember the day of his death. At that time I was in Jackson, Mississippi. Catholics constituted no more than two percent of the state's total population. The Catholic Church was not viewed kindly by many people.

Yet, it was as if the whole of Mississippi were gathered around the deathbed of a beloved grandfather. When his death came, strangers approached me on the street to express their sympathy.

Universally he was acknowledged as good and kind. By the act of his beatification the Church has confirmed this general impression. He was, indeed, a good man. He was a holy man.

This morning, when I offered Mass for the first time in remembrance of him, I was struck by how apt was the Gospel reading assigned for this Wednesday of the 27th week in Ordinary time. Jesus was asked by the disciples to teach them how to pray.

There is no more important request we can make of the Lord. The secret of Blessed John XXIII's goodness is in his life of prayer and in his constant quest to better learn how to pray. Jesus told his disciples that they should pray always. Our lives should be a prayer acceptable to God.

When Blessed John XXIII met a group of Jews and greeted them with the words, "I am Joseph, your brother," he was at prayer. By his own account, the convening of the Second Vatican Council was in response to an inspiration of the Holy Spirit which came to him in prayer. The Council itself was an intense experience of the Church's communion with God.

How fitting it is that Pope John Paul II wished to link the liturgical memorial of Blessed John XXIII with the Second Vatican Council by choosing October 11, the opening day of the Council, as the memorial of his blessed predecessor.

This past weekend the Holy Father led the bishops of the world in a special Jubilee observance. At the closing Mass we were more than seventy cardinals and fifteen hundred bishops. It was the largest concelebration of bishops in the history of the Church. The spirit of these days was a spirit of prayer. We began at the Basilica of Saint John Lateran with a moving penitential service.

On Saturday morning we went in pilgrimage to Saint Paul's Outside the Wall to reflect together on the missionary mandate of the Church. Later that day, the Holy Father received us in audience, and encouraged us in our ministry to one another.

Saturday evening, in Saint Peter's Square, we gathered with the Holy Father and thousands of other pilgrims from throughout the world to pray the Rosary before the statue of Our Lady of Fatima. How very Catholic that time of prayer was! Mary, now as always, urges those who love her to do whatever it is that Christ asks of us.

At the end of the Mass on Sunday, the Holy Father, with the bishops of the world united with him, consecrated the world to the Immaculate Heart of Mary. How mysterious and how powerful is the force of prayer. It is at that point of total dependence upon God that we are strengthened to be instruments of His will.

My prayer on Sunday brought before the Lord the terrible violence in the Holy Land, and I prayed for a just peace for Israel and the Palestinian people. I prayed for the Sudan, for freedom and justice in China, for Cuba, and for Yugoslavia and its neighbors. I prayed for our country, that the awesome power of the ballot be exercised in accord with an informed conscience, which is to say with a recognition of the claims of truth, of the Gospel of Life.

The Jubilee for Bishops was a fitting prelude to this first memorial of Blessed John XXIII. Our present Holy Father bears not only his name as a sign of continuity with his pontificate, but also shares the vision of his blessed predecessor for the Second Vatican Council. To understand well Vatican Council II and the Pope who convened it, one has but to study Pope John Paul II and his ministry as bishop and as successor of Saint Peter.

Pope John Paul II, kneeling before the statue of Our Lady of Fatima, pouring out his heart in prayer for the Church and for the world, leads in the manner of Blessed John XXIII.

Lord, teach us how to pray. Lord, help us to understand that the way we pray always is to see that every event, every thought, every desire, every word, every act is bathed with the light of grace. All life is of a single piece. Integrity means to live the whole of life as a prayer. Thank you for the gift of Blessed John XXIII. Thank you for showing us, through his life, what it means to be good, what it means to be holy. Lord, teach me how to pray.

78

✢

Our Buddhist Friends, You Are Very Welcome

Christmas Eve with Vietnamese Catholics

24 December 2000

What a special grace it is to celebrate this Mass each year with the Vietnamese community. Vietnamese Catholics in this Archdiocese and throughout the United States make a very significant contribution to the Church in this Country.

While greeting the Catholic Vietnamese community, I also wish to acknowledge the presence of our Buddhist friends. You are very welcome. It is a joy to have you join with us for this special Mass.

The birthday of Jesus is the occasion for us to reflect more deeply on the great mystery of the Incarnation. God is always beyond our ability to fully understand. Yet, at Christmas, we celebrate the birthday of Jesus, who is at once the Son of Mary and the Son of God. While God is beyond our ability to fully comprehend, we are able to touch God in the child born of Mary.

Pope St. Leo the Great, reflecting on the mystery of Christmas, the mystery of the Incarnation, wondered what might have been God's motive underlying the Incarnation. He answered his own question with insight that "the incomprehensible willed to be comprehended." God, incomprehensible in himself, wanted to be understood, to be known by the human mind. So it is that the Word was made flesh and dwelt among us.

When we look into the crib and are reminded of that first Christmas night when Mary wrapped her newborn son in swaddling clothes and laid

Cardinal Law and the Dalai Lama on a visit by the latter to Boston.

Him in a manger, we proclaim our faith in the wonderful, saving truth that God became man. Jesus is called Emmanuel, which means "God-is-with-us."

The mystery of the Incarnation does not only reveal God to us, however. Jesus also reveals to us all that we are called to be as human beings. Jesus is the new Adam. In him there is revealed the beginning of a new creation.

When we are baptized, we die to sin and rise to newness of life in Christ. With St. Paul we are able to say, "I live now, not I, but Christ lives in me." For us, to live is Christ.

Christmas, then, invites us to a deeper faith in God, who is revealed in Christ, and to a deeper appreciation of our baptismal dignity as persons called to live in Christ, who is God Incarnate.

The peace of God, which is the promise of the angels, will be ours if we strive with all our hearts to live in Christ. God's Christmas gift to us is His peace. It is ours if we strive to live in His Son, if we strive to be holy.

May Mary, the Mother of Jesus, pray for us. May her powerful intercession help us to echo her "fiat," to say "yes" to God's will with her generosity of heart. If we do that, then her song will be ever on our lips: "My being proclaims the greatness of the Lord."

79

✢

Let My Mouth Be Filled with Your Praise

Testimony to Dr. Theodore N. Marier

Choir School Master, 27 February 2001

Suzanne, Vincent, Robert, and each of you in the family who are gathered here, you are surrounded by a congregation that knew, appreciated, and loved your father, your grandfather. How appropriate it is that you have brought him here to Saint Paul's. For fifty years as organist and music director at Saint Paul's, he helped thousands upon thousands of worshippers to lift their minds and hearts to God. In a 1993 interview, Dr. Marier responded to a question concerning the meaning of the Choir School's motto. He said on that occasion: " 'Repleatur os meum lauda tua' means 'let my mouth be filled with your praise.' It is the first line of an antiphon proposed by Pope Pius XII as a unifying chant for all the choirs of the world. I thought this a singularly appropriate motto for the school."

Ted was, of course, correct, as he was in pitch and in all things! It *is* a great motto for the school. The motto also serves, however, to characterize his life and work. "Let my mouth be filled with your praise." What more fitting epitaph could we voice in an effort to evoke his faith-filled, loving, demanding, ebullient presence in our midst? He lived and died as a choir boy.

Our readings today help us to understand the human mystery that is death. With prophetic insight Isaiah points us to Calvary when he says: "On this mountain the Lord of hosts will provide for all peoples. On this mountain he will destroy the evil that veils all peoples, the web that is woven over all nations; he will destroy death forever."

Jesus, the Incarnate Son of God, did that. He destroyed death forever as he bore our sins and our death. He, the Lamb of God, died for us. In baptism, we are buried with Him, so that we might rise with Him to newness of life.

The ecstatic words of Revelation speak to us of that new life: "I saw a new heaven and a new earth. . . . I also saw the holy city, a new Jerusalem, coming down out of heaven from God. . . . Behold, I make all things new."

"What is essentially new about Christian death," says *The Catechism of the Catholic Church,* "is this: through baptism, the Christian has already 'died with Christ' sacramentally, in order to live a new life; and if we die in Christ's grace, physical death completes this 'dying with Christ' and so completes our incorporation into him in his redeeming act."

The Paschal Mystery, the Mystery of Christ's saving death and resurrection, is at the heart of the Church's liturgy. As a matter of fact, the Eucharist is the source and summit of the Church's life. Ted believed that, and was privileged to devote his entire life to help others appreciate and live that saving truth. I stand here as one of the thousands who have benefited by his gifts. Perhaps my most vivid memory is of the first celebration of the Restored Easter Vigil here at Saint Paul's. Ted, Joe Collins, and, of course, Monsignor Augustine F. Hickey, were responsible for unveiling the meaning of the Paschal Mystery through the beauty of the Easter Vigil. What a gift to the Church!

In this Eucharist we hear Jesus say to us: "I am the resurrection and the life; whoever believes in me, even if he dies, will live, and everyone who lives and believes in me will never die." We are consoled by the fact that Ted's life was so intimately linked to the proclamation of this saving truth. We pray for him in this Mass, that whatever might obscure his vision of God would be clarified, and that he, with his beloved Alice and all the faithful departed might sing forever the praise of God in the heavenly liturgy.

80

+

There Are No Strangers in the World of a Holy Person

Pastoral Guidance to the Archdiocese

10 March 2001

Let me begin with a few preliminary remarks. This convocation is focused on the future, a future which we view with hope. What I have to say in my talk, and, more importantly, what will take place in the focus sessions which will follow are intended to be of help to parish pastoral councils as you assist your pastors in developing mission plans. Finance councils should be helped in their responsibilities to make possible the funding of existing and new mission initiatives. I cannot emphasize enough the importance of these focus sessions.

You will also find the Parish Resource Fair a great help. And please be sure to visit each one because those who feel that they may not have the best place will be very upset with us if you don't all go to each one. My experience is that many persons in the Archdiocese are really unaware of the great resources available to assist parishes. Be sure that you browse through all of these displays, but please do so during free time.

A day like this does not happen without a great deal of planning. Key to the planning of this day have been Barbara Shine, Harry Foden, Sister Dorothea Masuret, C.S.J., Father Bob McMillan, S.J., Sister Marian Batho, C.S.J., and Bill Dittrich. They have been assisted by Barbara Horan, Barbara Richards, Fran Foden, Sister Eleanor Shea, C.S.J., and Sister Philomene Walsh, C.S.J. Join me in thanking this key leadership group.

This site is perfect for our purposes, but demands careful planning. We are blessed with the competence of Anne Cimini who has once again served as the Archdiocesan Site Coordinator, and I'd ask you to join me in thanking Anne, her husband and her children.

The World Trade Center has been most accommodating, and I acknowledge Tom Ridlon who has served as our liaison with and coordinator for the Center. Thank you, Tom.

Paul Kelly, principal of Saint Joseph Elementary School in Needham, serves as Coordinator of Music for our prayer. Paul, I am grateful to you and all the musicians for your help. Thank you so very much.

The choir that sang a moment ago and the choirs which sang earlier represent in a magnificent way the diversity that exists in the Archdiocese as indeed did those who were kind enough to bring the flags of their countries in procession. We thank you very, very much for that. Father O'Brien has indicated the wide diversity of background in this Archdiocese. Mass is celebrated each Sunday in twenty-six different languages. My words now are being simultaneously translated into Spanish, Vietnamese, Haitian Creole, Portuguese, and American Sign Language. Thank you, translators. What a gift are the various cultures, the various peoples, the various ethnic backgrounds woven together into a magnificent unity which is the mystery of the Church. Perhaps the Church's greatest gift to the world is our unity.

As I have done at other convocations, I will focus today on planning for mission. This planning takes place primarily at the parish level. Each Parish Pastoral Council has as its principal task to assist the pastor in developing a plan for mission for the next five years. My remarks and the focus sessions are intended to help you in that task.

Planning should also take place at the cluster level. Recently a pastor confessed to me, in conversation and not in the sacrament of penance, or I couldn't tell you, that he had come to a point of absolute frustration with cluster meetings, because nothing was ever decided. Does that sound familiar? He determined that the next meeting would be his last. Then the miracle happened. The cluster finally decided to do something together.

Clustering is a new concept for us, and it does take time to begin to see that there are certain things that can be done cooperatively to mutual advantage. Don't give up on clustering. It works.

Seventeen years ago this month I celebrated my first Mass as Archbishop of Boston. Time goes by very quickly when you're having fun. The opening prayer for that Mass voiced all the hope that was in my heart for this great Archdiocese as we began our life together. That prayer is in my heart again today as we look with hope to the future of this Archdiocese and of its 368 parishes. Pray with me now:

> God our Father,
> in all the churches scattered throughout
> the world

you show forth the One, Holy, Catholic and
Apostolic Church.
Through the Gospel and the Eucharist
bring your people together in the Holy Spirit
and guide us in your love.
Make us a sign of your love for all people,
and help us to show forth
the living presence of Christ in the world,
who lives and reigns with you and the
Holy Spirit,
One God, forever and ever.
Amen.

We gather here as Church. We are the Church. We cannot be defined by the buildings in which we worship. We cannot be defined by the many institutional expressions of our life together: schools, colleges, social service networks, hospitals, and whatever else. The Church is a mystery experienced, touched, in the corporate life of one billion men and women scattered throughout the world in dioceses such as our own. Together we show forth the One, Holy, Catholic and Apostolic Church.

Our life, the life of each one of us as members of the Church began in baptism. In the waters of that sacrament we were buried with Christ and we rose with Him to newness of life. Our baptism in the name of the Father, and of the Son, and of the Holy Spirit signifies that in Christ we share in the life of the All-Holy Triune God.

To be a Catholic means to live a new life in Christ. To be a Catholic means to be called to holiness of life. Jesus tells us that it is the very holiness of the Heavenly Father to which we are called.

It is good for us to begin our reflection on the mission of the Church centered in the mystery of the Church and the universal call to holiness. Whatever else may be our vocation, each one of us has been called by God in baptism to holiness of life.

In the final analysis, all that we are about as parishes, as clusters of parishes, as an Archdiocese should be directed towards our sanctification.

Lest we have the wrong idea, holiness does not mean a self-absorbed, inwardly-turned life. To be holy means to be a sign of God's love for all people, it means to show forth the living presence of Christ in the world. We are to do this in our individual lives, our families, our parishes, and as an Archdiocese.

I thank God for the ways in which His love is evident in the parishes of this Archdiocese. Last Sunday at the Holy Cross Cathedral we had the Rite of Election. On the First Sunday of Lent each year those seeking to be baptized or received into full communion with the Church gather with me at the Cathedral. More and more parishes or clusters of parishes have developed the Rite of Christian Initiation for Adults (the RCIA). My hope is that the RCIA will be an integral part of the life of each parish or cluster, and that the Cathedral Rite of Election will be participated in by all parishes.

The Rite of Election, like the Chrism Mass, is a privileged moment in our life together as an Archdiocese. Incidentally, let me put a plug in here for our patronal feast next Saturday. Saint Patrick is the patron of this Archdiocese, and at 12 noon at the Cathedral of the Holy Cross I will celebrate Mass there. You are all invited.

The development of the RCIA is not just a matter of providing a program for those who wish to enter into the Catholic Church. What is needed for the RCIA to succeed is for each of us to have a missionary spirit. It is the task of each one of us, of every parish, of every cluster of parishes to actively invite others to share with us the riches of our Catholic faith.

There is a great missionary tradition in this Archdiocese. It has inspired countless men and women to give themselves in loving service thousands of miles from home. It has inspired and continues so to do, an impressive generosity of prayer and monetary support through the Propagation of the Faith. It has given birth to the missionary Society of St. James the Apostle and Por Cristo. All of these are commendable activities which look to the needs of the Church in far-off places.

We must also be missionaries at home, however. Do we think that the great blessing of the Catholic Church is only for us? The Rite of Election last Sunday was a moving testimony to the compelling nature of Catholic faith. How I pray for the outpouring of God's Holy Spirit upon this Archdiocese so that each of us would be filled with the missionary zeal of St. Paul. There is no parish, no city, no town or neighborhood within this Archdiocese where there are not thousands of persons thirsting for what the Catholic Church has to offer.

I commend the effective efforts of so many to make our parishes welcoming communities of faith. I would hope that every parish council would place high on its agenda the issue of evangelization. The Office of Spiritual Development is a resource in this.

In 1999, the Bishops of the United States issued an important document on Adult Faith Formation entitled *Our Hearts Were Burning Within Us.* In it we called for a renewed commitment to adult faith formation. I want to underscore adult faith formation as a pivotal mission priority in every parish and cluster of parishes. We cannot have a missionary spirit without a sound faith formation. Let me quote from that document of the U.S. Bishops:

> We are filled with great joy and expectation as the third millennium of Christian history dawns. Before us, in the wonder of God's gracious plan, stretch new opportunities to proclaim the Good News of Jesus to all the world. . . .
>
> To do their part, adult Catholics must be mature in faith and well equipped to share the Gospel, promoting it in every family circle, in every church gathering, in every place of work, and in every public forum. . . .

> To grow in discipleship throughout life, all believers need and are called to build vibrant parish and diocesan communities of faith and service. Such communities cannot exist without a strong, complete, and systematic catechesis for all its members. By "complete and systematic",

the bishops go on to explain,

> "we mean a catechesis that nurtures a profound, lifelong conversion of the whole person and sets forth a comprehensive, contemporary synthesis of the faith, as presented in The Catechism of the Catholic Church." . . .
>
> Adult faith formation, by which people consciously grow in the life of Christ through experience, reflection, prayer and study must be "the central task in this catechetical enterprise," becoming the "axis around which revolves the catechesis of childhood and adolescence as well as that of old age."

I have quoted at length to emphasize the pivotal importance of adult faith formation in planning for mission. This is, of course, without prejudice to all that we do in religious instruction and formation of children and adolescents. Thank God for every one of our Catholic schools, and their nearly four thousand teachers. No religious education program can match the benefit of a Catholic school. It is my hope to begin an endowment fund to augment the salaries of teachers in parochial schools and in central high schools. At the same time, we should all work to provide relief to parents of Catholic school students through tax credits or some other measure which will introduce equity into a presently unjust system. Parents have the primary right and obligation as teachers of their children, and the government should recognize that right.

In 1988, we concluded the Eighth Synod of the Archdiocese. So many of you here helped to work on that. I acknowledge in a special way the work of Monsignor Paul McInerny, and Sister Mary Ann Doyle of the Sisters of St. Joseph. The Synod said, concerning Catholic Schools: "The Synod upholds the position of the American bishops who . . . have stated that the Catholic school is 'the most effective means available to the Church for the education of children and young people' as they grow into Christian adulthood. The Archbishop of Boston has consistently expressed his own support and endorsement of our Catholic schools, but the Synod realizes that similar support must be forthcoming from the laity, religious, and clergy of the Archdiocese."

It is good to recall these words of the Synod. I am encouraged by recent efforts at recruitment for and support of Catholic schools. I do not believe that we have all the Catholic schools necessary in this Archdiocese. Planning for mission at the parish and cluster level should consider the possibility of a Catholic school where such does not exist. Where there are heavy concentrations of new peoples special efforts must be made for recruitment of such students for our Catholic schools.

Most of our children, however, attend government schools. How grateful all of us are to the nearly sixteen thousand catechists who assist in the religious education and formation of these children. Join me in thanking them.

What an excellent work is done by these catechists. They have a very limited number of hours available each year for classes, they must contend with the negative aspects of the dominant culture, and often parents lack an adequate faith formation themselves to be supportive of what goes on in the religious education classes. My gratitude goes out to all our catechists, to the DREs, and to all who assist them. The Archdiocesan Institute for Ministry, or AIM, was developed with them in mind. I urge you to encourage and facilitate participation in the courses of AIM on the part of your parish catechists.

AIM is not limited in its scope to catechists, however. It is, itself, a means of adult faith formation. Parish and finance council members, thousands of volunteers in a wide variety of works, and every Catholic adult could benefit by the courses provided through AIM. In planning for mission, there should be a systematic audit of the degree to which parish members have availed themselves of the courses offered by AIM over the past two years. Promotion of AIM is an excellent way to foster adult faith formation. This year alone, AIM is offering 101 courses at 41 different locations around the Archdiocese. Over 700 of the 1,300 registrations so far this year are people taking an AIM course for the first time. That's very encouraging. And allow me to speak directly a word to our Hispanic brothers and sisters concerning a new initiative of an AIM course in Spanish.

Tengo una informacion muy importante y urgente que compartir con la comunidad Hispana aqui presente.

El próximo sábado, 17 de Marzo, vamos a inagurar en la Archidiocesis el "Instituto de formacion de laicos."

Es este un proyecto muy deseado y apoyado por mi.

Encarezco a los parrocos y sacerdotes encargados de las distintas parroquias que inviten a sus feligreses a participar en el programa para que, preparandose mejor, puedan servir mas eficazmente como laicos en las parroquias y en la Arquidiocesis.

En la mesa de la oficina de ministerios pueden solicitar informacion y recoger los programas con todos los detalles.

Les repito, es un programa muy querido de mi corazon porque, como Arzobispo de Boston, veo la urgente necesidad de formar a muchos laicos Hispanos que se unan a la evangelizacion y al servicio de todos nuestros hermanos en la Arquidiocesis de Boston.

We also have inaugurated a Master's Program in Theology at Saint John's Seminary. I see that Father Paul Ritt, who is director of that effort, is with us today. We have the marvelous cooperation of the faculty of Saint John's Seminary and of others in making this program possible, and we have subscribed beyond our dreams for the first year. This is another effort in adult faith formation.

St. Anthony's parish in Lowell, as part of the parish's efforts in adult faith formation, began four years ago supporting parishioners attending AIM. In 1997, 24 parishioners participated. To date, there have been over 250 registrations from this one parish. Gerry McDonald, the DRE, says: "The wealth they bring back to the parish is immeasurable."

The focus on adult faith formation is a kind of Copernican revolution in catechetics. All too often our focus is limited to the young. Even in a primary focus on the young, however, it is immediately evident that we teach best by the example of our lives. We need adult faith formation so we can give better examples to our young.

Uncatechized and spiritually underdeveloped adults are the greatest obstacle to the Church's efforts to evangelize. Faith illiteracy weakens our missionary efforts.

I am encouraged by the efforts at adult faith formation focused on couples preparing for marriage. How important are these programs. St. Margaret's in Burlington, working with a team of married leaders and a spiritual director, has developed a program with ten contact hours with engaged couples. The topics touched include the nature of the sacrament of marriage, Natural Family Planning, which should be an integral part of every marriage program, communication, parenting and family finances, domestic abuse, and addictions. Typical of the responses from engaged couples is this: "We didn't want to come at first, but we are glad we did in the end." The married couples on the team report that they themselves "feel affirmed" in their own marriages as they assist the engaged couples.

In planning for mission, it is helpful to review what is presently provided by parishes for engaged couples preparing for marriage, and also, what is provided for parents of children about to be baptized. It very often happens that parents of infants are both faith illiterate and inactive Catholics. The baptism of a child provides a splendid opportunity to minister to these parents. The fact that they wish their children to be baptized is itself a very positive thing, and a good starting point. If we are serious about planning for the future, we must be concerned about the faith formation of these young parents. We need to develop programs of faith formation which accompany young parents with mentor couples. By the time a child is confirmed, the faith of his or her parents should have been developed by a sustained program of faith formation. Yes, this is a challenging ideal. It is one, however, which we must strive to meet.

The Mothers' Group in St. Mary's, Franklin, is a great example of informal adult faith formation. In a setting of friendship and support, mothers are afforded an opportunity for spiritual development and their children have an opportunity to play with new friends. Both Bible study and service opportunities are provided, as well as support for new mothers.

The challenge of youth ministry is always before us. The Eighth Synod lifted this up as a necessary mission priority, and almost every parish visitation report includes this among its priorities. St. Joseph Parish in Kingston has seen steady growth in the development of a Comprehensive Youth Ministry. The parish makes full use of Archdiocesan resources in developing personnel, programming, and support needed to make the parish a youth-friendly community.

My own experiences with Pilgrimage 2000 and with the World Youth Day in Rome convince me that the young people of this Archdiocese are ready to be challenged by the faith. The message of the Cross, which is the message of sacrificial love, is a message they are ready to hear, and which they deserve to hear.

Young Adult Ministry in this Archdiocese has also come into its own in recent years. Mr. Jim Breen, Director of our Archdiocesan Young Adult Ministry Office, along with volunteer young adult leaders have done an outstanding job of assisting parishes and clusters of parishes developing their own programs. It is always dangerous to single out parishes, but just as examples of many others let me mention Quincy Catholic Young Adults, including Quincy parishes clustered around St. Joseph, 7 Ups (the seven United Parishes of Southie), St. Ignatius, Chestnut Hill; St. Patrick, Stoneham; St. Patrick, Natick; St. Mary, Chelmsford. These parishes are successful in integrating young adults into all aspects of parish life, not just as a young adult group. Rather than develop new programs for young adults, existing programs were expanded by the participation and energy of young adult members of the parish.

As you assist your pastors in developing plans for mission for the parishes and clusters of this Archdiocese, utilize the resources of the Archdiocese and build on the good results of programs and initiatives in other parishes. AIM offers an excellent session on Parish Pastoral Council Training. Our Lady of Good Counsel, Lawrence, which recently went through the process of reconfiguration, and St. John's in Peabody, with a new pastor, recently participated in this AIM session with both pastors and council members.

I am impressed by the fact that the Lawrence Collaborative, which includes nine parishes of Lawrence, has scheduled its own Convocation for March 31, 2001, as a follow-up of this Archdiocesan Convocation. The objective which the Collaborative has set for that convocation is to develop a mission plan which takes into account the urban, multicultural and social justice demands of the city of Lawrence.

As many of you know from my letters following your parish visitations, I see Stewardship as an essential part of planning for the future. The concept of stewardship in our Archdiocesan program is spiritually based and focuses on time and talent as well as treasure. To illustrate the effectiveness of this program, listen to the results at St. Joseph Parish in Salem: There are now four new committees: Prayer Ministry, Home Visits, Landscaping, Coffee after Mass, and five expanded committees: food pantry, giving tree, music, altar servers, and lectors. There are through this stewardship program 236 new parish volunteers. This in itself, in terms of time and talent, makes the Stewardship program worthwhile. Besides all this, the weekly income at St. Joseph's has increased by $1,275.00.

It is impossible for me to enumerate specific programs without mentioning one of my favorites: a parish-based health care ministry program. Recently I visited Diane Walsh at St. Margaret's Pavilion at St. Elizabeth Medical Center. Diane and Jim are the proud parents of their fourth child, Julia. Diane explained to me that she did not know what she and Jim would have done without the help of the health care ministry program at St. Mary's Parish in Franklin. For three weeks, in a systematic way, parishioners provided an array of services which lifted strain and worry from this young family.

St. Bridget's in Framingham and an ever-increasing number of parishes are developing outreach to the sick and homebound beyond the all-important sacramental ministry. Given the direction of health care today and ever-shorter hospital stays, a parish-based health care ministry program is very much needed.

What I have attempted to do thus far is give some examples as to how the mission of the Church can be implemented at the parish and cluster level. These examples are drawn from the experience of our parishes. We began with a reflection on the Church's mission and then moved to concrete examples. Now let me conclude with an echo of what Pope John Paul II has set before us as a plan for mission for the new millennium. He has done this in a remarkable document entitled, *Novo Millennio Ineunte* (At the Beginning of the New Millennium). *"Duc in altum,"* "Put out into the deep," he tells us. He draws these words from the time when Jesus urged Simon to push out from shore and lower his nets for a catch. Peter had already done that, as the experienced fisherman he was, and had come back to shore with nothing to show for it. One can almost hear Peter's internal thoughts as Jesus is telling him to push out from shore: "This won't work. I am familiar with these waters. This is a useless exercise." Sound familiar? Nonetheless, Peter did put out into the deep at Jesus' words, and was amazed at the result.

"Duc in altum (Put out into the deep)!" The Holy Father goes on to say: "These words ring out for us today, and they invite us to remember the past with gratitude, to live the present with enthusiasm, and to look forward to the future with confidence: 'Jesus Christ is the same yesterday, today and forever.'"

I commend this document to your prayerful reading. It contains a magnificent review of the events of the Great Jubilee 2000, and distills the grace of the Jubilee as a call for us to seek the face of Christ in every person and in all we do.

Then the Holy Father points us to that future for which we must plan as parishes and as an Archdiocese. He begins again by quoting Jesus: "I am with you always, to the close of the age." Then he continues:

> "This assurance, dear brothers and sisters, has accompanied the Church for two thousand years, and has now been renewed in our hearts by the celebration of the Jubilee. . . . Conscious of the Risen Lord's presence among us, we ask ourselves today the same question put to Peter in Jerusalem immediately after his Pentecost speech: "What must we do?"
>
> We put the question with trusting optimism, but without underestimating the problems we face. We are certainly not seduced by the naïve expectation that, faced with the great challenges of our time, we shall find some magic formula. No, we shall not be saved by a formula but by a Person, and the assurance which He gives us: "I am with you."
>
> It is not therefore a matter of inventing a "new program,"

he tells us. The 'program' already exists: it is the plan found in the Gospel and in the living tradition, it is the same as ever. . . .

"But it must be translated into pastoral initiatives adapted to the circumstances of each community."

Then the Holy Father highlights what must be a part of all pastoral plans:

- A focus on the universal call to holiness,
- Prayer,
- The Sunday Eucharist,
- The Sacrament of Reconciliation,
- The primacy of grace,
- Listening to the Word,
- Proclaiming the Word,
- A Spirituality of Communion, which incidentally is what we celebrate in this place today,
- The diversity of vocations,
- Ecumenical commitment,
- A commitment to practical and concrete love for every human being.

It is my strong recommendation that at each meeting of your parish pastoral council a portion of time, at the beginning, be allotted to a prayerful study of *Novo Millennio Ineunte.* I am asking the planning group of this Convocation to prepare a simple study guide for that purpose. It will take more than a year to get through the document in this way. The time will be well spent, however, and will help us to keep the focus on the mystery of the Church.

A cursory look at these eleven mission emphases underscores the importance of adult faith formation. Focusing first on the universal call to holiness ensures that our parish planning is going in the right direction. Much of what follows are ways to help us grow in holiness. Holiness is not a call to focus inwardly, although that is important. Holiness is most clearly evident in a life of love, a life turned outward towards God and towards neighbor. There are no strangers in the world of a holy person; every person, from the first moment of conception to the last moment of natural death and every moment in between, is recognized as a brother, as a sister, as a child of God made in His image and likeness.

How grateful we are for the works of Catholic Charities providing the single largest array of social services to those in need of any agency in this Commonwealth, with the exception of the government itself. We should celebrate that fact.

In his call to love, the Holy Father urges us to dialogue with those of other religions. In our Archdiocese, this must come to include more and more Moslems and Buddhists. We have a very special relation with our Jewish brothers and sisters. This dialogue was nurtured in a personal way by Cardinal Cushing. We have an obligation to model Catholic-Jewish relations in this Archdiocese, and I would hope that parish pastoral plans would keep this in mind.

The Sunday Eucharist is central to our life as Church. It is gratifying to note that Sunday Mass attendance has increased slightly the last several years. Nonetheless, far too many Catholics do not appreciate the obligation and the incomparable blessing of the Sunday Eucharist. Our parish planning must focus on the quality of our liturgical celebrations and on our outreach to inactive Catholics.

The Holy Father urges us to focus on the diversity of vocations. We do this always in the context of the universal call to holiness. I have been most encouraged by the yearly weekend retreats which have afforded men the opportunity to prayerfully discern a vocation to priesthood. I give those retreats and in the seminary today 45 percent of our seminarians have been through that retreat prior to entering the seminary. Our parish planning must include vocation promotion through prayer and other means. I particularly commend specific times for adoration before the Blessed Sacrament for the expressed intention of an increase of vocations to priesthood and to religious life. Nothing would please me more than to have times of adoration in every parish of this Archdiocese for that intention. We are blessed with a diversity of vocations in this Archdiocese: married couples, dedicated single laypersons, consecrated virgins, religious priests, sisters, and brothers, permanent deacons, diocesan priests and bishops. Each of us, however, has first been called to holiness of life.

I see a clear parallel between these eleven emphases for mission of the Holy Father and the prayer with which we began.

We prayed: "Through the Gospel and the Eucharist bring your people together in the Holy Spirit and guide us in your love." This, certainly, implies the universal call to holiness. Then we prayed that we might be a sign of God's love for all people, and we asked God's help that we might show forth the living presence of Christ in the world.

I give thanks to God for the many ways in which this is done through our parishes and through Archdiocesan efforts. Holy Redeemer Parish in East Boston, a predominantly Hispanic parish, was the first to respond to the victims of earthquakes in El Salvador. This parish of working-class people has raised $35,000 for this special appeal. Incidentally, there are 3,235 worshippers at Mass each weekend at Holy Redeemer.

The parishes of the Archdiocese have been exceptional in their cooperation with the In Support of Life program concerning end-of-life issues.

I would hope that all in the Archdiocese would join me in advocacy for affordable housing. We also need to give clear and consistent voice in support of the poor and in support of the family.

Our social agenda as Catholics can be simply stated:

We are pro-life,
We are pro-family,
We are pro-poor.

The three go together. Each position should animate the ways in which we seek to express our respect and love for every human being. To be holy means to link together faith and life. A holy life is an integral life. For example, we cannot be pro-life personally but supportive of abortion rights publicly. This spiritual schizophrenia is incompatible to our call to holiness.

The dominant culture in which we are immersed is in so many ways inimical to the truths of faith. Our starting point is the love of God for all people. We must fearlessly speak the truth in love. We know that Jesus Christ is the same yesterday, today, and forever. We know that He will remain with the Church until the end of time. We know that Mary, Mother of the Church, intercedes for us as she did for the early Church on the eve of the first Pentecost.

So with an indomitable hope born of faith, we set out into the deep as we plan for mission in our parishes, in our clusters, and in our Archdiocese.

81

✣

But the Souls of the Just Are in the Hands of God

Month's Mind Mass for Victims of September 11 Attacks

11 October 2001

We come to this altar to join our hearts to the grief sustained by those whose loved ones were victims of the terrorist acts of September 11. We come as a people of faith. We know that in Christ Jesus, God has destroyed death forever. We know that for those who die in the love of God the moment of death brings to completion what was begun in Baptism when first we died to sin and death. We are comforted by John who reminds us that we are, in fact, God's children even now, and that after death the blessed are destined to be like God, for we shall see Him as He is.

Today, the national and international crisis which absorbs the world is experienced in this cathedral in personal terms, in the terms of husbands and wives who have lost their spouses; parents who mourn children and children bereft of mother or father or both; siblings who grieve for brothers and sisters; friends and colleagues numbed by the suddenness of it all.

We gather here as Church, conscious that we have been made one in Christ through grace. To live in Christ is to be bound together by His love. We take strength from one another in our holy communion with the Risen Lord.

The Prophet Isaiah, with poetic insight, describes our day and every day that is shrouded by the violence and death wrought by sin. He speaks of "the veil that veils all people, the web that is woven over all nations. . . ." He names that veil "death." It has other names as well: hate, injustice, prejudice. It bore the name of terrorism as it shattered our lives on September 11.

Isaiah voices a hope that the Lord God will wipe way the tears from all faces when He will destroy death forever. He points to "this mountain" where the Lord of Hosts will provide for all people.

That mountain is the hill of Calvary where Christ's cross stretched up to heaven. The Evangelist Luke brings us there in the powerful words of today's Gospel: "It was around midday, and darkness came over the whole land until mid-afternoon with an eclipse of the sun. The curtain in the sanctuary was torn in two. Jesus uttered a loud cry and said: 'Father, into Your hands I commend My spirit.' After He had said this, He expired."

It is as though we were experiencing an eclipse of the sun in the darkness of grief which has come over us. In that eclipse, our faith brings us to the mystery of the cross, to this holy mountain, to this altar where God has destroyed death forever, to the dawn of Easter.

In this Eucharist, under the appearance of bread and wine, we show forth the saving death of the Lord until He comes again in glory. The Lord has truly risen from the dead. In His rising, He has destroyed death forever.

When we leave this world in death, our souls go before God in judgment. The souls of the just are even now in the glory and peace of heaven. They do not need our prayers. Our prayers can assist the souls of those in purgatory, however, Purgatory is a place of preparation for the Beatific Vision. To be able to offer prayers for these souls is itself a consolation.

John strengthens us when he says:

"See what love the Father has bestowed on us in letting us be called children of God! Yet, that is what we are."

While our gathering here is in the context of a Catholic celebration of the Eucharist, we understand the saving power of Christ's death on the cross as universal in its application. God's love revealed in Christ Jesus is a love for every human being. We trust in God's providential love for all persons of good will even as we seek to share the riches of our faith with others. Jesus Christ laid down His life for us all; to acknowledge Him and His saving death and resurrection brings with it the greatest of blessings.

So, we have come to this altar to proclaim the mystery of faith. May our prayers hasten our beloved dead to the glory of heaven. May our solidarity with you here present and all those bearing the grief of September 11 in personal loss be a source of strength, consolation, and peace.

Photo Credits

Bernard "Padrecito" Law in Ecuador with *Por Cristo*, an organization he helped found to provide primary health care and reduce infant mortality (cover photo): Lisa Kessler; Cardinal Law and Pope John Paul II (p.xxix): Felici; Cardinal Law and summer campers in Boston (p. 1): Richard R. Maclone; Listening to Mother Teresa (p. 56): Sarah Merians & Company; Cardinal with ailing child (p. 94): William T. Lane; Cardinal with children (p. 132): Michael Fein; Presentation of the New Catechism (p. 228): *L'Osservatore Romano*; A Visit to Poland (p. 254): Frederic J. LeBlanc. All other photographs courtesy of Lisa Kessler and the Law family.